Domenico Quaranta

In
Your
Computer

Domenico Quaranta
In Your Computer

Publisher: LINK Editions, Brescia 2011
www.linkartcenter.eu

Translation and editing: Anna Rosemary Carruthers

Printed and distributed by: Lulu.com
www.lulu.com

ISBN 978-1-4467-6021-5

« There is this hacker slogan: "We love your computer."
We also get inside people's computers.
And we are honored to be in somebody's computer.
You are very close to a person when you are on his desktop. »

_ Jodi, 1997

Domenico Quaranta is an art critic and curator. His previous publications include **Gamescenes. Art in the Age of Videogames** (2006, co-edited with Matteo Bittanti) and **Media, New Media, Postmedia** (2010). He curated various shows, including **Holy Fire. Art of the Digital Age** (2008, with Yves Bernard) and **Playlist. Playing Games, Music, Art** (2009 - 2010). He is the founding Director of the MINI Museum of XXI Century Arts and a co-founder of the Link Center for the Arts of the Information Age. http://domenicoquaranta.com

Contents

Acknowledgments

This book is a collection of texts written between 2005 and 2010 for exhibition catalogues, printed magazines and online reviews. In the beginning, the idea was simply to experiment with print-on-demand publishing, and to offer a printed, or printer-friendly version of a series of texts that, while mostly available online, for some reason are not that accessible. Some of them were simply too long to be read online, and too badly formatted to be printed; others were badly translated; and others were simply invisible in that Library of Babel that is the World Wide Web, hidden among hundreds of documents on the wrong shelf, or buried under a stack of dead links.

Unfortunately I soon realized that if I didn't want to make a 400 page, expensive, unreadable book, I had to be selective. As I was editing my own work, the risk was that of creating an authorized, celebratory portrait of myself and my recent past. I did my best to avoid it, and to shift the focus from myself to the wonderful people I've been in contact with in recent years. Still, this book is a pocket version of what, among my work, I would save from the universal flood, in a world without computers. Most of the fields of research I have developed in the last few years are represented: from Net Art to Software Art and videogames, from biotechnologies to the debate around curating and the positioning of New Media Art in the contemporary landscape, and back to Net Art again.

The prevalence of recent texts – most of them were written between 2008 and 2010 – is not just the consequence of an error of perspective (like anybody else in their thirties, I like my present and tend to dismiss my past), but also of my working conditions. I still write bad English and have more to learn than to teach, but I have friends from all over the world asking me to put pen to paper.

My gratitude goes to them all, for allowing me to have these texts published and then re-published in this book. I also have to thank my good friend and comrade Fabio Paris, for his invaluable advice and his great work for the cover design of this book; my wife, Elena, and our little monkey, Dante; Anna Rosemary Carruthers, for editing some of these texts in a way that makes them look better than they actually are; all the hardware and software I have used and abused over the years, and, last but not least, all the wonderful artists that got inside my computer and used it to put a virus in my brain. It's still there, and I love it.

Brescia, March 2011

Introduction

«What the modern means of reproduction have done is to destroy the authority of art and to remove it - or, rather, remove its images which they reproduce — from any preserve. For the first time ever, images of art have become ephemeral, ubiquitous, insubstantial, available, valueless, free. They surround us in the same way as a language surrounds us. They have entered the mainstream of life over which they no longer, in themselves, have power». [1]

At the beginning of the last decade of the Twentieth Century, some pioneering artists discovered that they could not only use their computers to make art, but also that they could deliver it, through the Internet, to many other online computers. In other words, they could bypass any system of selection, mediation, contextualization and filtering, and address viewers directly, making their way into their computer screens and using them like a Trojan horse to break into their minds. They also discovered that this very process could become their work of art, and that the viewer could be involved in it, and thus become something more than a simple user.

The same thing happened to all other cultural objects, beyond art. It began with academic papers and information resources. Then came images, music, video and cinema, personal and corporate information, creative writing, material items. But for art it was different. At that time, if we exclude street art and a few media stunts, there was only one way for an artist to reach an audience: the exhibition space. Galleries, temporary exhibitions, art fairs and museums. You had to go through a tough selection process, and for what? To show your work on the same white walls, and always to the same select few. Then came the internet.

I was definitely not one of the first people to be reached by an artist through my computer screen. When this practice started, I didn't even have a computer. I didn't need it. As a teen, I played some arcade games, without enjoying them that much. I was a nerd, but not that kind of nerd. At high school, the math teacher taught me Turbo Pascal. I still hate them both (math and the math teacher). Then, in 1997, my uncle got out of prison, and for some unknown reason, bought me a computer. At the time I was 18 years old, and at university I discovered that a computer could be used for more than just math and videogames. Moreover, my uncle was the charismatic kind of criminal and, when I was a child, he had enchanted me by sending me some wonderful matchstick ships from prison. So, if he thought I needed a computer, I probably did. I no longer admire my uncle, but I still think that a computer is just as fascinating as a matchstick galleon.

Anyway, it took me another couple of years to discover that this particular vessel could bring art right into my bedroom. Not reproductions, but the real thing, and this distinction was very important to me at the time. It was exciting. This matchstick ship proved to be an underwater relic, full of recent, yet already classic, masterpieces. I intuitively felt I was witnessing the very beginning of an extraordinary development in the production and circulation of art, and I wanted to be part of it.

I talked with my contemporary art teacher and advisor, Luciano Caramel, who had been a militant art critic and curator in the Sixties. He understood and supported me. I wrote my MA thesis about äda'web, a pioneering website active between 1994 and 1998 that commissioned online works from established, as well as young artists, and I started writing for a couple of online Italian art magazines.

These are the antecedents of this book, whose timeline starts in 2005. In these years I've witnessed the goings on in the realm of art, for most of the time through this small, rectangular window that has grown in size and resolution over time. Of course, I have also attended conferences and exhibitions, traveled as much as possible, met some of the artists I first encountered in my computer and enjoyed a beer with them. Yet most of my experience of art has been mediated by a screen.

But it wasn't just me. And it wasn't just the people who appreciated so-called "Net Art". Any art professional would probably say the same. Even those who don't know that computers and the internet can be a medium for art, if they still exist. They too read online magazines and blogs. They too Google the names of artists for info, works and faces. They too get most press releases via email or e-Flux. They too watch videos on Ubuweb, Youtube and Vimeo. They too read online portfolios.

Yet, a difference between me and them remains: between those who have learned to enjoy their computers as the site for a legitimate, direct, authentic experience of art and those who still perceive them as conveying a mediated, indirect experience of art; between those who understand the strange mix of intimacy – it's here, on my screen – and monumentality – it's out there, in the public domain, accessible to everyone – that all online artworks possess; and those who still prefer to buy art in print form, or as an editioned video.

This difference is not connected to some kind of quality judgment – I'm better than they are – or with the ability to keep up to date – I'm open to the new, they are obsolete. It is more likely the kind of difference that distinguishes the community you belong to when you have a strong experience of any kind: when you fall in love, save a life, see somebody die, take psychedelic drugs. You simply see the world in a different way. And you would like other people to see it that way too.

This book collects a series of texts I have written in the last five years, about some of the things that made me look at art in a different way. While it might also be of interest to people who are already interested in what they can find on their computer screens, it has been conceived for those who still have some problems with it, and feel more comfortable in traditional exhibition venues, among traditional art objects.

So the question is: why? Why should you look at the world in a different way? And how might this book help you to do so? After all, many of the things featured in here seem to belong to a utopian past; and some of the perspectives discussed in these essays may look out of date. The quote that I used as an epigraph for this book, and that inspired its title, came from Jodi, the pioneering net.art duo, in 1997.

They said:

> When a viewer looks at our work, we are inside his computer. There is this hacker slogan: "We love your computer." We also get inside people's computers. And we are honored to be in somebody's computer. You are very close to a person when you are on his desktop. I think the computer is a device to get into someone's mind. We replace this mythological notion of a virtual society on the net or whatever with our own work. We put our own personality there. [2]

Exactly ten years later, their comrade Olia Lialina said:

> For a long time it did not make sense to show net art in real space: museums or galleries. For good reasons you had to experience works of net artists on your own *connected* computer. Yesterday for me as an artist it made sense only to talk to people in front of their computers, today I can easily imagine to apply to visitors in the gallery because in their majority they will just have gotten up from their computers. They have the necessary experience and understanding of the medium to get the ideas, jokes, enjoy the works and buy them. [3]

Lialina was explaining why, in 2007, she was making gallery work, and she felt comfortable with a context that was previously contested by so-called Net Art. At the time, Net Art as a movement was over, and many former Net artists had started showing their works in gallery space. So, was it a case of the revolution being over and the art world managing to absorb and normalize the winds of change, as it usually does?

I think it would be prosaic and ingenuous to sum things up this way. Revolutions are not successful when everybody becomes as radical as the revolutionaries; they are successful when they bring about a permanent change in the general mindset, even if less radically. Luckily, the French revolution didn't turn everybody into a Robespierre. But today, nobody would dare question the ideals it was inspired by. Freedom, equality and fraternity are values shared by everybody, at least in name only.

In other words, the revolution has only just begun, and it will take a long time to reach completion. Art is the first to envision the change, and the last to change. The shift that Lialina noticed in the gallery audience is permanent, but it is just one step in the right direction. Along with her, many former Net artists started bringing their works – and their ideas – in front of them. Many of them are still highly active on the net, together with many artists – some of them very successful – who have never defined themselves as net artists. Think, for example, of Paul Chan, Cory Arcangel, Seth Price. And of course, younger generations of artists – the so-called digital natives – are pushing this process even further.

This is changing little in the contemporary art world. Again: art is the first to envision the change, and the last to change. People are getting used to immaterial money, immaterial books and immaterial labor, but they still think that an artwork should be a unique, valuable object they can hang on their wall. At the same time, however, they are getting used to a new culture, and new ideas. Sooner or later, they will understand the absurdity of their attachment to a concept of art that is rooted in the industrial age, and they will be ready for the upgrade.

Let's take another example. At the beginning of this book, I look at a trend called "generative art". Basically, it's about artists programming their computers to make them generate an infinite flow of images that are unlike any kind of image that could be produced by the human hand. Even if there is something "old fashioned" in this practice – images and animations are often selected according to their beauty – the practice itself, in the way it subverts the traditional process of art making, is revolutionary. Unfortunately, it never took off in the art world, and while some of its practitioners became designers or architects, others – such as Casey Reas – successfully entered the art world by reconnecting to the conceptual tradition of art based on instructions. The term "generative art" no longer makes sense as an art label. But was it a complete failure? The fact is that in the last ten years, we have gotten more and more used to, on one hand, the aesthetics of information and on the other, the idea of artist-machine collaboration. So, today we are not that surprised when, entering an art fair, we see a beautiful piece of generative art hanging next to a print by Marina Abramovic. Of course, it is not called by that name. The piece I'm talking about is a work by the successful German photographer Thomas Ruff, from his series *Zycles* (2008). Ruff has always been interested in the presumed objectivity of the photographic medium, and in the ambiguous relationship between representation and reality. The *Zycles* are photographs of mathematical formulas, discovered in some «antiquated 19th century books on electro-magnetism» [4], translated into a 3D software environment, recorded from different points of view and then printed on huge canvases. Again, the revolution has only just begun. These images are still turned into expensive objects and sold for a high price by a mainstream art gallery. But the seed has been planted – how much time will it take to grow into a tree?

We are in the midst of a major change. At the end of the process, not only the way we live, work, travel and communicate, but also the political and economical structures and the social organization we are used to will probably be fundamentally different from how they are now. In art, this change will be complete when the way we make, circulate and understand art is completely different from the way we do it now; and when the way we understand the difference between copies and original and between art and non-art will have adapted to the new models created by the information age. The most we can do now is to take our time, adapt to our new living conditions, be aware of the process going on and look to the most radical propositions around for signals of what is to come. In the awareness that we probably don't have to look that far: these signals are already here, in our computers.

[1] John Berger, *Ways of Seeing*, The British Broadcasting Corporation and Penguin Books, London 1972, p. 32.

[2] Tilman Baumgärtel, "Interview with Jodi", in *Telepolis*, 1997, online at www.heise.de/tp/r4/artikel/6/6187/1.html.

[3] Olia Lialina, "Flat against the wall", 2007, online at http://art.teleportacia.org/observation/flat_against_the_wall/.

[4] From the press release of the show at the Mai 36 Galerie in Zurich, Switzerland (September 12 – October 18 2008).

The legend of net.art

This text was written in 2005 for the catalogue of the show CONNESSIONI LEGGENDARIE. NET.ART 1995 – 2005, conceived by Luca Lampo ([epidemiC]) and organized in Milan by Luca Lampo, Marco Deseriis, 0100101110101101.org and myself. It was the first large-scale exhibition I was involved in, and I'm still profoundly indebted to it and the brand new perspective it proposed. CONNESSIONI LEGGENDARIE was probably the first serious attempt to talk about net.art as an avant-garde, and to tell and document its stories instead of devitalizing it by bringing bits and pieces of it into gallery space. Unfortunately the catalogue was in Italian, and the exhibition did not reach the international audience it was meant for.

Mythology has always played a vital role in art and its narration. From Leonardo to Duchamp, Caravaggio to De Chirico, Shakespeare to Jarry, all the greatest artists have knowingly encouraged the creation of a legendary superstructure around their identities, with the active participation of historians, narrators and contemporaries. Few of them have managed to live out their legends to the full: more often than not they have cleverly manipulated reality using the means of communication at their disposal, effortlessly donning their carefully constructed personalities on all public occasions and jealously guarding their private lives, concealing their own fragile truths behind an armor of mystification.

The historic avant-garde movements painstakingly perfected the weaponry of mystification, constructing solid castles on foundations of thin air: just think of Arthur Cravan, the anarchic dadaist performer, or Jacques Vaché, a posthumous legend created by the surrealists out of an epistolary exchange. The avant-garde movements get the credit for having transferred mythology from the individual plane of "genius" to the collective arena, lending the narration of the legend an unassailable coherence.

From this point of view, dada is a case in point: the narrative constructions overlap, intersect, and contradict each other, but the historic truths they conceal remain out of reach. And it was precisely this that transformed a group of mischief-makers, with little to contribute on the aesthetic front, into the most disruptive avant-garde movement of the 20th century. It would obviously be meaningless to explore dadaism apart from the legendary superstructure it created around itself: the mythopoesis is an integral part of the oeuvre, and one cannot exist without the other. If I was a more sophisticated critic I would go so far as to say that the construction of a legend becomes a necessity from the moment in which a work of art loses its "aura": the alternative is becoming a mere product, without any kind of added value.

Throughout the twentieth century mythopoesis was the strategy of choice used by all the movements which opposed the other great mechanism for the legitimization of art without an aura: the market and the museum. And strangely enough, as the myth-making machine perfected its tactics, it went increasingly underground, taking us from Dadaism to Fluxus to Situationism, Punk, Neoism and Luther Blissett. Meanwhile, contemporary art was getting ever more prosaic and incapable of forging superstructures. The exception that confirms the rule is Young British Art: a weak legend built around the stereotype of a group of "mad, bad and dangerous" young artists by a talented advertising executive in the service of a precise financial strategy.

All of which leads us to the fact that, at the beginning of the nineties, when a small group of artists scattered around the globe began experimenting with the internet, they found themselves in an ideal position to fashion a new legend. And they exploited the situation to perfection, giving rise to the greatest artistic set-up of the 20th century. Net.art, to be precise. But one thing at a time.

Working in an accessible, distributed medium, where the concepts of copy and original no longer have meaning, and property does not exist, the first net.artists were in no position to rely on the legitimization mechanisms of trade and exhibiting, which in any case they had a number of reservations about. On the other hand, however, they had got their hands on an extraordinary means of distribution and communication which forged a direct link between sender and receiver, which enabled them to reach the public at large with great ease, and manipulate people, the other media and the main vehicles of information with equal ease. Here was a medium that went so far as to encourage the creation of fictitious identities, because «on the web, no-one knows you're a dog». A medium that had already showed its potential to spawn legends like Condor, the elusive hacker Kevin Mitnick. And a medium that enabled people to work in networks, giving a small group of ground-breaking artists global connotations, and lending their work unprecedented impact.

The result is that, browsing through the "deposits" of net.art today, namely the archives of historic newsletters like Nettime, 7-11, Rhizome and Syndicate, the art historian gets the impression of perusing a heroic age recounted in real time by scores of poets who constructed their own legends piece by piece. This was done with a sense of irony befitting a post-modern avant-garde movement, which merely multiplied the levels of mystification. And they did it with the active participation of militant criticism, which robs anyone attempting a reliable reconstruction of events of even the barest glimmer of truth. Every e-mail, every essay, every interview, is another piece in the puzzle. As this book is.

Net.art produced and challenged the legend of its own genesis, the phrase «automatically generated by a piece of malfunctioning software» [1]; and recounted its first faltering steps, the meeting in Trieste (May 1996) and the London conferences in 1996 and 1997. It laid claim to founding fathers without ever taking a paternity test, and it told us its own story, step by step, presenting us with a conveniently pre-packaged version; it predicted the outcome of its encounter with the art world, and its own precocious gallery debut; it told of its own death and built itself an impregnable mausoleum, where its mortal remains attempt to crumble into dust, because this is the only way to ensure a legend true staying power.

Inconsistencies and contradictions, as we learned from dada, are an integral part of this hall of mirrors: enabling Alexei Shulgin to pronounce net.art dead, but continue to produce unforgettable projects; allowing 0100101110101101.ORG to hide their identity behind a series of zeros and ones all the while adopting a form of explicit openness that borders on the pornographic, in the project *Life Sharing* (2000), which granted the viewer complete access to their computer, and giving Vuk Cosic the opportunity to write:

> «My next idea is to set up an initiative where the greatest number of finished works by net.artists will be collected on a DVD and given to web masters to create mirror sites. At the same time I am starting my career as an artist, which makes this project impossible». [2]

As the legend was a collective invention, it is obviously impossible to identify the contributions of single individuals. We focus on a few, from which it is possible to select a number of particularly meaningful examples. Vuk Cosic, allegedly responsible for coining the term "net.art" – allegedly, because as a self-respecting dadaist he did not invent the term but came across it – has adopted a Duchampian attitude that has taken him from his first brilliant experiments to almost total inactivity. And we had been warned: «I go to the conferences. That is what net.art is». [3] The former archeologist turned net.artist and media archeologist turns out speeches on net.art with the same nonchalance that Duchamp made art playing chess. And he is in excellent company in this ironic form of self-historicization. Alexei Shulgin has inscribed his definition of net.art, his story, rules and even his future on genuine Tables of the Law, erecting a monument "aere perennius", as Horace would have put it. When net.art first made it into the galleries, Olia Lialina responded by setting up her very own made-to-measure museum online. While Jodi, the first mythological creature of net.art, the black hole that terrified, exalted and amused thousands of internet users, studied ways of getting their own legend into real-life gallery and museum venues. 0100101110101101.ORG, with the collaboration of a wider network known as d-i-n-a, organized events inviting the tutelary deities of their own highly (im)personal pantheon, under the telling title of the "Influencers". And in 2003, less than a decade from the beginning of the story we are telling, Josephine Bosma was already talking about a kind of nostalgic revival of net.art's "heroic period", in the context of a show meaningfully entitled "An archaeology of net.art". [4]

Like every self-respecting legend, net.art obviously has its heroic episodes, which are well-represented here: the theft of the Documenta X site, perpetrated by Vuk Cosic; the *Digital Hijack* etoy used to reveal itself to the world; the stunt pulled off by Cornelia Sollfrank, who managed to con one of the first institutional attempts to get a hold on net.art, by generating more than 200 female net.artists out of thin air. And the *Toywar*, in which net.art won its battle against the corporation baddies, then the series of masterful thefts by means of which 0100101110101101.ORG captured international attention in the space of a few months, becoming the Bonnie and Clyde of net.art, not to mention the front page stories of the feats of The Yes Men and *Vote-auction*.

Before concluding, there is one last question to answer: is net.art really dead? Obviously not. Its death, like its birth, is part of the legend, and the reality is very different. There are no movements that are born and then die, and what we have here is an oscillating flow of experimentation with the media and new technologies which spans the second half of the 20th century and extends into the new millennium. A flow made up of isolated experiences, key encounters and episodes of networking, with heroic battles and other times when things fell more into line with market forces. A flow in which the legend of net.art represents the great, indisputable masterpiece.

First published in: Luca Lampo, Marco Deseriis, Domenico Quaranta, *CONNESSIONI LEGGENDARIE. NET.ART 1995 – 2005*, catalogue of the exhibition, Mediateca Santa Teresa, Milan, 20 October – 10 November 2005. Ready-Made, Milan 2005. Translated by Anna Carruthers.

[1] Alexei Shulgin, "Net.art, The Origin", in *Nettime*, 18 March 1997.
[2] Vuk Cosic, "One Artist One Art System", in *net_condition*, 1999, http://on1.zkm.de/netcondition/projects/project15/bio_e
[3] Vuk Cosic, in Josephine Bosma, "Vuk Cosic Interview: net.art per se", in *Nettime*, 29 September 1997.
[4] Josephine Bosma, "The Dot on a Velvet Pillow – Net.art Nostalgia and net art today", 2003. In Per Platou (ed.), *Skrevet i stein. En net.art arkeologi [Written in Stone. A net.art archaeology]*, exhibition catalogue, Museet for Samtidskunst, Oslo, 22 March – 25 May 2003.

0100101110101101.ORG

This previously unpublished text was written in 2009 and talks about some of the first works of the net.art duo Eva and Franco Mattes, also known as 0100101110101101.ORG. The text focuses on the concept of identity theft and identity construction, two of the major issues raised by the work of the Italian couple.

«Jesus, strength and wisdom of God, awaken in us the love of the Holy Scriptures, where resounds the Father's voice, that illuminates and blares up, that feeds and comforts». Pope John Paul II, Prayer for the preparation of the Grand Jubilee 2000

When the collective 0100101110101101.ORG burst onto the scene between 1999 and 2000, it was like a firework exploding in the intricate mesh of the net, or as if a dozen snipers had suddenly started firing at the same target from different positions. It was difficult to establish their identity, but one thing for sure was that behind that codename there was a team, a fast-acting, extremely talented team. Their statements and interviews always featured different names. They inhabited the web as if it was their natural element. It was evident that they had been in training for a long time, before firing their first shot. They knew what to aim for and they always hit their target. They bombarded mailing lists and got the media in a flap, like the Gauls among the Capitoline geese. They began with a series of thefts, and claimed responsibility for two colossal hoaxes, one attacking the art system, the other the Vatican. Their links with Luther Blissett, their accents and the geographic location of the Darko Maver project placed them in Italy, in Bologna to be precise, but their roots were as mobile as their cultural references, which ranged from the American pranksters to the Balkan avant-garde Neue Slowenische Kunst. In time the aura of mystery gradually lifted, not least thanks to the total transparency of later works, *Life_Sharing* (2000 – 2003) and *Vopos* (2002). Then they themselves decided to clear up the identity question once and for all, or rather, flesh out two of their many fictitious identities, presenting themselves as Eva and Franco Mattes.

Their first public action dates back to February 1999: in a spectacular stunt, 0100101110101101.ORG downloaded the entire contents of Hell.com and published them on their own site, with one minor change to the interface which subverted the whole concept of the site. Hell.com was a private platform for artistic experimentation, like an online workshop closed to the public. Entrance was invitation-only, on a private basis, or on rare public occasions, such as the exhibition *Surface*, which opened in February 1999 and was reserved to the community of Rhizome. Which 0100101110101101.ORG just happened to be members of. In June 1999 it was the turn of Art.Teleportacia, the newly opened web gallery belonging to Russian artist Olia Lialina; then in September Jodi.org, one of the acknowledged masterpieces of net.art, was cloned.

A private site, an online gallery, a web-based work of art: 0100101110101101.ORG's heists wove a complex statement about the contradictions entailed in producing culture on the net, in a context characterized by the persistence of copyright but also the perfect reproducibility of data; all the hype surrounding interactivity, but also the 'closed' nature of works; attempts at commercialization, but also the death of the unique work of art. As they explained, naturally plagiarizing someone else:

> «Copies are more important than their original, although they do not differ from them. Copies contain not only all the parameters of the work that is being copied, but a lot more: the idea itself and the act of copying».
> [1]

Appropriating a work of art means interacting with it, using it in ways not foreseen by the artist. This can range from simple plagiary to the collage-based operation *Hybrids* (1998 - 1999), developed in that period, which restored the original revolutionary nature of the collage.

Initially, the way in which 0100101110101101.ORG used key techniques such as culture jamming, guerrilla communication, plagiarism and defacement had very little in common with other instances of media hacktivism. And 0100101110101101.ORG intentionally distanced itself from those:

> «If you do what we do with a work of art, the operation has a value in itself... If you steal the Disney site, you are acting against Disney... we are not interested in doing this kind of hacktivism. We work on other contradictions like originality and reproduction, authorship and network, copyright and plagiarism». [2]

The "copy trilogy" was completed in December 2001 with a work entitled *FTPermutations*, making way for another series dedicated to the theme of transparency (glasnost) of data and the omnipresence of surveillance. Like its predecessors, *FTPermutations* was a minimal piece of "performance" art which had an explosive effect. Having been invited to participate in the Korea Web Art Festival in Seoul, 0100101110101101.ORG uploaded its files on the show's FTP server as requested, but the night before the opening the collective changed the names of all the directories, thus dissociating the names of the artists (linked from the homepage) from their works. The artists mutinied, and the curator was fired. The collective, on the other hand, chose to see this as "permutation" rather than sabotage. They were asked for web art, digital products, and they made net.art, manipulating network protocols. "We have never produced anything. 0100101110101101.ORG only moves packages of information from one point to another, diverts their flow, observes changes, and eventually profits from them", they later explained. [3]

In the meantime their notoriety was growing, thanks also to having claimed responsibility for two spectacular projects ongoing since 1998: the *Darko Maver* operation and the project *Vaticano.org*, considered to be the very first internet coup. 0100101110101101.ORG purchased the domain www.vaticano.org, which at the time was still available, and published the entire contents of the Papacy's official site, www.vaticano.va there. They then got to work on a major edit, an operation midway between satire and what the Yes Men call "identity correction". Between learned quotes from the holy scriptures, the Pope and other high prelates they appropriated pop songs, and exalted free love, "brotherly intolerance" between religions, the oblivion of the senses and "international friendships". They invoked the success of student movements and claimed their own "duty to civil and electronic disobedience". In the *Intermediatic Decree on Communications Tools*, the "Great Cathodic Church" explained its "Total Domination Plan", in terms of "Technomoral Law", "Telesalvation", and "Holy Public Opinion", coolly referencing the anathemas of "Father" Mcluhan. Yet the power of the interface – that the Vatican, in a nod to tradition, has maintained intact up till now – was such that it fooled around 200,000 viewers in the space of a year (December 1998 – December 1999), who put in a total of 50,000 hours of navigation.

In December 1999 the Vatican, in a genuine operation of international espionage, put two and two together, but 0100101110101101.ORG managed to ensure that the silence in which the act of censorship was carried out was a deafening one.

Out of all 0100101110101101.ORG's works, *Vaticano.org* is probably the project which comes closest to politically-based media hacktivism. Yet once again, politics and ideology appear alien to the Italian collective. When asked «Can you change politics and social behaviour with your art work?» the answer was: «I don't care. My only responsibility is to be irresponsible». [4]

Vaticano.org was an act of pure narration, an identity appropriation designed to create a new subject, a new spectacular entity: "a Free Spirit Jubilee." In their words, «The Internet Coup is a spectacle for the Netizens, a hit performance for the masses, online for a year, every day and every night, this is Media Rock 'n' Roll!» [5]

This stance emerged with even greater clarity in two of the group's most recent creations: *Nikeground* (2003 - 2004) and *United We Stand* (2005 - 2006). In the former, at various levels of action (urban performance and net-based communications), they donned the guise of a giant multinational company – Nike – in the process of taking over a public urban area. The latter, meanwhile, was in the form of a marketing campaign to promote a non-existent film. While in the first media impact was sought, and achieved, thanks also to the reaction from Nike (who reported the artists for breach of copyright), in the second this dimension disappears, so much so that the project was exhibited in galleries (first in Bologna then in New York), as a work substantially in line with the public performance. In narrowing the gap between action and claim 0100101110101101.ORG revealed that its real objective was not media impact, but the production of meaning, the construction of a narration or a performance-based situation exploring one of the key themes of their oeuvre: identity as a narrative construct, a pile of symbols which can be infinitely manipulated, and if need be plagiarized, the fruit of the interweaving of different flows of information. In their works identity can be built from scratch using a few narrative stereotypes (*artist maudit* Darko Maver), or a corporate image (Nike, the Vatican) which is both highly distinctive and powerfully conditioning, to be subverted and rewritten. A tenuous identity (Europe) can be unmasked when seen through the narrative stereotypes and iconography of a Hollywood action blockbuster, while the personal identity of Eva and Franco Mattes, also known as 0100101110101101.ORG, actually becomes more elusive the more details are added, and, paradoxically, the more 'constructed' it appears, the more authentic it feels.

[1] Uri Pasovsky, "Life imitates art and art imitates itself", in *Haaretz*, 19 Sept 2000.
[2] Tilman Baumgärtel, "No Artists, just Spectators. An interview with the artist group 0100101110101101.ORG which became famous for copying art websites", in *Telepolis*, 9 Dec 1999.
[3] Jaka Zeleznikar, "Now you're in my computer. Interview with 0100101110101101.ORG", in *Mladina*, January 2001.
[4] Alain Bieber, "How to provoke today? Alain Bieber interviews 0100101110101101.ORG on Nike Ground", in *Rebel:Art Magazine*, 1 April 2004.
[5] [0100101110101101.ORG], "Vaticano.org: The First Internet Coup", online at http://0100101110101101.org/home/vaticano.org/story.html

Generative Ars

This text was written in 2006 for the first edition of the festival C.STEM, a first (and, unfortunately, short-lived) attempt to create an event showcasing recent experiments with software and generative processes on Italian soil. Playing on the ambiguity of the label "Generative Art", the text defines it as a technique (ars, not art), that attempts to bring international debate onto more solid ground.

Almost fifty years since the term first appeared, for the art audience Generative Art is still a mystery. Not that it is difficult to understand, the opposite is actually more the case. The real problem seems to be finding a place for it on the contemporary art scene. Artists like Casey Reas, Ben Fry, Joshua Davis, Yugo Nakamura, Marius Watz, John Maeda, Philip Galanter and Golan Levin, who move freely from art to pure programming to visual design and back, keep astonishing the public, and the fact that the term "Generative Art" is used also in relation to music, poetry, architecture and industrial design doesn't help either.

I believe that the problem resides in the term, or, more precisely, in the way it is usually understood. The succession of art labels such as Pop Art, Minimal Art, Conceptual Art, Digital Art and so on, throughout the 20th century, make us think that Generative Art should be interpreted in the same way: as a style definition, a trend or an art movement. Yet, in order to understand Generative Art, you need to step back, to consider terms like "ars combinatoria" or, more in general, to consider the Latin meaning of the word "ars" rather than the present meaning of it. Like the Greek "techné", the Latin word "ars" indicates a technique, a structured set of rules and acts that allow somebody to produce something. Generative Art is, in fact, a technique, a method, a practice, a way of proceeding. This element is present in all definitions of Generative Art, but it probably deserves to be highlighted. Take the seminal definition proposed by Philip Galanter in 2003, for instance:

> «Generative art refers to any art practice where the artist uses a system, such as a set of natural language rules, a computer program, a machine, or other procedural invention, which is set into motion with some degree of autonomy, contributing to or resulting in a completed work of art.» [1]

This definition, which is appreciable under many aspects, still places too much emphasis on the term "art" to be considered really comprehensive, but is nevertheless a good start.

A technique, then: which can be variously used by artists, musicians, architects, scientists and designers. Sometimes, all these roles converge on the same person, but we must be careful: as Marius Watz says, «I work and think very differently when creating art and design» [2]. A technique which is based on the application of a system's internal rules – as Galanter observes, ordered, unordered or complex – in order to produce something. A technique which pre-exists the computer era, but which has received crucial input from its inception. A technique which has often re-appeared in the art world, and which artists have contributed to defining, but also a technique which is not only artistic; and which, in its present version, derives from a gathering of different fields, from algorithmic composition to digital animation, from the underground rave scene and vj culture to architecture. A technique – and for those who attribute derogatory connotations to the word, this needs to be said– which is above all a philosophy and an instrument of knowledge.

At this point, we can narrow it down and specify that from here on in we will be talking about the artistic use of generative methods, and, in particular, about those artistic practices where the instructions consist of digital code and where the performer is a computer. This brings us to our first question: is the work of art the process or the result? The generative program or the generated work? This is a difficult question. My answer is: the first, the second, or both, according to the author's wishes. As Philip Galanter notes, «what generative artists have in common is how they make their work, but not why they make their work or even why they choose to use generative systems in their art practice.» [3] Galanter, like others, insists on the process, linking Generative Art to the long tradition of procedural art; others point to the result, yet the best stance is one that includes both possibilities. As Marius Watz puts it: «The artist describes a rule-based system external to him/herself that either produces works of art or is itself a work of art» [4].

For this reason, the use of generative methods is essentially neutral, and does not have any particular ideological implications. Nevertheless, this practice challenges contemporary art in a very interesting way, pushing it towards profound innovation.

First of all, the use of generative methods tends to cast the figure of the author in a completely new light. We have said that Generative Art is based on a process which, «set into motion with some degree of autonomy» [5], produces a complete work of art. In other words, there are two acts of creation, one following the other, and two distinct "authors": the person who chooses the system that will be used and writes the program – the set of instructions, the algorithm – to be performed; and the person – or the thing – that materially performs the program. The person that we, albeit it with reservations, continue to view as "the author", only writes the instructions, that are performed – with a margin of interpretation which can be considered relevant – by somebody or something else. The author, therefore, sets in motion a process which develops autonomously, and often unpredictably. It is less like dealing with an artist, in terms of our usual conception of artist, and more like observing a lesser god, who activates a system and then sits back and watches it come to life.

In effect this is not far from truth. After many centuries, Generative Art returns to the idea of art as an "imitation of life", imitating not so much life's external appearance, but its dynamics. We must go back to the initial problem, the question of an author who seems to share his or her role with a machine, and sometimes hand it over completely. Which of the two is the artist? And, above all: can a machine produce a work of art?

There is an interesting piece by Casey Reas that can help answer this question.

MicroImage, presented at Ars Electronica in 2003, is an installation that features the same code running on three machines, positioned side by side. The code is the same, but the output is completely different, because it changes every time it is performed. The artist has written the code, but the machine has a wide margin of operative freedom. Nevertheless, the artwork is neither the code written by the artist, nor one of the endless outputs proposed by the machine: it is the combination of the idea, the code and the output, organized in the form of an installation. At least in this case: because Casey Reas can choose – as he did – to isolate an image, decide that this has an autonomous aesthetic value, print it and sell it as a work of art; or record one of the endless productions of the code and show it as a video animation. Or even, as Sol LeWitt used to do with his *Wall Drawings*, say that the idea – captured in a certain form through a given set of instructions – and not one of its many possible realizations, is the work of art. The author is dead, long live the author!

If the author delegates the tangible implementation of the program to the machine, we might be led to believe that the author does not actually require any particular artistic talent. In these terms, Generative Art could be seen as the culmination of the "deskilling" process started by Duchamp and developed by contemporary art. Nevertheless, if you really think about it, generative artists have to be skilled, and to a high degree: all the artists who use generative methods are skilled programmers, and proud of it. The code that they write is not hidden, but prominently flaunted. What emerges once more is the figure of the artist as an artisan and attention to the manual side of contemporary art. This manual aspect is rooted in in-depth knowledge that entails a reflection on complex systems, computer theory, and so on. In other words, Generative Art bridges the gap between theory and practice, between the "bête comme un peintre" and the figure of the philosopher artist that has dominated the 20th century.

Finally there is another system of values, rejected by 20th century art, which the use of generative methods has revalued: art as a search for beauty, as a reflection on form, as a process of knowledge. Aesthetic judgments are often present in Generative Art, in relation to both the code and the final result. Generative Art seems to have learned from pop culture – one of the spheres where it has its roots, thanks to electronic music, animation and vj culture – what art, for a century, has tried to forget: that work on form is not a sterile aestheticism, an escape from reality, something fashionably superficial, but an extraordinarily powerful way of investigating our time. Beauty is also about the beauty of nature: generative processes often imitate natural mechanisms, and offer insight into them, showing us that «the universe itself is a generative system», as Galanter puts it [6].

All these considerations about Generative Art in general can be verified in the practices of the artists present at the first C.STEM event. All of these artists operate in the intersections between different creative fields, and most have a difficult relationship with the world of traditional art. This is due both to contemporary art's jaded view of new media experimentalism, and to the aforementioned difficulties in defining the place of Generative Art. The innovative elements we have explored paradoxically make this art to some extent more hedonistic, more radical (and more difficult to understand) than the art which uses the new media in a more conceptual, ideological way. Perhaps the contemporary art world will only be able to accept Generative Art when it is able to appreciate the profound connection between these artists and the work of famous masters like John Cage, Sol LeWitt and Hans Haacke, and understand their innovative power.

In the meantime, the artists are not wasting their time complaining. Marius Watz is a Norwegian artist who started working at the beginning of the Nineties, creating visual animations for rave concerts. This practice, and his activity as a designer, have given rise to his exaggerated, baroque aesthetic – something deeply different from the majority of Generative Art, which, aesthetically speaking, looks mainly to Minimalism and the tradition of geometric abstraction. Set against Philip Galanter's proposal for «a maximal art with minimal means» [7], we have Watz's caustic aphorisms: «more is more» and «there is no culture like pop culture» [8]; he flaunts superficiality and hedonism, but under this surface there is an awareness that makes his work less a mirror of his culture of reference, and more a distillation, a reflection on it:

> «My visual style tends towards extremes, taking color strategies and form systems that clearly have an origin in the pop culture, but are exaggerated to the point where conventional aesthetic expectations break down. I work with code as a way to create visual systems, exploring the material qualities of different algorithmic approaches, seeking to surprise myself as much as anyone else.» [9]

Surprise is an important component in the poetics of Generative Art, where the artist, as we have seen, is often the enchanted observer of a process which develops in unpredictable directions. This emerges even more when, as in the case of Fabio Franchino, the casual components of the process are underlined. The project *Kinetoh* consists of a series of studies on sign, form and color, producing ultra high definition images. Franchino activates the process and leaves it to develop slowly on his computer screen, hour after hour. From time to time, he goes back to observe it, and if he finds a particularly surprising, or just beautiful, configuration, he fixes it on a frame, then transforms it into an autonomous artwork. The artist keeps for himself the world which came into being before his eyes, offering us only a few fragments which, for him, represent the most significant images. In the introduction to the project, Franchino quotes Edward de Bono: «Chance doesn't have limits, the imagination, on the other hand, does.» *Kinetoh* is a collection of memories of a voyage to an unknown land situated on the border between imagination and the potential of chance.

If Watz's work is loud and excessive, Alessandro Capozzo's reveals a sober, rigorous, minimal aesthetic. The chromatic aspect is pared down, with a preference for pale colors, often set against brighter ones (but always a two-color selection). Forms position themselves in meshes, aggregations of lines, arborescent patterns, and often develop following organic dynamics, obtained through the use of artificial life algorithms. Capozzo's aesthetic is that of the code, but while, on one hand it displays its mathematical and algebraic nature, on the other it reveals a delicate musicality, a poetry of the ephemeral, which arises from a detailed observation of life: like in *Exuvia* (2006), an installation created in collaboration with Katja

Noppes, that plays on the uncertain limit between life and its pale "shroud", and whose title refers to the exoskeleton of a larva.

The dimension of the installation also appears to suit Limiteazero (Paolo Rigamonti and Silvio Mondino), who define themselves as a studio of architecture, media art and media design. Interested in mediation between virtual and real space, Limiteazero occasionally uses generative methods in order to give life to "active metaphors" - to quote the title of one of their works - that enable the senses to perceive the constituent elements and structures of immaterial spaces through sounds, forms and colors. Again, the frame of reference is life, even if here organic life is replaced by the life of the network and the world beyond the mirror that is, for us, the space of bits.

First published in Domenico Quaranta (ed), *C.STEM. Art Electronic Systems and Software Art*, Teknemedia, Turin 2006.

[1] In Philip Galanter, "What is Generative Art? Complexity Theory as a Context for Art Theory", in *Generative Art Proceedings*, Milan 2003. Online at www.philipgalanter.com/downloads/ga2003_paper.pdf.
[2] In Domenico Quaranta, "GENERATIVE (INTER)VIEWS. Recombinant conversation with four software artists", in D. Quaranta (ed), *C.STEM. Art Electronic Systems and Software Art*, Teknemedia, Turin 2006.
[3] In Philip Galanter, "Complexism and evolutionary art", in Juan J. Romero, Penousal Machado (eds.), *The Art of Artificial Evolution*, Springer 2008, p. 320.
[4] In Thomas Petersen, "Generative Art Now. An Interview with Marius Watz", in *Artificial.dk*, 20 September 2005. Online at www.artificial.dk/articles/watz.htm.
[5] P. Galanter 2003.
[6] Ivi.
[7] Thomas Petersen and Kristine Ploug, "'Generative art is as old as art'. An interview with Philip Galanter", in *Artificial.dk*, September 6 2004. Online at www.artificial.dk/articles/galanter.htm.
[8] T. Petersen 2005.
[9] Ivi.

LeWitt's Ideal Children

This article was written for an Italian contemporary art magazine in 2005, in an attempt to introduce a topic prevalent in the international debate to the local audience: Software Art and its connections with early conceptual art. Despite its popular approach and some juvenile naivety, the article is original in its attempt to collate various scattered notes into a "theory". Today, "Software Art" as a category is no longer fashionable, but much computer-based art can still benefit from this approach.

I

«... in a way we are Duchamp's ideal children», the Slovenian artist Vuk Cosic declared [1] in an interview back in 1997. It would be hard to find a better summary of one of Net Art criticism's core concepts: namely the belief that Net Art has its roots in Dadaism, passing through Fluxus, Situationism, the Neo Avant-garde movements of the 60s and Conceptual Art. No doubt strategy played an important role in this genealogical statement. Yet this alone does not account for a phenomenon that was entirely unforeseeable in the mid-nineties. A phenomenon – Net Art – that didn't have anything to do with the post-modern refinement of the digital media of the time, or with what was happening in the art world. The internet seemed to convey expectations that had long been considered dead: a general rejection of the art system and of those persistent dogmas such as the uniqueness and non-reproducibility of the work of art; the deconstruction of the medium; the dematerialization of art; a new political inspiration. In short, only the profound nature of the medium can help explain this "Modernism revisited in color", to quote Mario Schifano's famous tribute to Futurism. Like it or not, if we can still talk about political art, appropriation, process, open work and new moderns, it is largely thanks to the advent of the World Wide Web.

Software Art grew out of this situation, and unsurprisingly inherited its genealogy, or rather, the tendency to reconstruct its own family tree. It is interesting to note how, in Software Art theory, the formulation of a definition continually interweaves with this retrospective investigation. Of course this is only natural: the hypothesis to be proven is that software – namely an encoded sequence of formal instructions – can be art; and what better than a precedent could save us from a lot of useless complications? Hence, Florian Cramer's famous statement that *Composition 1961 Nr 1, January 1,* a piece of paper bearing the phrase "Draw a straight line and follow it" by the Fluxus artist La Monte Young, can be viewed as a perfect example of Software Art. Clearly, through La Monte Young, this recognition extends to all art based on the execution of a formally encoded process. And it was again Cramer who, in his seminal essay "Concepts, Notations, Software, Art" [2], quotes Tristan Tzara's instructions for writing a Dada poem and mentions John Cage and Sol LeWitt, artists we will return to shortly.

The most interesting thing in this framework is that it is not at all a matter of misappropriation. In other words, we are not confronted with a son who recognizes a father who, in turn, if he were to find out, would immediately disown him; on the contrary, it is a question of a completely verifiable pedigree that is attested by some important events. Let's give it a go: Software Art is conceptual art's acknowledged son, its sole heir, able not only to fully take on its heritage but also to solve some of its perplexing difficulties.

Jewish Museum, New York 1970. Jack Burnham, an American theoretician and curator, organizes an exhibition featuring some conceptual artists alongside representatives of the creative research on computer technology. Joseph Kosuth, Vito Acconci, John Baldessari, Les Levine and Hans Haacke share the playground with Theodor H. Nelson (the inventor of hypertext) and the Architecture Machine Group, directed by Nicholas Negroponte. The exhibition, called *Software: Information Technology: Its New Meaning for Art*, aims to highlight the effects of the newborn information age on artistic production. In the catalogue Burnham stresses the fact that «the public can personally respond to programmatic situations structured by artists» [3], with or without using computers. As Edward A. Shanken wrote about him:

> «*Software* was predicated on the ideas of "software" and "information technology" as metaphors for art. He conceived of "software" as parallel to the aesthetic principles, concepts, or programs that underlie the formal embodiment of the actual art objects, which in turn parallel "hardware".» [4]

Software was neither the first nor the only declaration of a relationship between the advent of conceptual art and the rising information age: that very same year, the Museum of Modern Art in New York proposed a show on conceptual art curated by Kynaston McShine, and significantly entitled *Information*. Yet, today Burnham's idea of software as "metaphor for art", and his emphasis on process, sound like a prophecy about the future rise of Software Art.

A year before *Software*, in January 1969, Sol LeWitt published his "Sentences on Conceptual Art". This seminal text included statements such as:

> «10. Ideas can be works of art; they are in a chain of development that may eventually find some form. All ideas need not be made physical. [...] 27. The concept of a work of art may involve the matter of the piece or the process in which it is made. [...] 29. The process is mechanical and should not be tampered with. It should run its course.» [5]

LeWitt's *Wall Drawings* are the perfect application of these theories: art exists as instruction, idea put on paper; its execution is a purely mechanical process that does not depend on the artist, but can be entrusted to an executor.

Thirty five years later, in June 2004, the American artist and programmer Casey Reas wondered: why not entrust art to a machine, then? His reasoning was simple:

> «The relation between LeWitt and his draftsperson is often compared to the relation between a composer and performer, but I think it's also

valid to look at the comparison between a programmer and the entity of execution. LeWitt writes programs for people to execute and interpret rather than for machines.» [6]

Taking these ideas to an extreme, Reas created *[software] structures* (2004), a project exhibited on Artport, the online gallery of the Whitney Museum. With LeWitt's consent, Reas converted three of his *Wall Drawings* into a form that could be interpreted by a program, but sought to keep the inevitable ambiguity of natural language; he then introduced a human variable, asking three artist friends to interpret the same "structure", and a formal one, using two different languages to display the code. The passage from human language to machine language involved some corrections. But, as Reas stated, «If this is a work of conceptual art, the concept should remain regardless of the medium.» [7]

As everybody knows, the greatest revolution of conceptual art was the rejection of the art object and the introduction of a totally dematerialized art (Lucy Lippard), made up of ideas and processes. At that time, a statement like that could not last for long. Collectors and museums soon began to confuse the work with its very execution: LeWitt's wall paintings made us forget the concept they represent, Art & Language archives became, as "installations", more important than the documents they hosted, and Lawrence Wiener's statements gained such visual majesty that the fact that they were originally purely spoken phrases became of secondary importance. Conceptual art had lost its radicalism, and the reaction was not long in coming.

[software] structures came about with the aim of answering a simple question: «Is the history of conceptual art relevant to the idea of software as art?» [8] At this point, it could make sense to reverse this question, and ask: «Is the idea of software as art relevant to the history of conceptual art?» The answer is yes. Software art brings immateriality back to conceptual art; the prevalence of the idea over the product, of the process over the result, of the code over the output. By turning the executor into a machine, any doubt about the artistic nature of the finished product is removed. Art must be sought elsewhere: in the "code", the modern reincarnation of the "concept" in the digital age.

Software Art picks up the conceptual path at the point where it entered a dead end; and the medium it uses ensures that the crisis won't be repeated.

I have called Software Art conceptual art's "acknowledged son". Sol LeWitt's recent career itself seems to lend credit to this thesis. In 1998 the Sandra Gering Art Gallery of New York organized a group show entitled *Formulations*, setting the work of LeWitt alongside that of Hanne Darboven and the software artist John F. Simon, Jr. Furthermore, his latest sculptures, called *Splotches* (2005), are molded out of fiberglass and painted by a machine that follows a set of instructions able to regulate both the shape and distribution of color over their surface. It's a pity that the instructions are not publicly available anymore: in that case, another executor might be able to re-enact the process that created these fascinating colored blobs. All we can do is hope that the next *Splotches* will be open source.

II

In May 2002 the first edition of the Read_me Festival – the first festival entirely dedicated to Software Art – took place in Moscow. A year later, in January 2003, the platform Runme.org, the largest available online artistic software "storehouse", was launched. On awarding the prizes, the Festival jury formulated a definition which was to become a classic: «We consider Software Art to be art whose material is algorithmic instruction code and / or which addresses cultural concepts of software.» [9] Two years later, in a seminal paper again debated at Read_me, the Danish art critic Jacob Lillemose [10] stated that the slash dividing the two sentences, instead of acting as a link between the two definitions, seemed to open a break: on the one hand formalistic research focused on the algorithm and its dynamics, while on the other what he termed a "cultural vision" which roots software in the socio-political context it emerges from. In 2003, Florian Cramer [11] also noticed the existence of two distinct trends in Software Art, that he called "Software Formalism" and "Software Culturalism"; yet Lillemose went a little further, going back to two different historical roots that he singled out in two ramifications of Conceptual Art.

The first trend, focusing on the aesthetics of code and programming languages, describes code as a process to analyze, a series of instructions to apply or the starting point for a visual work taking place on the interface. This trend has affinities with two very different ramifications of Conceptual Art, namely the linguistic trend of Joseph Kosuth and Sol LeWitt and the process-oriented work by John Cage and La Monte Young. And as we noted in the first chapter of this text, it is above all LeWitt who seems to represent the missing link in the chain.

In 1997 the American artist John F. Simon Jr. made *Every Icon*, a simple Java Applet whose function was to show every icon displayable within a 32 x 32 square grid (the standard size of a desktop icon). Rather than being a conceptual-inspired work of Software Art, *Every Icon* could be described as the last conceptual masterpiece, a proper sublimation of the process: its mission is easy, but the rigor with which it is observed opens a never-ending process, that turns into a reflection on time and eternity, comparable to Roman Opalka's work. Besides, the work's interface is so simple that *Every Icon* – formalized by Simon either as an on-line work or as a single object inclusive of hardware (an LCD display) and software – functions entirely as a describable and recordable concept: «Given: A 32x32 Grid; Allowed: Any element of the grid to be black or white; Shown: Every Icon.» As the artist states,

> «While *Every Icon* is resolved conceptually, it is irresolvable in practice. In some ways the theoretical possibilities outdistance the time scales of both evolution and imagination.» [12]

Simon's engagement with the formalistic trend of Software Art becomes evident in the minimal aesthetics of his following work, again aimed at creating abstract interfaces – prints, drawings or hardware panels assembled by the artist himself – which display an algorithmic operation, and going back from Minimalism to older models, but not for that any less attractive, such as Piet Mondrian and Paul Klee.

Simon pays homage above all to the latter in his latest work, which is both the summing up of twenty years of work, a drawing tool everyone can use, and a reflection on the way a fluid medium like software enables various avant-garde intuitions to be brought up to date. Published by Printed Matter, Inc. in collaboration with the Whitney Museum of New York – which offers some of the tools on its site – *Mobility Agents. A Computational Sketchbook v1.0* (2005) [13] is a CD-rom accompanied by a booklet. There, Simon describes the birth of the three tools that make up the software, capable of creating complex shapes starting from very simple input: a point, a curved or straight line drawn at different speeds. The anomaly lies in the fact that these instruments are subordinated to the gesture, to the impulsive nature of the improvised sketch, and that instead of imitating traditional painting tools (brush, spray can) they are oriented toward representative drawing or photo-realistic graphics, encouraging abstract research.

Simon has not written software which draws, but software to draw, making it possible to work on both levels: programming (which here should be read as "creative writing", since it actually creates) and abstract drawing. Code – the same tool which initiated *Every Icon*'s radical Conceptualism – now allows him to be a "painter" again without denying any of those premises: after having delved into the catalogue of possibilities, he has simply made his choice.

The other Software Art trend is in a diametrically opposite direction, that of Cramer's "Software Culturalism". On one hand, it has its origins in the world of alternative software and "software as culture" (Matthew Fuller), namely the belief that software is not a neutral tool, but the fruit of a specific culture and ideology; while on the other hand, as Lillemose points out, it refers to two other inflexions of Conceptual Art: the political stance of Hans Haacke, Dan Graham, Victor Burgin, Gordon Matta-Clark, and the performance-based work of Vito Acconci, Bruce Nauman and Chris Burden. Making use of the term "contextual art", theorized by Peter Weibel in the 70s and taken up again in 1993 for the exhibition *Contextual Art. Art of the 90s*, Lillemose states that "Software Culturalism" belongs to the "contextual family", inaugurated by Conceptual Art, which «criticized the art institution, a.k.a. the white cube, as an oppressive and restrictive space that only accepted a certain type of art and a certain type of aesthetics.» [14]

Of course, Software Art is not specifically criticizing the art world, as the institutional critique did; its target is, more broadly, the current social and political situation, against which it sets radical, alternative, or subversive instruments, capable of subverting social practices and cultural forms. In this sense the software projects by the Austrian duo UBERMORGEN.COM can be considered particularly emblematic.

Based in Vienna, UBERMORGEN.COM was born as a dotcom devoted to a particularly virulent form of media activism, renamed "Media Aktionism" in homage to the Viennese Actionism of the 70s. In 2000, UBERMORGEN.COM achieved international visibility with *Vote-Auction*, a website that, during the American elections, offered citizens the chance to put their vote up for auction to the highest bidder, turning the undoubted economic value of a vote into real money. The project, unfortunately, garnered not only an entire episode of *Burden of Proof*, the CNN legal program, but also a slew of charges, and a series of injunctions sent by an (American) court to the group's (Swiss) server to close the site down (as promptly happened). *The Injunction Generator* (2003) is a sarcastic denunciation of this paradoxical situation (American jurisdiction does not cover Switzerland, and neither can an injunction be sent by e-mail) transforming the injustice which UBERMORGEN.COM suffered into a public service: everyone can go on the project's site and fill in an online form, addressing it to the server of a site that one wants to delete from the Web. The software sends out an official injunction, and informs us whether our attack was successful or not. The work is a masterpiece of dark humor, formally moderate but conceptually explosive in its depiction of the internet as a no-man's land where the law of the jungle is in force, and turning the illegality it uses against the law itself. Highly skilled at creating false business identities, UBERMORGEN.COM declared that the work was a project by IP-NIC (Internet Partnership for No Internet Content); in turn, the generated documents were "[F]originals", forged original documents (at this point, it is almost superfluous to mention the authenticity certificates by the pre-conceptual artist Piero Manzoni): exactly like the bank statements generated by the *Bank Statement Generator* (2005), a software which keeps us up to date, in a rather unorthodox way, with our account. In the belief that authenticity is a collective hallucination, UBERMORGEN.COM sows the seeds of doubt in the faith we place in a highly unreliable banking system.

Lastly, the very recent *GWEI* (*Google Will Eat Itself*, 2005), made in collaboration with Alessandro Ludovico and Paolo Cirio, shows how it is possible to turn business into an instrument of struggle against the establishment. The project uses the Google Adsense advertisement tool: a system that, when requested by the user, inserts various links to potentially interesting businesses in the user's site. When a visitor clicks on one of these links, the site owner earns a small sum which can become considerable if the site is a popular one. In the case of *GWEI*, real users and artificially simulated users raise the site's earnings, and when Google's checks arrive they are immediately reinvested in Google shares. In other words, *GWEI* is a slow but infallible system to devour Google using of its own money, and eat away at one of the strongest businesses in the world through advertising. It may or may not function: what matters is its critical and imaginative power, the celibate machine that, in a surprising way, turns capitalism and advertising into absurd instruments of struggle. In other words, the concept. Also known as software.

At this point, we are far removed from LeWitt. But Software Art is as varied as Conceptual Art, whose complex family tree Software Art references through the voices of artists and critics. We may or may not believe in this rhizomatic pedigree that is also, as we have said, a precise cultural strategy aimed at enabling Software Art to come out from the isolation that the art world persists in relegating it to. Of course, the artists already have some documents ready to prove it: forged original documents.

First published in two parts in the Italian magazine *Arte e Critica* (Issue 44, December 2005 and Issue 45, March 2006); an English version was published in the online review *Hz Journal*, (January 9, 2007).

[1] In Tilman Baumgaertel, "Interview with Vuk Cosic", in *Nettime*, June 30, 1997.

[2] Florian Cramer, "Concepts, Notations, Software, Art", March 23, 2003, online at http://userpage.fu-berlin.de/~cantsin.

[3] Jack Burnham, "Notes on Art and Information Processing", in Jack Burnham (ed.), *Software: Information Technology: Its New Meaning for Art*, exhibition catalogue, New York, Jewish Museum 1970.

[4] Edward A. Shanken, "The House That Jack Built: Jack Burnham's Concept of 'Software' as a Metaphor for Art", in *Leonardo*, Volume 6, Number 10, November 1998.

[5] Sol LeWitt, "Sentences on Conceptual Art", in *0-9*, New York, no. 5, January 1969.

[6] Casey Reas, "[software] structures", June 2004, online at http://artport.whitney.org/commissions/softwarestructures/.

[7] Ivi.

[8] Ivi.

[9] AAVV, "Read_Me 1.2 Jury Statement", May 2002, online at www.runme.org/project/+statement/.

[10] Jacob Lillemose, "A Re-declaration of Dependence. Software art in a cultural context it can't get out of", in *Read_me 2004*, online at www.artnode.org/art/lillemose/readme2004.html.

[11] Florian Cramer, Op. cit.

[12] John F. Simon Jr., "Every Icon Statement", in *Parachute*, January 1997, online at www.numeral.com/articles/paraicon/paraicon.html.

[13] John F. Simon Jr., *Mobility Agents. A Computational Sketchbook v1.0*, Whitney Museum & Printed Matter, Inc., New York, 2005.

[14] Jacob Lillemose, Op. cit.

F for Fake: Or how I Learned to Manipulate the Media to Tell the Truth

Media manipulation is probably one of the greatest issues of the new millennium. Now more than ever, the truth is unstable, nebulous and difficult to grasp, hidden under layers and layers of information. But if the media manipulate truth, they in turn can be manipulated to interfere with the flow of information, so as to make it clearer or even denser. This article aims to explain the rules at play in today's European net art, and reflect on the relationship between reality and fiction, information and manipulation, the artificial and the authentic, drawing on the latest striking fake by 0100101110101101.org (United We Stand), UBERMORGEN.COM's [F]originals (forged originals) and the cruel hyper-realism of the Where-next website (Molleindustria + Guerrigliamarketing).

Branding and identity

I am a European citizen. I vote for the European parliament, I can travel freely among the countries of the Union, I pay for my cigarettes in Euro. My European identity has millennia of history behind it, yet there is something lacking. I don't have a football team that sings the European anthem, hand on heart, and the sight of the European flag fails to strike a chord in me. The fact is that since it became a federation, Europe, which has always existed, has not succeeded in manufacturing any foundation mythology. There was no long march towards Europe, no European resistance, no European war of independence. Not that a war is necessary. We are in the 21st century and companies like Nike and Coca Cola have had all the time needed to teach us that there are other ways to get people to identify completely with a symbol, a lifestyle, an idea. It is due to this that it seems perfectly legitimate to do away with the historic identity of one of the key public areas in Europe – Karlsplatz in Vienna – and replace it with the "brand identity" of one of the world's most famous multinational companies.

It was in September 2003 that the hoax news of the transformation of Karlsplatz into Nikeplatz spread around the globe, and the creators of the spoof – Eva and Franco Mattes aka 0100101110101101.ORG – found themselves embroiled in a risky law suit with the multinational, that they ended up winning.

In 2004, shortly after their victory, they declared:

> «Nike, like all the modern multinationals, is not a company, but an idea. An idea represented by a brand. It is an intangible entity, an abstract message, and an enormous advertising machine... And because it is so intangible, what really counts is how people perceive Nike. Its profits depend on its popularity, its success depends on the image that people have of it, not on the quality of the products it sells». [1]

The project *United We Stand*, also launched by 0100101110101101.ORG, at the end of 2005, can be seen as the flip-side of this concept. Instead of tackling the intangible aura of a multinational company, 0100101110101101.ORG attempted to promote a product without an aura: Europe. Throughout the twentieth century the film industry, and Hollywood in particular, has proved to be an extraordinary tool for mythopoeia and propaganda, capable of imposing an ideal way of life (the American way of life) on the entire planet, along with a new Mount Olympus peopled by film stars. This is why it seemed like a natural choice to use the medium of film to perform the important mission of giving Europe a soul and an identity.

The twentieth century is over. The film industry is losing its importance in the media world, and its ability to embody, and renew, some of the great collective legends. This is why United We Stand looks faintly ridiculous, as does the European flag flying in the middle of the poster [2]. It is not the production of an actual film, but a promotional campaign for a film that doesn't exist. «Working on an imaginary film is the best way to talk about an imaginary concept: Europe», the duo declared [3]. The result was a massive marketing campaign which invaded public areas – with posters up around the cities of Berlin, Brussels, Barcelona, Bologna, Bangalore and New York – and media space, publicizing a media object that did not exist, but was perfectly capable of generating noise. An empty space makes its presence felt by means of communication strategies, forcing us to take a long hard look at the problems with something else which doesn't exist: Europe.

Forged originals

As Bruce Sterling [4] points out, «fake projects, like protesters' street puppets, are so common they threaten to become a genre». Manipulating the media is not the exclusive preserve of artists, quite the contrary. While Eva and Franco Mattes are the heirs of a long tradition, from American pranksters to the Luther Blissett network, lobbies, political parties, corporations and even the institutions are now increasingly resorting to manipulating the media. Now that traditional marketing and propaganda tools are proving to be increasingly ineffective, media manipulation is turning into the real media tool of the 21st century. Media manipulation has brought us fictitious proof for justifying a war, and put out low resolution video messages on the web to keep the war going; it is present in tapped phone conversations handed over to the newspapers, which are completely genuine, but which contain a mixture of meaning and crackle, chit chat and crime, capable of eliciting some startling responses. One recent episode in Italy shows just how widespread it is. In order to support the position of the centre-right coalition in a referendum, the Mediaset group broadcast a commercial that entirely resembled an official broadcast but provided only partial information about the referendum. This little masterpiece of modern-day political propaganda sits perfectly with the definition of "[F]original" (forged original) which was dreamt up by the Austrian duo UBERMORGEN.COM (Lizvlx/Hans Bernhard) to describe almost all their works:

«forged original document; either forged or authentic document or forged and authentic: a [F]original is always original and unique. [F]originals are pixels on screens or substance on material [i.e. ink on paper]. [F]originals are not pragmatic - they are absurd. They do not tell you whether they are real or forged - there is no original but also no fully forged / faked document. Foriginals can be human or machine generated; Foriginals are digital or analogue». [5]

This concept came to light after the masterful operation *Vote Auction* (2000), during which UBERMORGEN.COM received an avalanche of legal injunctions by email from the USA: documents of dubious authenticity as they are easy to fake, and in any case without legal standing outside the United States, but which succeeded in getting the project site shut down several times. UBERMORGEN.COM responded to this absurd situation by creating "legal art", and their *Injunction Generator* (2003): a software program that takes the data entered by the user to generate and send to the designated victim an injunction identical in form to those received by Hans Bernhard for *Vote Auction*.

In the ongoing work of UBERMORGEN.COM, the [F]original offers up a system (and a theory) for the long tradition of media fakes to which the *Vote Auction* project itself belongs, asserting the death of the concept of "originality". UBERMORGEN.COM sets up companies and generates legal documents, bank statements and medical prescriptions with the same freedom (and the same means) with which it designs logos and seals, processes images stolen from the net (pixelpaintings) and manipulates the communications system to spread fictitious news stories. On May 2nd 2006 for example, an email titled "Police officer killed in Berlin?" was widely distributed. In the email Hans Bernhard appears to be forwarding a message received from a certain Barbara Alex, who has attached a video filmed on a cell phone in Berlin during the May 1st demonstrations: a blurred, low resolution scene, where you can just make out hooded figures savagely beating up a policeman in a Berlin street. UBERMORGEN.COM claimed this apparent "found footage" as a work of art, a sort of readymade titled *[F]original Media Hack no. 1, Web 2.0*. The actual story of the video, which unsettled many viewers, and was published on Google Videos and Youtube, is rather different. The operation was planned by UBERMORGEN.COM in collaboration with Alister Mazzotti of Mazzotti Action, a team of stuntmen. While Mazzotti Action made the video, Hans Bernhard plotted the media action, invented a fictional character (Barbara Alex), explored the blogosphere and wrote the email. In the end he decided to pass off the video "trouvée" as a work of art, ably sidestepping the reader who might be led to view it as a media fake, due to the involvement of UBERMORGEN.COM. And in this way, using an email, a cell phone and knowledge of how the net works you can outwit the media:

«Pure Media Hacking: No ethics, no content, no message. With the action "[F]original Media Hack No. 1" we follow a simple instruction on how to infiltrate mass media with low-tech devices such as email, mobile-phones, web/blog and ambiguous data. This action is a clean and simple execution and broad experiment within this conceptual setting. It is an amalgamation of fact and fiction». [6]

Are we really sure that UBERMORGEN.COM are the only people aware of this opportunity?

Faked reality

Since 9-11 the world media and its consumers have been bombarded fairly regularly with threats, news of possible attacks, and information about the detection of groups of terrorists ready to swing into action. For the most part we have only witnessed these thanks to the media. This does not stop them from creating fear, and keeping civil society in a state of permanent terror that has made us accept all sorts of things: limitations of our freedom of expression, the war in Iraq, Guantanamo Bay and the CIA abductions in Europe. The chilling, pitiless hyper-realism of *Where-next* (2005) is rooted in this climate, where fear gives way to numbness. *Where-next* is a perverse gambling game that invites users to guess the place and date of the next terrorist attack using Google maps. Every time an attack occurs in the real world the creators of the site identify the nearest guess and award the winner a t-shirt with a photo of the attack, emblazoned with the words I PREDICTED IT. Alongside the map the site shows a banner with the World Trade Center still standing, with the macabre phrase «This space is for rent!» and «Your ad HERE» printed in front of the Twin Towers. The fact that the entire thing was viewed as utterly contemptible was maybe what led the people behind the site to come out from behind their media invention and reveal the ideological structure of the project: a bitter, sarcastic critique of capitalism, which gambles with our lives.

The site was created by Molleindustria and Guerrigliamarketing, both real companies. One is a studio that produces political video games, the other a marketing agency connected to the Luther Blissett Project, responsible for some of the most sensational media hoaxes of the 1990s. In a mischievous masterstroke, *Where-next* has incorporated two icons of capitalism and the new economy, Google and eBay, into its interface, and even put its banner space up for auction on eBay. *Where-next* sets out to be the freewheeling heir of these corporations, liberated from hypocritical ethics, in a process of "identity correction" which has a lot in common with the work of the Yes Men, the US group which impersonates corporations and institutions on public occasions after forging their websites. Despite the obvious intention to shock, both the press and art critics have been harsh: first attacking, then censoring it.

This attitude should come as no surprise, as media hacking uses the same arsenal as its enemy: the dark, fickle mood of our era, the lack of ethics which spares no one. To be really effective, it has to adopt the philosophy of UBERMORGEN.COM: «No ethics, no content, no message». It must hide its ideology, or be so violent that its ideology is unclear. It must not reveal the truth, but help us develop the tools to defend ourselves from the attack of the media. To do this, what better way than inoculating us with the virus itself?

First published in Emma McRae and Maria Rizzo (eds.), *MESH 19. Global/Regional Perspectives*, Australia, September 2006, available online at www.experimenta.org/mesh/mesh19/. Translated from Italian by Anna Rosemary Carruthers.

[1] Valentina Tanni and Domenico Quaranta, "0100101110101101.ORG - Nike Ground", in *Exibart*, April 27, 2004, online at www.exibart.com.
[2] Ironically, as Eva Mattes points out, no one ridicules the American flag on Peter Fonda's jacket in the iconic 1969 film *Easy Rider*.
[3] Domenico Quaranta, "Zero incassi al botteghino!", in *Flash Art*, April 2006.
[4] Bruce Sterling, "The Power of Fake. Exploring Net.art's new frontier", in *Modern Painters*, April 2006, pages 34 – 35.
[5] UBERMORGEN.COM, "[F]original Definition", www.foriginal.com.
[6] www.foriginal.com/no1/protocol/PROTOCOL.htm.

Interview with UBERMORGEN.COM

This interview was done by e-mail in November 2008 for the Italian webzine Digimag, and focuses on the last project released by UBERMORGEN.COM at the time, The Sound of eBay. *The project, which converts user data from eBay into electronic music, with an interface based on Teletext porn, is the third part of the so-called* EKMRZ Trilogy (2005 – 2008), *an exploration of e-commerce after the dotcom crash. In the interview, we talk about consensual hallucinations and corporations, media hacking and affirmative subversion, pop culture and bombs.*

"WE LOVE IT!", YOU SAY ABOUT EBAY. AND I LOVE THIS AFFIRMATIVE APPROACH. OBVIOUS CRITICISM IS SO BORING! ANYWAY, I CAN'T BUT WONDER: HOW MUCH YOUR AFFIRMATION IS SUBVERSIVE? AND HOW MUCH LOVING EBAY IS LIKE, IN KUBRICK'S WORDS, LOVING THE BOMB?

One thing after the other: thanks for loving it – and absolutely yes, obvious criticism can be so incredibly boring and thus useless and actually further the issues of the critique. Here is the link to the project: http://www.Sound-of-eBay.com – if someone kinda missed out on that... The nice thing about affirmation is that one can never tell if it is at all subversive, nor if it can or should be interpreted as such. And then, it is always a good idea to love the bomb 'coz you sure don't want to be on the losers' side once the big battles are over and won, right? You can never ever love enough. Especially not a nice, beautiful and lovely platform such as eBay! We are bomb lovers, literally, so we use eBay in our daily lives and we are not cynical about our love. The subversion starts where the affirmation tilts, and this is individual, a question of perception. The user can decide on her/his own on which level s/he wants to go to. This reminds me a bit about the situation of the humans in Pixar/Disney's animation movie *Wall-E* (2008), the slightest disruption of the flow of reality (consensual hallucination) can create life-changing moments, but it does not have to, it is just an option. We are non-judgmental about this, we are plain simple affirmative in a normal way – although we are both psychos, but this ain't no contradiction. All there is left to enjoy with stock traded corporations nowadays is lifestyle and surface glamour and entertainment – as one cannot make money anymore...

BESIDES THAT, THE WHOLE *EKMRZ TRILOGY* DISPLAYS QUITE UNUSUAL STRATEGIES. IN *GWEI - GOOGLE WILL EAT ITSELF* (2005 – 2008), YOU ADOPT A DAVID VS GOLIATH APPROACH: THE PROCESS IS FANTASTIC, BUT THE DAMAGE IS MINIMAL. IN *AMAZON NOIR - THE BIG BOOK CRIME* (2006 – 2007), THE NOIR NARRATIVE DESCRIBES YOU AS THE "BAD GUYS". AND NOW, IN *THE SOUND OF EBAY* IMPOSSIBLE FIGHT AND ROBBERY BECOMES AFFIRMATIVE CELEBRATION. CAN YOU EXPLAIN THE MEDIA HACKING ELEMENT OF THE *EKMRZ TRILOGY*?

We have never enjoyed the wanna-believe David vs Goliath story: there is a big guy and he kills everybody and nobody wants to challenge him anymore and then there comes this little guy and it is supposed to be something special that he shoots him with a very low-tech gun. Is that not the thing we call terrorism now? So, let's get real – if one really wants to be an underdog, one loses – the underdog is not the winner in real life, c'mon – David also would have needed about 300 billion stones to be thrown in order to kill the beast... So it is basically still the same method, the intrusion into mass media with lo-tech such as web, email, sms & texting, mobiles, phones, fax, posters etc. We use sophisticated technology behind the web-interfaces, but the core of the action, the core of the Media Hack is the crisp story and its distribution in to the global network of mass media. We have chosen three different approaches on how to infiltrate news-media, the blogosphere and art publications. Each project was launched individually with an experimental twist and a very different strategy... For *GWEI* we used a bottom-up/top-down mixed strategy, with *Amazon Noir* we were forced to use the hardcore top-down method and with *The Sound of eBay* we use the – for us classical – approach of widely distributed spam. All three methods have similar goals, to have high frequency and reach in classical mass media channels... We target the art clientele on the one side, the nerd community as well as a global audience of news consumers of all different ages, social backgrounds and interests on the other...

> IN THE *EKMRZ TRILOGY*, YOUR TARGETS ARE THE HEROES OF THE POST-DOT-COM-CRASH RENAISSANCE: THREE GIANT CORPORATIONS WITH A GOOD-LOOKING, FRIENDLY INTERFACE. WE ARE FAR REMOVED FROM THE TIMES WHEN YOU COULD HEAR PEOPLE SAY THAT THE DEVIL WEARS BLUE (A COMMON JOKE ABOUT IBM). WHAT HAS HAPPENED IN THE LAST FEW YEARS? IS IT JUST GOOD PROPAGANDA? OR ARE THEY REALLY "GOOD GUYS"?

They may be good-looking but hell not sexy... except Google Maps to be honest. The thing is: they are neither good or bad, because "they" do not exist. That is the great thing about Google: one cannot even phone them up in a normal fashion, Google does not even pretend to exist. Corporations do not exist, they cannot be good or bad, that is something only humans and mosquitoes are free to decide upon. We are not dealing with this "problem". All judgments about good and bad, evil or saints, are purely superficial and propagandistic. Our method is experimental, we use the corporations, their platforms and technologies as a playing field for our lust and perversion. One problem we have is that the best jokes, the most perverted ideas and the hardest images are destined for an audience of just two people, namely lizvlx and Hans Bernhard. Here we sit in the same boat as Andy Kaufman and his acolyte Bob Zmuda, doing enormously funny jokes, but the fun is just for themselves and can not be communicated or understood by outsiders... A rather user-unfriendly concept.

> WITH THE *EKMRZ TRILOGY*, YOU SEEM TO SAY THAT THE EPIC OF THE NET IS, MORE OR LESS, A CORPORATIVE EPIC. DO YOU AGREE?

I don't even want to answer this question as it is so poetic. Seriously – WELL YES OF COURSE! There are two levels to the Internet nowadays for sure: the whole Web 2.0 thing – TV on demand alias YouTube, Facebook alias social life surrogate; and the corporate consumer product heavens – "where buyers become deciders!™". We have now only focused on the good ol' consumer markets, because

– well, because the whole world was just literally screaming at the top of its lungs the whole time about how great the extension of consumerism into the private (home/computer) was. And then baboom, it all implodes with one big dotcom bang. And even though millions of people had predicted that for extremely obvious reasons, everybody was like "wow, ohmygod". Everybody except the richer crowd that is of course. And now the thing is repeating itself in the financial markets – because financial assets have become consumer products to bankers just as much – that was something we worked on with the *BANKSTATEMENTGENERATOR* in 2005. What we wanna say is: Yes, we are clearly living in a governmental-corporate environment and our privacy has become a commodity of its own. We personally do not care about that, privacy is the natural enemy of fame and we choose the latter. In the mid 1990s, it was a nice moment to contemplate during the rush and to think about the non-criminal subversive potential of these popularized technologies, but it was pure wishful thinking.

LIKE *CARNIVORE* [1], *THE SOUND OF EBAY* CAN BE DESCRIBED AS A FORM OF DATA PORNOGRAPHY. YOUR ROBOTS SUCK UP SENSITIVE AND NON-SENSITIVE DATA, AND YOU TRANSLATE IT INTO SOMETHING ELSE: SOUNDS, VISUALS. SEXY LINGERIE. BUT LIKE *CARNIVORE*, *THE SOUND OF EBAY* MAY RAISE THE QUESTION: WHAT IS THE POINT?

Oh, it is a mere mirror of the nonsensical behaviorism that web 2.0 users show on a daily basis. As much fun as it is to do projects that have a very clear vision and goal – as much those projects always risk being just preachy boring stuff (none of our projects though – I must admit that we really have mastered avoiding this mistake). But are you really asking what the point of combining porn, music and sales data is? If so - stop it!!! there is no point in music and sex – there has absolutely never been a point to databases filled with extremely unnecessarily data gathered from uninteresting users (myself included, I tell you...). You say sexy lingerie, I say please relax and let your mind and body wander... UBERMORGEN.COM might always be trying to combine some nice entertainment with very intellectual European subversive art, but God Christ, we need to relax sometime and sell Google ad space on eBay and write a book about it and sell that on Amazon and twitter everybody about it and be totally modern, postmodern and lostmodern.

MEANINGFUL OR NOT, *THE SOUND OF EBAY* IS PRETTY "POP" - MUCH MORE THAN *GWEI* AND *AMAZON NOIR*, WHICH ARE VERY CONCEPTUAL WORKS, BOTH IN THE PROCESS AND THE AESTHETICS. YOU SEEM TO BE SAYING: STOP THINKING, ENJOY OUR MUSIC AND OUR OLD-FASHIONED PORNOGRAPHY. IS ENTERTAINMENT THE ULTIMATE SUBVERSION?

After having produced both *GWEI* and *Amazon Noir* together with Alessandro Ludovico and Paolo Cirio, we decided to finish the trilogy with a subtle affirmative UBERMORGEN.COM-only feathery project working freely with pixel/data-material. Tackle the third entity of the rat pack of the corporate web – eBay – loose from interpretation, just mere lust coupled with entertaining data transformed into a series for song and dance. Now, talking about real hardcore entertainment, just look at the Bush administration – they have turned the USA into a pre-fascist nation and are super-openly using medieval methods of torture shock all around the globe where deemed "profitable" - and then look at their performance *in personam* and via the media: all sitcom style with a little James Bond here & there – especially when things might actually become a bit realistic... Thus, entertainment products are ultimately subversive works of art, politics becomes entertainment but we do entertainment that becomes politics, even something soft and corny like *The Sound of eBay*. We are constantly tilting back and forth between the art world and mass media entertainment. E-monsters such as Robbie Williams, Madonna, Britney Spears or former boy-band The Backstreet Boys create(ed) highly self-referential and subversive products and shoot them at very content and context-sensitive global audiences. Consumers are not stupid and with high-end forms of entertainment you communicate through the gut and not via the brain. Intuitively the recipient understands the vibe and becomes partially schizophrenic by enjoying the comfy feeling of the beat while feeling the psycho vibe.

WHY DID YOU CHOOSE A LOW-RES, TELETEXT-BASED AESTHETIC FOR THE PROJECT? IS THERE ANY ANALOGY BETWEEN EBAY, WHICH SURVIVED THE DOT-COM CRASH, AND TELETEXT, A TECHNOLOGY THAT HAS BRILLIANTLY SURVIVED THE INTERNET AGE?

That is a sweet analogy. Might be the reason. It just seemed the right thing to do. We have waited for almost a decade to find a perfect project to work with the aesthetics of teletext. *The Sound of eBay* (here is the link again, just in case you haven't checked it out yet: http://www.Sound-of-eBay.com) was ideal for that, it had no obvious link to pornography or any kind of related topic such as gender issues, sex, S&M style... After we finished the design and released *The Sound of eBay 1.0* Dragan Espenschied (Drx) sent us a link of a way cool project he did in 2001 named *Teletext Babez* [2]. The lo-tech/res aesthetic also corresponds with our Media Hacking strategy, stating that we can have enormous reach and frequency (hundreds of millions of people) with plain simple low-tech/res tools such as mobile phones, email and html. And also, a very strong YES to tech-sustainability, teletext is a parasite of television, incubated in the mid 1970s in the UK and at the beginning of the 1980s in central Europe – we love it, and even better, we use it every day.

READING YOUR PRESS RELEASE, I WONDERED WHY YOU PUT SO MUCH EMPHASIS ON THE DISTRIBUTED, NETWORKED NATURE OF THE CREATIVE PROCESS. YOU SAY: «NETWORKING IS WORKING... THE DIFFERENT PARTS OF *THE SOUND OF EBAY* WERE COMPILED IN VARIOUS GEOTECHNICAL-LOCATIONS... THERE WAS ONE REAL-LIFE MEETING IN VIENNA; ALL OTHER COMMUNICATION TOOK PLACE IN VARIOUS SKYPE CONFERENCES, VIA EMAIL AND THROUGH PHONE CONVERSATIONS». SINCE THIS IS QUITE USUAL TO OUR CURRENT WAY OF WORKING, I'M WONDERING IF THIS IS IMPORTANT IN ORDER TO UNDERSTAND THE WORK.

Honestly, sometimes we are just amazed about our very new methods of working. Working processes have been revolutionized in the last ten years and we want remind ourselves, take a look back and enjoy the convergence of communication. Before the age of global internet usage we were not able to cooperate and work at the same speed and with the same methods (flat hierarchies, instant global simultaneous production, sampled concepts, access to vast database resources, etc.) we use today. The core team of *The Sound of eBay* was living within a radius of 3 km in the city center of Vienna (Soundcoder Stefan Nussbaumer, lizvlx and Hans Bernhard, Theorycoder Grischinka Teufl and Visualcoder LIA). And, the essential data-grabbing robot comes from Erich Kachel, a guy we don't know. We don't know who he is, we don't know where he (or she) lives, we have no reference to her/him, we find no references on the Web except some strange coding tutorial web-sites. We have never talked to or seen a picture of her/him... S/he is a phantom, a positive intruder and one more possible spy in a row of spies we have been exposed to in the last ten years. Always remember: «Hate your neighbor!» - that was a standard declaration by Prof. Peter Weibel in all his lectures during our studies with him in Vienna.

> YOU WORK WITH OTHER PEOPLE, YOU USE OPEN SOURCE SOFTWARE, YOU WANT TO RELEASE THE GENERATOR UNDER A GNU PUBLIC LICENSE... AND IN THE MEANTIME YOU SELL WORKS IN THE ART MARKET. TWO THINGS THAT SOME YEARS AGO WERE SEEN AS CONFLICTUAL ARE NOW WORKING PERFECTLY TOGETHER. DO YOU THINK THAT A MARKET OF PRECIOUS, UNIQUE OR LIMITED EDITION FETISH OBJECTS IS STILL POSSIBLE IN THE AGE OF OPEN SOURCE AND COLLABORATIVE AUTHORSHIP?

Yes. We strongly believe in that. There is no conflict. The only overlapping would be in the merchandise sector. But the art collectors (individuals and institutions) have such a defining power that in collaboration with auction houses and galleries, the market-players will just decide what they consider high-end art and unique for them and the market. The certificate will become the defining power and the main limited and unique piece. It will become the license to print an image or (re)produce an installation. The production process might shift from artist-producer to collector-producer, from gallerist-distributor to artist-distributor... We are working on that. But please don't wait for us!

First published in Italian in *Digimag*, Issue 39, November 2008 with the title "It's lustful entertainment, baby! Interview with UBERMORGEN.COM".

[1] *Carnivore* (http://r-s-g.org/carnivore/) is a project launched in 2001 by the Radical Software Group (RSG), and inspired by DCS1000, a piece of software used by the FBI to perform electronic wiretaps. Using the server application made available by the RSG, many artists developed "clients" which display an ever different visualization of the data sniffed by the surveillance software.
[2] The project is still documented at
http://drx.a-blast.org/~drx/projects/teletext/.

Remediations. Art in Second Life

Around 2006, virtual worlds entered the peak of their hype cycle. One of the pupils of the mass media was Second Life, a synthetic environment that gave its users a high level of freedom, in terms of both design and in-world activity. Unsurprisingly, many of these users were artists and creatives, who used virtual worlds as a new field of experimentation and as a new distribution platform. A small but extremely dynamic art world developed in Second Life, including artists, art critics, galleries and no-profit organizations. That same year, I designed my own avatar (which, by a strange coincidence, bore my very same name) and some months later, I launched "Spawn of the Surreal" (http://spawnofthesurreal.blogspot.com/), a blog that featured the results of my explorations of what I called "the dumpster of the imaginary". My first post on "Spawn of the Surreal" dates back to July 4, 2007; the last one being written on September 9, 2009, even though it stopped being a regularly updated blog some months before. That is when, more or less, at least to me, Second Life stopped being an interesting playground for radical artistic experimentation.

Of course this doesn't mean that nothing interesting is happening out there any more. What went in 2008, and is gone today, was the "community": the feeling of being a happy few, conquering a temporarily autonomous zone where there were no rules, no institutions, no definitions, no boundaries. Written in 2007, this text chronicles that lost moment, and the ongoing debate on the performative nature of art in virtual worlds.

Second Life [1]: hardly a day goes by without it being talked about. The media success of the virtual world launched in 2003 by the Californian company Linden Labs appears to be on a par only with its user popularity (around 10 million residents as I write) and commercial success. These three things are obviously closely connected: people flock to SL, companies follow, the media talk about it and this attracts new people and new companies.

The hype – which strangely enough, as activist and media critic Geert Lovink [2] notes, is fed by «old school broadcast and print media and the wannabe cool corporations» is starting to show its first cracks [3], and while on the one hand it has served to make concepts like "avatar", "virtual worlds" and "social networks" popular, on the other, with its uncritical enthusiasm and superficiality, it has created false expectations that risk leading to an equally uncritical condemnation of a context that does have its problems, but is undeniably rich in potential.

It's all true: the habitual users of SL represent a ludicrously tiny percentage of the 10 million curious visitors who set up an account for a single visit, without ever following it up; the only returns on the million dollar investments made by the big companies have been in terms of publicity, while their virtual headquarters are usually deserted; SL's graphic engine and scripting language are vastly inferior to those of other virtual worlds; its world is built around a trashy, kitsch aesthetic; the prevalent image is that of «a mega milkshake of pop culture» [4], and life revolves mainly around the banal repetition of real-life rituals (having sex, going dancing, and attending parties, openings and conferences) and the same principles: private property, wealth and consumption. As Paolo Pedercini writes:

> «There is something terribly dystopic about a universe that is so vast and engaging, yet at the same time so privatized and privatizing. This is more than just a nice dream to buy into, more than yet another incarnation of the panopticon... Every day and in an increasing manner this virtual world lays claim to around three and a half years of the intellectual activity of the users who contribute to making it bigger, more dynamic and more attractive» [5].

Many view SL as a superficial, hedonistic, phoney bandwagon, a world which is alienating, self-perpetuating, closed off from life, dedicated to profit and the pleasures of the flesh (in a virtual sense, obviously); it lives off the unpaid creativity of its users and its consumerist aspect is like an endemic cancer at the heart of the system (it has been estimated that an avatar consumes as much energy as the average Brazilian citizen) [6]; both its technological infrastructure and the social structure it has spawned are frustratingly limited, and last but by no means least, it is tedious, utterly tedious.

This type of criticism often crops up in online artistic communities. At times it springs from mere prejudice, but in many cases it comes from people who have a fairly broad experience of life "in-world". The American artist G. H. Hovagimyan, one of the pioneers of Net art, asserts, «When you allow an engineer to dictate how you are creative and what form that takes then you have given up your artistic freedom. This is the case in SL». [7]

Yet despite this, SL is literally teeming with artists. No other virtual world can boast such a variegated, complex and rich artistic community, and it is probably the only virtual world to have succeeded in focusing global attention on contemporary art, thanks to artists such as Eva and Franco Mattes (0100101110101101.ORG) and Cao Fei, who took her virtual alter-ego China Tracy to the Venice Biennale.

Art in Second Life

Talking about art in SL means, in the first place, working out exactly what it is we are talking about, which doesn't exactly simplify things. What I want to talk about is not SL as a place where a rapidly expanding artistic community meets and networks, or SL as a place which is developing a new art system and market: both interesting phenomena, but for the time being, decidedly over-rated, in view of the fact that the advent of a sustainable art economy is still far off, and as yet there are no players on the horizon capable of changing the rules of a game where works of art go for a handful of Linden dollars (the currency in SL, which can also be changed into real dollars) [8].

What I want to talk about is SL as a venue for practising art. SL describes itself as «an online 3D digital world imagined, created and possessed by its residents». [9] In other words, in SL design is by far the prevailing activity, and so-called "creativity" is the top-rated resource [10].

From avatars to houses, everything that we are not able (or don't wish) to buy has to be designed, and everything you design is subjected to the appraisal of others. The alternatives are anonymity and boredom. This, it could be said, is the curse of SL: there's no way to have fun unless you make it yourself. In this world of "creative" people, the word art is frequently misappropriated: this is the first word of warning we would give to the art tourist who decides to venture among the isles of the Metaverse [11].

The second is that SL – like the internet – is often used as a showcase by artists in search of the success which seems to elude them in the real-world art system; in other words, in SL you often come across the same old art, but without that initial selection filter that the art world appears to guarantee. Thirdly, in a world which sees itself as the virtual "double" of the real one, art proliferates in all its possible forms, but with the difference that these levels, distinctly separate in real life, are all mixed together in the virtual world. In other words this means that in most of the hundreds of "art galleries" that abound in SL, figurative kitsch lies alongside late informal, street market paintings jostle with photography, graffiti, abstract works, digital images produced by Photoshop wizards, monumental sculpture and multimedia installations. The temple of this variegated art scene is Second Louvre, which hosts a wide selection of the artworks produced by SL residents. Sanguine sketches, paintings and photographs sit alongside *Achilles 2006*, a monumental sculpture by Starax Statosky, SL's very first (self-declared) native artist. That of Statosky is a curious case, but one which offers a useful starting point for delving into the complexities of the concept of "art in virtual worlds".

Most of his works are "traditional sculptures", namely monumental sculptures of neoclassical inspiration modeled in 3D; however the techniques he uses are anything but "traditional", being more similar to that of a programmer than a sculptor. Moreover, Statosky's art is not limited to his sculptures, but extends to his avatar, and his maverick biography, including committing 'suicide' (that is, abandoning SL) when a program update rendered one of his works unusable. In SL, in other words, in the first place it is impossible to make any kind of distinction between traditional media and digital media, and secondly, everything (even the most apparently traditional practices) can be the result of a precise, knowing, artistic design.

This comes to the fore in the case of Fau Ferdinand, one of the most famous "painters" in SL. In actual fact, her paintings, characterized by an eclectic style which buries echoes of surrealism and expressionism among a rich pop substratum – are decidedly less interesting than the whole "Fau Ferdinand project", which encompasses her avatar, her house/gallery inspired by the design of a particle accelerator, and her in-world life. All of this applies in the real world too, but in SL it is taken to extremes. To hark back to one of 0100101110101101.org's historic projects, we could say that every SL artist is a budding Darko Maver – a "fictitious" character waiting to be acknowledged as "real". Or, if you prefer, a convincing Roberta Breitmore, to reference the pioneering work of Lynn Hershman Leeson and her constructed persona (who, needlessly to say, recently landed on SL, thanks to Stanford University) [12].

And, as if all this wasn't enough to be going on with, in a world which abuses the word art, we are often forced to reconsider as "art" initiatives which set out with another intent. In an interview with Mario Gerosa, the artist Gazira Babeli quotes the example of Travis Curry, «a Texan guy who crossed the whole of SL on foot. If he had said, "I see this as an artistic project, something which I will document and communicate", no-one would have objected» [13].

Having said this, if art in SL was limited to the situation described above, it would not be entirely wrong to second the view that all of us, artists and critics included, have fallen victim to the hype, and that beyond purely documentary interest, there is no future for art in SL. Not even the widespread, undoubtedly appealing genre of the multimedia installation appears to challenge Hovagimyan's observation: the works of renowned artists such as AngryBeth Shortbread (Annabeth Robinson), DanCoyote Antonelli (DC Spensley), AldoManutio Abruzzo, Juria Yoshikawa and Adam Ramona (the Australian Adam Nash) certainly represent highly effective explorations of the sense of space, time and identity in a virtual world, and sound out the acoustic and aesthetic potential of SL, yet it is hard to get away from the idea that, like any kind of architecture, they are little more than stylistic exercises exploring the potential of a good graphic engine, going no further than the limits set by its program designers. In internet terms, we could liken many of these works to high quality experimental web design [14].

This comparison is not casual. Strangely enough, what is happening in SL resembles the situation at the dawn of Net art. The uncritical enthusiasm for the medium at most gives rise to some excellent craftsmanship, but art lies elsewhere, specifically among the artists who apply a critical approach to the medium, not in order to avoid tackling it, but in order to develop works which challenge and address its technical, cultural and ideological limits. This concept was expressed extremely well by the artist Man Michinaga:

> «I got very tired of feeling like I had to jump on every new piece of tech, and I am trying to focus more on critical content, less on tech... But I saw SL as a new community with a lot of excitement... One thing that I wanted to do was to actually do something that was REAL in SL, not empty hype...» [15]

Man Michinaga is Patrick Lichty: American artist, curator, media critic and lecturer. In SL he is one of the founding members of Second Front, a collective of performers which re-presents the logic of Fluxus events in-world, in performances which are often staged in public areas unannounced, improvised and with a high level of audience participation. One of the most memorable was *Spawn of the Surreal* (February 2007), where the group used a kind of virus to deform the avatars present, drawing them into a sort of improvised dance: thus hitting the audience in what it holds most dear, and challenging the worship of physical beauty that reigns in this hedonistic world. Meanwhile *The Last Supper* (January 2007) was a re-enactment of the Last Supper which challenged the prevailing popularity of classic masterpieces in SL, packed as it is with reproductions of famous paintings and sculptures. The members of the collective staged Leonardo's *Last Supper* before profaning it with an improbable punk twist.

Re-enactment, or as Lichty prefers to call it, "remediation", is one of the most popular, interesting avenues in art in SL. The most famous examples are probably the performances of Eva and Franco Mattes, who stage versions of historic pieces from the sixties and seventies. The Mattes specifically select performances destined to appear paradoxical in the setting of a virtual world, given the strange twists that concepts like the body, space, violence and the setting take in a universe made of polygons. In this way, their re-enactments represent both a radical challenge to Performance Art, and to that of the concept of a "second life". For instance, in *Joseph Beuys' 7000 Oaks*, Beuys' ecological operation becomes a "conceptual virus" which invades a world characterized by high energy consumption, therefore highly polluting.

Another artist who works a lot with the concept of remediation [16] is Gazira Babeli, an Italian performer who has been creating radical, irreverent works in SL for over a year, which, combined with her alluring persona and insistence on concealing her true identity, have helped make her a cult figure. In actual fact this concealment has a specific purpose: Gazira Babeli is a project in her own right, the construction of a narrative identity that feels increasingly real the more it appears to remain independent of any kind of author. Everything that Gazira does, from her performances to the installations presented in her first retrospective [17], from the cult-movie *Gaz' of the Desert* (2007) to her involvement in Second Front, contributes, first and foremost, to bring her persona to life. And this is a character that exists only in what could be termed a "repository of the imaginary", that lives off culture, as we can see in her frantic cans of *Campbell's Soup*, her hailstorm of pop icons, her live performances of Bacon's masterpieces and Duchamp's *Nude Descending A Staircase*, and her spectacular *Omaggio a Luciano Fabro*.

Taking this approach to extremes, Patrick Lichty has come up with the project *(re)constructing Cicciolina* (2007), which he terms a "remediation of the artist as object". What is being offered here is a post modern icon, which immediately raises a comparison with a culture (that of media manipulation) and an aesthetic (devotion to a synthetic, exaggerated form of beauty), which have greatly conditioned the history of SL.

Leaving Second Life

The situation described up to now could not exist without a context to feed and support it, offering it a setting and opportunities to unfurl. The main centers that support this "native" art include Ars Virtua, Odyssey and NMC Campus. The first is a "new media center", founded in November 2005 by James Morgan, which as well as hosting key shows (from Eva and Franco Mattes to the virtual extension of the project *77 Million Paintings* by Brian Eno) has also created an artist residency program. By working in partnership with "real" exhibition venues, Ars Virtua aims to give rise to projects which also have a physical presence. NMC Campus is an experimental platform connected to the New Media Consortium, an international partnership that numbers around 250 bodies. In view of its highly institutional nature and solid links with Linden Labs, NMC Campus lends particular support to creative efforts aimed at making "positive" use of the technical potential of SL, with less attention to the development of critiques of the platform. These abound above all in Odyssey, an island run by Sugar Seville and founded by the Dynamis Corporation. The main appeal of Odyssey lies in the fact that, while it is not a strictly art-related context, what it offers is a free arena open to discussion and experimentation. This openness has led to the creation of a large community of artists, and the organization of events that are already part of the history of the SL community.

But while the development of a home-grown form of art is the most interesting aspect of art in SL, there is still one big question that needs to be answered: to what extent can such art still have a meaning outside the "niche" it is created in, and the context it relates to? How can it be viewed in relation to contemporary art?

First of all, it has to be said that whatever the future holds for SL, the issues regarding "screen life" which have been lurking in the background throughout the nineties, and which have now come to the fore in the context of virtual worlds, are set to be a dominant theme in daily life for a long time to come. And should this not be the case, it is undoubtedly a dominant theme at present. This has been shown by the Mattes and their avatars; and by the Chinese artist Cao Fei, who presented her work *i.Mirror* at the last Venice Biennale, a wide-ranging three-part documentary regarding the setting, the people and the stories that are woven every day in virtual worlds like SL.

As for native art, the position of Second Front is fairly emblematic. The collective claims that its in-world performances do not represent the full extent of its oeuvre, but are merely a point of departure in a wide-ranging vision of performance art which takes them from communications media (and the web in particular) to real space, in the form of re-presenting videos, digital prints and so on. The same can be said for Gazira Babeli, whose movie and videos have made it out of SL, and who is currently looking at ways to stage some of her most provocative works in real life.

The Port community is looking at another option with its project *Objects of Virtual Desire*, which «explores immaterial production in a virtual world, and if and how this can be transferred into an economy of material production». In other words, the collective has identified a number of objects that the avatars of SL attach great sentimental value to, and has translated these into real objects. The German artist Aram Bartholl has also developed a number of projects that translate typical virtual world conventions and objects into reality. In *Tree*, backed by the Berlin Department for Culture, Bartholl transports a tree created as it would be in a virtual world, into a real setting, simulating its three-dimensional nature with overlapping orthogonal planes. All that remains to be seen is whether these portents actually do, as they would appear to, herald an increasing level of exploration of "virtual life" in contemporary art.

First published in *HZ Journal*, issue 11, December 2007, online at www.hz-journal.org/n11/. A shorter version has been published in Italian in *Flash Art*, Issue 266, October - November 2007. Translated from Italian by Anna Rosemary Carruthers.

[1] From here on in, SL.
[2] In a message sent to the mailing list *Fibreculture* on 14 June 2007: http://fibreculture.org/pipermail/list_fibreculture.org/2007-June/000286.html.
[3] I refer to a recent article in *Wired*, which after generously contributing to the hype, seriously challenges the point of investing financially in the virtual world: see Frank Rose, "How Madison Avenue Is Wasting Millions on a Deserted Second Life", in *Wired*, 24 July 2007, online at www.wired.com/techbiz/media/magazine/15-08/ff_sheep.
[4] Paolo Pedercini, "Sette giorni in una Seconda Vita. Reportage da un mondo virtuale", in *Molleindustria.it*, September 2005.
[5] Ibid.
[6] See Nicholas Carr, "Avatars consume as much electricity as Brazilians", in *Rough Type*, 5 December 2006, online at www.roughtype.com/archives/2006/12/avatars_consume.php.
[7] In a message sent to the mailing list *-empyre-* 18 August 2007: https://mail.cofa.unsw.edu.au/pipermail/empyre/2007-August/msg00156.html.
[8] With regards to this, see Helen Stoilas, "Art makes a scene on Second Life", in *The Art Newspaper*, 4 July 2007.
[9] From the site www.secondlife.com.
[10] Talking about SL the anthropologist Tom Boellstroff uses the term "creationist capitalism". Quoted in Mario Gerosa, *Second Life*, Meltemi, Milan 2007.
[11] This term, coined by the sci-fi writer Neal Stephenson in his novel *Snow Crash* (1992), is very popular with residents as a synonym for SL.
[12] See http://presence.stanford.edu:3455/Collaboratory/346.
[13] Mario Gerosa, in *Second Life*, quoted, p. 142.
[14] This comparison is actually a little simplistic, as these projects go deeper than exercises in style, experimenting with the concept of identity. While DC Spensley is a mature artist, his virtual persona is young, enterprising and ambitious. Lance Shields is a Tokyo-based, male multimedia artist and designer, while Juria Yoshikawa, his avatar, is a Japanese girl with blue hair. Another issue revolves around the fact that, when you create a sculpture, a multimedia installation or a kinetic space in SL, you are not simply designing an information space, but a living space that can be experienced by other people in the form of avatars. Yet, Hovagimyan's criticism still applies: these artists are just exploiting the potential of a medium designed by someone else, without the value added by its evolution into a social space.

[15] Email to the author, 17 August 2007.

[16] Truth be told, Gazira is actually fairly critical of the concept of remediation. After a shorter version of this article was published in *Flash Art*, she wrote to me: «This increasing consensus regarding the idea of "remediation" has been troubling me for at least a year. If I played with it, it was just to deny or ridicule it, because it sounds really like a sense of guilt and/or impotence over the past... and art... When I came out with the word "performance", I understood that there were two possible attitudes: as a commentary (if defined in the art history sense) or speculative (as in the common usage: "performative = an utterance by means of which the speaker performs a particular act"). I am more interested in action than remediation». Email to the author, October 2007.

[17] *Gazira Babeli: [Collateral Damage]*, ExhibitA, Odyssey, 16 April 2007.

Gazira Babeli

This text was written as a catalogue text for Gazira Babeli's retrospective exhibition in Second Life. The exhibition, called "Gazira Babeli – [Collateral Damage]", was set up in the land of Odyssey, in a brand new exhibition space called ExhibitA, and was curated by Sugar Seville and Beavis Palowakski, the visionary founders of Odyssey. The catalogue was a red book that awaited the visitor on the exhibition's entrance desk; clicking on it, the text was displayed in a pop up window. The exhibition ran from April 16 to May 30, 2007, and showed the performative work developed by the artist through the previous year in the form of large scale, active installations. To the uninitiated, one year might seem a very short period of time for a show that has been described as a "retrospective". But in a virtual environment, one year can be enough to develop a whole artistic career. And that's what happened to Gazira, who was born in March 2006, reached her artistic maturity in 2007 and got recognition from the art system in the next couple of years. As I write,there are rumors that she retired.

Gazira Babeli is an artist who was born in Second Life on March 31 2006. Tall and willowy, her expressionless eyes hidden behind a pair of dark glasses, she exudes a strange allure somewhere between voodoo priestess, drag queen and X-men heroine. Of mixed race, she almost always appears dressed in black, usually alternating between her performance outfit (a severe-looking long black coat), and her more casual everyday look (t-shirt, mini-skirt, fishnets and Doctor Marten boots). One thing she is never without, not even when she takes everything else off, is her outlandish cone-shaped head gear, a key part of her get-up, which as we will see, also has its own precise function.

Now we would not have concentrated for so long on Gazira's appearance if we had not read quite so much on the grey attire of Joseph Beuys, his felt hat, and his shaman-like presence. Gazira, who sees herself first and foremost as a performance artist, is well aware of the fact that, from Beuys to Orlan, the body represents any performer's first work of art, and that the construction of one's persona is not a sideline, but a key part of the oeuvre. No details must be overlooked. Life and art are one. But here there is also another level to consider. Gazira Babeli lives and works in Second Life, a 3D virtual world launched by the Californian company Linden Lab in 2003, and entirely constructed, owned and run by its residents. The latter are conscious that their avatars are their first, true creations, and dedicate much of their attention to their appearances. In other words the specific characteristics of an artistic genre (in this case performance art) are inextricably bound up with the internal logic of the universe that hosts it, giving rise to a succession of superimposed layers we will often come back to.

Living in Second Life

> «We still don't understand what 'life' is and yet, we are talking about a second one. One life at a time, please! Maybe these lives (RL and SL) are not so different: symbolic abstractions and virtuality are common attributes.» [1]

Having said this, we should however note that Gazira's existence in Second Life is radically different from that of all other residents. Second Life is an alluring metaphor which aims to offer exactly that to its residents. If our "first lives" are those in the real world, our second lives are played out in a virtual world by our digital representations, or avatars. The latter exist in a simulated world which largely reproduces the dynamics of the real world: avatars go shopping, look after their houses and appearances, work, have sex and travel. Most of the residents do all this in total acceptance of the simulation, namely without realizing they are inhabiting an interface made up of data, a world held together by code and script. When this awareness comes to the fore, we can talk about a "third life", as Matteo Bittanti termed it in a recent essay. In Bittanti's view, the third life is «the set of activities carried out by a subject acting in Second Life through an avatar»: «a subject boosted by analogical and digital extensions and prostheses such as an avatar, computer, keyboard and monitor.» [2]

This subject is constantly overlaying practices of social life and programming practices or 3D modeling, constantly combining the two levels of reality he or she inhabits: «the analogical plane (first life) and digital plane (second life)». Gazira Babeli operates on yet another level of life (and awareness). She does this, first and foremost, by doing away with the first life: for Gazira, the subject – be it a man or a woman – that created her, is not her 'real' alter ego, but simply the stupid deity that manipulates the interface she lives in, the mysterious being that governs her actions from on high. In this way, Second Life becomes her real plane of action, and it is from this perspective that her radical identification between social life and manipulation of code acquires meaning. Living in any world means acting with an awareness of the rules that govern that world. But the social conventions that rule the virtual world of Second Life, just like the linguistic conventions that support its interface, only work on the surface: the world that Gazira has chosen for herself is based on other laws, those written in programming code.

This is why her performances are not based on acting – like any normal avatar – on the Second Life platform, but on manipulating and activating its code. She is not a performer, but a "code performer". She does not pretend, like everyone else, to be in a world made of objects and atoms, but is aware of inhabiting a world made of code, and being made of code herself. Performance art is always a critique of the norms the surrounding world is based on. And Gazira operates precisely in this way, which is why she appears like some kind of bizarre shaman to those who see her. In all cultures, shamans have the power to enter into contact with the world of primitive forces and mediate those forces. Gazira runs scripts as if they were magic spells, unleashing earthquakes, natural disasters and invasions of pop icons like plagues of locusts.

And as in Second Life every fragment of code has to have its own "physical" location, Gazira keeps her scripts in her hat, her magic wand. She knows that the body is a construct, and enjoys deforming it or rendering it interchangeable. She knows that space is an illusion and she plays around with these contradictions. She knows that «reality depends on your graphic card», and never misses a chance to call attention to that. But she transfers everything onto the artistic plane, by means of what she terms "performances", "sculptures", and "paintings". In this way she introduces another level of action, another idiom to decodify and another set of rules to subvert: those of the art world.

Space

«Falling down from a height of 21,987,0987 meters is not so safe in RL...» [3]

In October 2006 a minor apocalypse hit a beach in Second Life, burying it under a flood of skipping Super Marios. In technical jargon this is called "grey goo", an expression used in nanotechnology and science fiction to describe a hypothetical apocalypse scenario in which self-replicating robots consume all living matter on the earth [4].

Although the cataclysm did generate a certain level of anxiety, Gazira appears to be more interested in sparking a mental short circuit than a genuine system collapse. This was why she populated the three-dimensional, baroque world of Second Life with the definitive icon of the 8-bit era.

This process is evident in *Kaspar Goo* (November 2006), where she asks an actor to play the part of Caspar David Friedrich's wanderer, going into raptures over the wonders of nature. It is dawn, and our wanderer, in his wide-brimmed hat, watches the sun come up over a fairy-tale scenario. The mimesis appears to be played out to perfection, till the traveler's doubts appear in concrete form, embodied as a shower of question marks sullying the horizon. A couple of days later Gazira showed up at the opening of a show held in Ars Virtua [5], an exhibition dedicated to avatar portraits by Eva and Franco Mattes (0100101110101101.org) [6]. At a certain point the venue filled up with bananas, and not just any old bananas, but a replica of the banana created by Andy Warhol for the cover of The Velvet Underground's first LP. It is hard to say whether this is a comment on the work of the Mattes (that's all pop!) or a competition over who is most "pop art" of all. But above and beyond this play of references, and observations about past art forms, which we will return to later, Gazira displays her desire to intervene on the surrounding space, in this case occupying it and revealing its conventional nature by inserting elements which are completely "foreign" to the three-dimensional illusion she lives in: out-sized two-dimensional objects borrowed from language (the question marks) or visual communications (Super Mario, Warhol's banana).

The spatial-temporal model of Second Life is a rather peculiar one. The force of gravity is present, but residents can fly. There are dimensions, distances, journey times and speed limits, but these can all be circumvented in an instant by teleporting. The latter practice, mutated from science fiction, is based on an implicit pact: the blind faith that, once activated, we will be teleported exactly where we want to go: a "real" place which can be physically identified on a map.

COME.TO.HEAVEN (July 2006) was a performance which explored a very simple hypothesis: what happens if, combating the force of gravity, I hurl my body (or someone else's) from millions of meters at extremely high speed? The result depends on the characteristics of the graphics board on the computer being used. In some cases the polygons shatter, and the result no longer has a human semblance, while in others the body appears to have gone through a kind of turbine, with limbs multiplying and breaking up, and the body becoming a messy pulp of flesh and hair. Exploiting the physical characteristics of her environment, Gazira appears to be exploring various strands of twentieth century art, and indeed she describes her work as a painting on the computer's graphic card. At the same time the frame of reference can only be that of an imaginary "flight" like Yves Klein's famous leap into the void.

Created on occasion of the exhibition "[Collateral Damage]", *U AreHere* (April 2007) consists in two sculptures which violate the pact of trust implicit in the practice of teleporting. Or rather, they represent an overly-literal application of the latter. The sculptures are two simple models on pedestals: the first represents a desert with some archeological ruins, the other a room with a window we can peep into to see what's inside: a banal-looking office with a clock, a desk and a computer. By clicking on the models we are transported into the setting in question: an arid, apparently infinite desert, or a closed room with no way out. Have we been shrunk or just taken hostage inside a "real" version of the setting represented by the two sculptures? We will never know, also in view of the fact that to get out we cannot fly, but have to use an internally-located device that we have to track down. But this is of little importance, for in any case the spatial/temporal model of Second Life has been violated. As for the office, for the time being we will only note that while Gazira views Second Life as a sort of Dickian replica of the world of Perky Pat [7], the real world (the room in which our real body is linked to the world) is none other than another imaginary dimension.

Earthquakes are another obvious way of manipulating space. Here, as in the various "grey goo" scenarios, it is fairly natural to think that Gazira is attempting a hack, or "griefing" as they say in Second Life. But while this is undoubtedly bound up with various attempts at artistically sabotaging a system – be it digital or social – we get the impression that in recreating a real-world phenomenon strangely absent from this virtual world which is so realistic in many other aspects, Gazira is once more playing around with its reality coefficient.

The Body

«My body can walk barefoot, but my avatar needs Prada shoes.» [8]

As well as taking center stage in performance art, in Second Life the body acquires some very particular characteristics. On the one hand the user is aware of dealing with a conventional representation of him or herself, a digital alter ego that enables him to interact with the surrounding space and the other beings present: nothing more or less than the little round faces used in the very first graphic chatrooms. On the other hand relations with one's avatar soon come to resemble those we have with our real bodies: it needs to be taken care of, dressed, groomed, kept satisfied (mostly in terms of sex and having drinks); it is inviolable and irreplaceable. In her work Gazira Babeli frees the body of the avatar from these restrictions, and invites us to see it for what it is: a representational convention that we are free to 'violate' at will. *Buy Gaz' 4 one Linden!* (April 2007) enables us, for the symbolic price of 1 Linden Dollar, to purchase Gazira Babeli's open source body: we remain ourselves but we can use (and abuse) her black coat, her body, even her hat.

Second Life is full of twins: the avatars of the greenest residents, who have not yet learned to personalize their bodies. This also recalls the world of Perky Pat, where the people, in their drug-induced state, identify with a limited number of people, ending up by being 'translated' into the body of Perky Pat or her boyfriend Walt. But this work was also a more general reflection on the concept of identity, something which is not only increasingly ambiguous, but which has now acquired such importance that in Second Life it is a kind of social divider, distinguishing crowds of newbies sharing the same stereotyped bodies, from an elite of experts capable of displaying their own individuality.

Meanwhile *Come Together* (April 2007) explored the concept of the fusion of bodies. The work is a pedestal surrounded by many colored balls, which in Second Life represent sexual relations. By clicking on these, the avatar is transported onto the pedestal, where it merges into the bodies of the other visitors, in a series of uncontrollable random movements. Once more symbols are subverted, and the parody of a real action (sex) is converted into a kind of fusion with synchronized movements only possible between avatars.

But the most radical violation is that of *Avatar on Canvas* (March 2007), a series of three Francis Bacon paintings where the main figure has been replaced by a three-dimensional chair. This is an implicit invitation to sit down, but when we do, our avatar is subjected to hideously violent deformations (thus completing the Bacon). At this point we can choose to leave Second Life and then come back with our usual appearance, or hang out in our new anamorphic but still entirely serviceable body.

Avatar on Canvas is in fact a watered-down version, in the guise of a work of art, of a theatrical performance by Second Front [9] (a group of which Gazira is an active member) entitled *Spawn of the Surreal* (February 11, 2007). On that occasion, Gazira incorporated her deforming code into a few of the chairs set up for the audience of the Second Front show. The audience members in question ended up being deformed without any prior warning, and their consequent panic and embarrassment reveals the – entirely irrational – sense of attachment that residents of Second Life have with regard to their virtual bodies, deemed sacred and inviolable exactly like our physical bodies.

Don't Say New Media!

«… a 'world in a valise'» [10]

Second Soup, performed in May 2006 (and recorded on video), sees Gazira tackling a giant can of Campbell's soup, another pop art icon. The artist is looking at it on a poster, when all of a sudden the can leaves its paper domain and grabs hold of her. From that moment on she just can't get rid of it. Gazira jumps, flies and runs, but the can always catches up with her. Pop art as an irksome deity, a cumbersome legacy that we just can't seem to shed? The penetrability of bodies in Second Life makes some of the scenes amusing, but Gazira doesn't appear to be enjoying herself much. "You love Pop Art – Pop Art hates you!", is the ironic subtitle to the piece.

In "[Collateral Damage]", *Second Soup* is presented as an installation of five soup cans that are activated when the spectator gets too close. Globally, this piece is a good starting point for considering the nature of Gazira's art. The performance dimension is undoubtedly a key element, but there is more to it than that. Gazira writes the code, runs it in person, and records her performances in photo and on video just like any performance artist, from Marina Abramovic to Vanessa Beecroft. But Gazira's performances are computing code, that the artist offers on her site under a Creative Commons license, so that anyone can use it. She operates in a network environment (Net Art?). She writes code (Software Art?). She uses legends and icons from pop culture (Pop Art?). In reality Gazira's work is above and beyond these categories, or rather it resides in a context where such distinctions no longer apply.

The comparison with Software Art would appear to be the most relevant in this case. In a 2004 essay the German critic Inke Arns introduced the concept of the performativity of code in software art, adapting it from John L. Austin's theory of the linguistic act. As Arns writes:

> «… this performativity is not to be understood as a purely technical performativity, i.e. it does not only happen in the context of a closed technical system, but affects the realm of the aesthetical, the political and the social. [...] Code thus becomes Law…» [11]

Arns concludes by observing that «software art directs our attention on the fact that our (media) environment is increasingly relying on programmed structures.» Gazira Babeli does more than just operate inside our media environment. She lives there. The code she writes transforms her environment, because her environment is made of code. In other words there is a shift from performative code to performance. When software artists write code they manipulate the environment of that medium. When Gazira Babeli writes code she manipulates the world she lives in, and undermines the illusion which that world is based on, the illusion that all the residents (artists included) take great pains to maintain. She reveals the secret behind the Perky Pat dolls and forces us to think about just why this doll's house attracts us so much.

The use of code is however where any resemblances between the work of

Gazira and New Media Art in general end. It is no coincidence that Gazira does not relate that much to the other artists in Second Life, and only if pressed will she reveal her relations with net.art. Her references are Friedrich, Warhol, Bacon and Duchamp. At the same time she always tries to link her works to traditional, recognized art forms: painting, sculpture, installation, video, performance.

In "[Collateral Damage]", this is self-evident: *Buy Gaz' 4 one Linden!* is a mural; *Avatar on Canvas* is a series of three paintings; *U AreHere* and *Second Soup* are sculptures, and so on. Simply put, Gazira exercises the right to "implement" these traditional forms using a series of possibilities embedded in the world she inhabits.

Nudes Descending a Staircase (April 2007) is an installation that ironically resolves the contradictions raised by exhibiting a painting in a setting like Second Life. It is a series of nudes printed on canvas, which fall off the wall and end up in a heap at the bottom of a staircase. Now this is obviously an animation in a virtual setting. And many of these works are interactive. But can we still talk about "new media" and "interactivity" when the world we live in is a software environment and the possibility to interact with things and people is one of its most natural characteristics, a given? For Gazira these are terms that should be banned from Second Life. But if you are tempted to use them, then just don't do it during the show: you could be swept away by the current version of *Don't Say Tornado*, a whirlwind that is activated when someone pronounces the words "new media". In its own way, another interactive multimedia installation…

Surreal Real

«…a portable desert» [12]

Another thing which really annoys Gazira, when it comes to Second Life and virtual worlds in general, is our inability to get over the interpretational models offered up thirty years ago by cyberpunk culture.

Constantly harking back to William Gibson's *Cyberspace* (1982) and Neal Stephenson's *Metaverse* (1992) [13] not only means hindering the development of new models, but also neglecting the numerous metaphors for 'elsewhere' that have also had a hand in shaping virtual worlds: from the Christian heaven to the island in *The Tempest*, from Moore's *Utopia* to Carroll's *Wonderland*. Gazira's works make constant references to these 'other' places (such as the heaven in *COME.TO.HEAVEN*, which in "[Collateral Damage]" is accessible to all, simply by typing "heaven me"). But it is in the short film *Gaz' of the desert* (2007), and the other works closely connected to this that references to a specific vision of 'elsewhere' are put forward with the force of a statement of poetics.

And this elsewhere is none other than the "surreality" conceived by the surrealists in 1924, and explicitly referenced in the title of the Second Front performance. In other words Gazira Babeli asserts that Second Life is a 3D manifestation of our collective subconscious, an imaginary sphere where body and space reveal a new dimension, where the notions of cause and effect cease to apply and where the succession of events is rapid, irrational and gratuitous, like a flow of thoughts. Second Life is a new mental space, where even an invasion of pizzas which spurt tomato sauce in all directions and sing "O Sole mio" when trodden on (*SingingPizza*, 2006) can be accepted; a dream-like landscape where space becomes animated, as in the installation *[Collateral Damage] = [Pizzaiolo!!!] + [Devil's Right Hand]* (2007), a stage where a pizza spatula and a guitar play ping pong with pizzas and vinyl records, which when they hit someone in the audience, project him or her to a space in front of an audience forced to applaud. This is a place where, like in our dreams, our bodies can undergo sudden metamorphoses, and an image or a sculpture can unexpectedly become a real space, an infinite desert that can be explored in all directions.

In this desert – the "portable set" of *Gaz' of the Desert*, which also appeared in *U AreHere* –, amid dawns and sunsets of overwhelming beauty, Gazira retreats, like Simeon the Stylite (the hermit who gave rise to that singular ascetic practice of spending a spiritual retreat seated atop a column) [14] to take on the temptations of the devil, interpreted in the film by the stunning Chi5 Shenzhou. Perched on her column in the driving rain, Gazira holds out for as long as she can, but in the end she is forced to give in. Only then are we catapulted into the anodyne setting of a call center (the office of *U AreHere*), where between calls Gazira appears to be busy putting together her story: imprisoned in the "world in a valise" she has chosen to live in, in her own surreal reality.

First published with the title "Gaz', Queen of the Desert" in the catalogue of the show "Gazira Babeli – [Collateral Damage]", ExhibitA, Odyssey, April 16 - May 30, 2007, curated by Sugar Seville and Beavis Palowakski.

[1] G. Babeli, in Wirxli Flimflam, "Gaza Stripped. Interview with Gazira Babeli", in *Slate Magazine*, January 2007.

[2] See Matteo Bittanti, "[Introduzione]", in Mario Gerosa, *Second Life*, Meltemi, Rome 2007, p. 14.

[3] G. Babeli, in W. Flimflam, quoted.

[4] See the definition of "Grey Goo" in *Wikipedia*: http://en.wikipedia.org/wiki/Grey_goo.

[5] http://arsvirtua.com.

[6] "13 Most Beautiful Avatars", curated by Marisa Olson.

[7] See Philip K. Dick, *The Three Stigmata of Palmer Eldritch*, 1964. In the novel the Perky Pat dolls are simulacra that, when associated with the use of a hallucinogenic drug, Can-D, enable earthlings deported to Mars to be temporarily "translated" into an imaginary world where they can experience an existence similar to their terrestrial lives through the body of Perky Pat, a Barbie-like doll.

[8] G. Babeli, in Tilman Baumgärtel, "'My body can walk barefoot, but my avatar needs Prada shoes'. Interview with Gazira Babeli", in *Nettime*, March 23, 2007.

[9] Second Front (http://secondfront.org) is an international collective of performance artists established in Second Life on November 23, 2006.

[10] G. Babeli, in W. Flimflam, quoted.

[11] Inke Arns, "Read_me, run_me, execute_me: Software and its discontents, or: It's the performativity of code, stupid!", in: Olga Goriunova / Alexei Shulgin (eds.), *Read_me. Software Art and Cultures Conference*, Aarhus, University of Aarhus 2004, pp. 176-193.

[12] G. Babeli, in T. Baumgärtel, quoted.

[13] Cf. William Gibson, "Burning Chrome", in *Omni*, July 1982 and Neal Stephenson, *Snow Crash*, Bantham Books 1992.

[14] Babeli took her inspiration from *Simón del desierto*, the 1965 Luis Buñuel film dedicated to Saint Simeon.

Interview with Second Front

The following interview was done by email in February 2007, and published on the online platform Rhizome. Since then, Second Front's performances have been shown live in New York, Los Angeles, Moscow, Brussels, Berlin, Vancouver and many other cities, and featured in magazines such as ArtForum and Art in America. Its current seven-member troupe includes Gazira Babeli (Italy), Fau Ferdinand aka Yael Gilks (London), Bibbe Oh aka Bibbe Hansen (New York), Tran Spire aka Doug Jarvis (Victoria), Great Escape aka Scott Kildall (San Francisco), Man Michinaga aka Patrick Lichty (Chicago) and Lizsolo Mathilde aka Liz Solo (St. Johns).

At first sight they might look like a pop hybrid between the X-men and the Four Horsemen of the Apocalypse, reviewed through the exaggerated and postmodern aesthetics of a virtual world such as Second Life. Quite the contrary. They are the first performance art group in Second Life: serious guys, practicing artists, curators and academics in real life, who decided to sound out the performative possibilities offered by a public virtual space that is growing at an impressive rate and being filled up by media agencies, stores, products, brands and inhabitants.

Second Front officially formed on November 23, 2006, gaining new members right up until the last few days. The current members are: Wirxli Flimflam aka Jeremy Owen Turner; Tea Chenille aka Tanya Skuce; Man Michinaga aka Patrick Lichty; Alise Iborg aka Penny Leong Browne; Tran Spire aka Doug Jarvis; Great Escape aka Scott Kildall; Lizsolo Mathilde aka Liz Pickard; Gazira Babeli aka CLASSIFIED.

The attention of "in-world" media came fast, even if Second Front doesn't seem to work much on communication: its very first performances were set up, unannounced, in public spaces, in front of a small, unwitting audience. Then, almost immediately (January 5, 2007) came the major intervention at Ars Virtua Gallery – the most famous contemporary art gallery in Second Life – for the opening of the visionary installation by the American artist John Craig Freeman (JC Fremont in Second Life). And many other performances...

Saying that Second Front is opening new paths in an unexplored territory is not rhetorical; and the loose, immodest and a slightly punkish way in which they do it is definitely unrhetorical. Their key feature is openness: openness and a plurality of visions and perspectives, which is quite blatant in this interview (where they all decided to give their own answers to the same question); they are open about a wide range of interventions, from reenactment to improvisation to code performing; open about different ways of shaping their work for the art audience, from prints to video to live broadcasting. They are growing up before our very eyes. And, rest assured, they hold good things in store.

WHAT IS SECOND FRONT?

Man Michinaga: Second Front is an international performance art group whose sole venue is the online world, Second Life. Second Front has members from Vancouver, St. Johns, Chicago, New Orleans, and Milan (to name a few), and works with numerous artists from around the world.

Wirxli Flimflam: As of January 14th, Second Front received official legitimacy from the *Ava-Star* tabloid (owned by *Die Zeit* in Germany) as the "first performance art group in Second Life". This basically makes us the in-world equivalent of Fluxus – perhaps we could also be nicknamed "SLuxus". This sudden rush from formation to celebrity has been quite fascinating since Second Front officially formed on November 23, 2006.

As for a more detailed idea of what Second Front is all about, some people in Second Life might confuse us with a "performing arts" group rather than a "performance arts" group. We are not a circus act nor a dance or theatre troupe, although our artistic practice might superficially resemble those other performing acts at times.

Tran Spire: Second Front is a network of performance-interested artists exploring new and different environments, specifically the online 3D animated game world of Second Life. The members have come together through a myriad of personal relationships that existed during the early days of the group's formation. This dynamic has morphed and mutated to include and involve variations on membership based on who is available and what presence they can perform with the others.

WHAT DOES IT MEAN, FOR YOU, TO STAGE PERFORMANCES IN SECOND LIFE? DO YOU REHEARSE OR DO YOU PREFER IMPROVISATION? DO YOU WORK WITH CODE OR DO YOU SIMPLY DO WHAT ALL THE OTHER AVATARS DO?

Alise Iborg: So far we have done both. I think it depends on what kind of performance we wish to stage. If it is better improvised we will probably do that. Each has its advantages and disadvantages. With prerecorded performances, we can fine-tune and edit out things we don't want the audience to see. But with improvised performances, the work takes on a life of its own fueled by the creative energy of our players which really shows through. Also, many times, it's the surprises and unintended actions that make the work really come alive!

Man Michinaga: Performing in Second Life gives Second Front the opportunity to work at a scale they would not normally be able to work on if done in the physical world, and play to a wider audience. Our level of preparedness is dependent on the context for the event. In regards to whether we use code or not, Second Front is using a growing set of code-based interventions in its performances, thanks to our techno-doyen, Mama Gaz Babeli. In regards to our avatars and props, almost nothing we use is 'standard', but some of us retain a few basic props like specific wings, or even old beginner's props like hair as a sign of their past as newcomers to Second Life.

Wirxli Flimflam: When we rehearse and plan scripts for major public performance events, we still have to rely on individual improvisation. Nothing is ever entirely scripted so each member can do their "own thing" and have breathing room yet at the same time not be confused as to what they should be doing. We use scripts and rehearsals etc. as a guide to help the performing member to feel secure with the thematic manner with which they wish to improvise. This allows for group cohesion both on an optical and practical level.

Great Escape: Second Life offers a unique space for performance. Without the normal constraints of the body – the usual center of performance – and without a traditional audience, we can try and do things that have been previously thought to be impossible.

Tran Spire: Performing in Second Life introduces variables and situations that complement and push further the understanding and comprehension that the members of the group share as a sense of what is real. By engaging with the contrived space of an online gaming environment, the challenges to perform are exaggerated by the parameters that persist as they interface with the context, the others members of the group, audiences and the templates of performance as an art medium. All of the tropes of performance are available to the group to use at will, hopefully to ends beyond the surface of what may appear evident around us.

Gazira Babeli: The real performance starts with login, the rest is performance record. The avatar just tries to forget being a code.

DO YOU PREFER PUBLIC SPACES OR ART VENUES FOR YOUR PERFORMANCES?

Man Michinaga: Second Front chooses its venues to fit the context of the piece and the performance. In the case of *Border Control*, it was done at Ars Virtua, therefore the context was that of an art space. For our *Breaking News* and *Abject Apocalypse* pieces, these were context specific (the Reuters building and the Star over the Christmas Tree at the US's NBC Rockefeller Plaza), and were performed in situ, with the product being the documentation.

Wirxli Flimflam: Personally, I prefer a large and well-known public venue that is not usually within the context of high-art. So for example, IBM, Sears, American Apparel, Wired, and Reuters are all great examples of the kind of venues I think are really inspirational for me. Again, this is a personal preference and not necessarily reflective of Second Front as a group.

Great Escape: It depends on the nature of the performance. An art venue is interesting because it brings Second Life into the physical space. I think it is ideal to broadcast the performance at an art venue while engaging with a specific site in Second Life.

Gazira Babeli: In art venues you can be welcomed with cheers, in public spaces with bullets. I prefer the latter, as death doesn't exist.

WHAT KIND OF AUDIENCE ARE YOU LOOKING FOR? DO YOU THINK THAT A PERFORMANCE IN SECOND LIFE COULD ALSO BE DISPLAYED IN THE REAL WORLD?

Man Michinaga: We are interested in reaching out to audiences who are interested in Second Life, and we are curious about the possibilities that avatar-based performance art can have. Currently, Second Front is performing in hybrid venues, such as simultaneous events in its home, the BitFactory in Han Loso, and in physical spaces, like Vancouver's Western Front, and Chicago's Gallery 416. We do hope that in addition to our performances in Second Life, Second Front can have exhibitions of its performances, imagery, video, and ephemera in the physical domain as well as any and all possible media. We do not wish to be limited by media, and also wish to spread our curiosity to the widest possible audience.

Great Escape: One thing I think we're looking to do is to question the underlying assumptions of Second Life and what it means to be a virtual being in that space. A dominant trend in Second Life is to shop, make friends online and participate in a virtual economy. We think this can be a venue for unique artistic expression. In this way, anyone in Second Life is an appropriate audience. The possibilities of the space haven't been fully explored as of yet and so I think people are much more receptive to performances than they might be in real life. Because it is so new, we can have a huge effect on people's thinking.

Tran Spire: I like the idea that the notion of an audience is being blurred by my own participation in this group. I am conscious of the fact that during all the stages of our performances, from pre-production planning emails to after-party videos, I am both a performer with the group and an audience to the many things taking place. Anything that contributes to challenging this space and dichotomy between creator and audience I think is an interesting thing to pursue.

Alise Iborg: We are looking for open-minded audiences who are not afraid to be part of the performance. And absolutely, Second Front could be displayed in the real world. The term that I use to describe this intervention in the real world, is 'virtual leakage'. I define virtual leakage as a two-way exchange between the virtual and the real, through which new hybrid meanings can be made. Meaning-making can no longer operate within the hermetic cases of the real vs. virtual, but instead, becomes a back and forth exchange in which ideas migrate by osmosis. While we as Second Life avatars become more real in the virtual world, so too, do we as human inhabitants of the real world become more virtual. In my opinion, there is an amazing opportunity for Virtual Reality (VR) to stake its own territory, but in order for VR to produce meaning that breaks with the real and from past artistic social practices, and to become a medium that produces singular works, the binary of the real vs virtual must be dismantled. Only then, will we be able to look at VR not as a simulation of the real, but as a simulation of itself.

Gazira Babeli: I prefer an unaware audience, an audience who does not necessarily have to understand what's going on. Second Life is a real world.

CAN YOU TELL ME SOMETHING ABOUT THE PERFORMANCES YOU HAVE STAGED TO DATE? HOW HAS YOUR APPROACH CHANGED FROM THE FIRST ONE?

Man Michinaga: Like any experimental troupe, we are always learning, and this affects our performance process. In addition, for *Breaking News*, many of us were only recently active, so our first performance was a really interesting experience. In short, *Breaking News* was an absurdist play on the 18th century idea of the Town Crier, played out in the latest of 21st Century news facilities. By shouting out non-sequitur, moment-to-moment headlines, Second Front hoped to perhaps jam the usual flow of information in the Reuters space, and possibly (ridiculously enough) barge into Adam Reuters' office itself! On the second occasion, we did get an audience, as passers-by stopped and sat to listen to our tabloid headlines. Of course (we assume) they did not take us seriously. For *Border Control*, we knew we would have an audience, and that we would need to fill a fairly set period of time with detailed orchestration, so we experimented at the BitFactory, rehearsing a series of vignettes that fit the context of JC Fremont & Rain Coalcliff's Mexican Border installation. The first act, "Border Patrol" was a Dada-esque performance of the increasing militarization of the borders throughout North America. Following that, "Red Rover" was a play on the creation of a border in the traditional children's game, but in our case the border decided to break down the audience instead of the other way around. Lastly, the final act, "Danger Room" was a piece that was intended to inspire a gestalt of danger and chaos in the age of Terror, but unexpectedly, chaos erupted and the sim actually crashed, whether by our actions or a combination of us and the audience isn't really clear. The approaches for the two pieces are quite different, as one is ad-hoc and the other follows a set choreography and set. Are we changing? Of course; it wouldn't be interesting if we weren't. We learn new things each performance, and while certain things get easier, we then try to push the envelope harder in other areas.

Tran Spire: I like to think that part of the script of each performance is written in the code of the place or environment in which it is situated. This lets the content be influenced by not only the art or non-art context but also by the different terrains that can exist in real life as well as in Second Life.

WHAT DO YOU THINK ABOUT ART IN SECOND LIFE? IS PERFORMANCE THE ONLY POSSIBLE WAY TO MAKE ART OUT THERE?

Man Michinaga: Absolutely not. While Second Life has limitations like any medium, the members of Second Front are excited to see individuals working in many different forms of expression, such as live music, 'painting', sculpture, even fireworks and aerial ballet. While Second Life is relatively new, the possibilities for expression in virtual worlds has yet to be fully explored. That's why Second Front was created!

Wirxli Flimflam: Context is extremely important here. Part of what makes Second Life itself is the fact that every moment seems like part of a performance. The fact that everything can be customizable in Second Life as well as the fact that just about any object can be wearable enhances my personal impression that performance art is the most "authentic" medium of Second Life in that Greenberghian sense.

Great Escape: Right now, the Second Life galleries are mostly replicating paintings and sculpture, enhanced with visual effects in Second Life. This is what you'd expect with the first generation of art-making in any new medium. I think that what we've seen so far in Second Life is only a glimpse of what the future holds.

Alise Iborg: Absolutely not. Second Life has offered the ability for anyone to create in VR which means that there are boundless possibilities for creativity and unprecedented work. In my opinion, VR is in itself a new medium but what is unique about VR is that through its technology, it can create work that can free itself from past art practices, though there are also amazing avenues of creation by referencing precedent artists and works, For instance, our *Last Supper* performance appropriates one of the most canonic religious events by producing an event of binging and purging art itself!

Gazira Babeli: Second Life is a frame-space which can include all sorts of artistic perversion. I call it performance, anyway. But if you find a better definition, please let me know.

WHAT IS YOUR RELATIONSHIP WITH YOUR REAL LIFE COUNTERPART?

Man Michinaga: There really is none. Patrick Lichty does not exist. Only I am real, and I control him. On a more serious note, the relationship between Man and Patrick is completely in line with my RL life. I am very sensitive to context, and the way I act in one context may be very different from another. In Second Life I feel that one has to be "Larger than Life", and that's what Man is – he's a big dark, figure – part angel, part rock star, part architect, part actor. That is, all the things that Second Life gives the individual more freedom to be if they so desire. I think that most of Second Front do this with great effectiveness and aplomb. My greatest concern is "the risk of the Artist"; that is, the bleed between worlds that I take by making potentially controversial art in Second Life. I think that Second Life is the first place where we can say that sometimes our actions online DO matter, and this is very perplexing.

Great Escape: I think that the avatar Great Escape occupies a strange nook in my subconscious. In many ways, Second Life operates as a fantastical dream state. We can fly, teleport and pick up houses and cars. My avatar has purple skin and fire out of his hair. When I go to sleep at night, images of the other Second Front members often fill my head. So for me, my avatar is embedded in my psyche, rather than an extension of my self.

Wirxli Flimflam: In a lot of ways, the relationship between Wirxli and Jeremy is much closer than one might think from first seeing me. I did intentionally want to make Wirxli more alien than human or perhaps a kind of first-generation "post-human". I was also reading up about the stereotypical shaman in most cultures who is gender-ambiguous... so in this case, there is a slight departure here from my Real Life self.

Tran Spire: I prefer to triangulate, dimensionally shift my relationship to each of the entities constituting themselves as versions of me. Therefore, I am waiting for the two to have a discussion and then ask me to join the conversation. I am interested to hear what they come up with and how they define themselves in regards to existence in a spatio-temporal plane, and whether they recognize each other.

Gazira Babeli: My body can walk barefoot, but my avatar needs shoes.

This interview was commissioned by and first published in *Rhizome.org* on March 1, 2007, with the title "A Leap Into the Void: Interview with Second Front".

Holy Fire, or My Last New Media Art Exhibition

The following text was written in 2008 for the catalogue of the exhibition Holy Fire. Art of the Digital Age, that I curated with Yves Bernard at the iMAL Center for Digital Cultures and Technology in Bruxelles. The exhibition sparked heated debate, that can still be followed by the reader on websites such as Rhizome and Fluctuat. In the framework of this book, this text introduces the issues of the positioning of New Media Art in the contemporary art field and the current uselessness of the label "New Media Art", and contributes to the international debate about new media curating, better addressed in the following text.

Holy Fire is an exhibition that could appear strange to the layperson, whatever the religion professed. Strange to the art fair visitor, being invited to an anomalous area, a "Center for Digital Cultures and Technology", to visit an exhibition of works with no common denominator between them, except for belonging to an alleged "Digital Age". Strange for a member of the so-called New Media Art community, coming to iMAL and finding something very different from his or her customary field: an exhibition of objects, some of which are "computer-based", but many more undeniably "traditional" – and once more with little in common between them. To both, *Holy Fire* might seem like "an exhibition without a concept". *Touché.*

Holy Fire is an exhibition which started life as a challenge: to organize an exhibition of New Media Art featuring works present on the art market. The aim of this essay is to explore how a routine operation in the art world actually becomes a cultural strategy (a "concept") in this context.

An Exhibition without a Concept?

Once upon a time there was the sixties. Extraordinary years, which laid the foundations for most of the art around today. Years in which artists, freed from the restrictions of formalism, began working with everything they could get their hands on: archived documents, organic materials, photographs, video devices, and the first computers. They defined new forms of art, and often bound themselves to a new brand of formalism. Video Art, Computer Art... artists worked on the specific characteristics of their medium, addressing that medium. We could call it "the curse of Greenberg": new media, the main thing to come out of that widening of artistic styles which became possible when someone decided to violate Greenberg's "flatness", always undergo a period of fierce formalism. But that's another story.

Video Art went on to follow the destiny we all know: after a brief spell of incubation, during which video was "the vacation of art" (Shigeko Kubota), it became a fully-fledged art medium, and started being used by artists who did not view themselves as video artists; even those who first donned the title of Video Art Curator began questioning whether the term "Video Art" had any meaning beyond a mere classification of materials. Now the term is only used nostalgically, but video is ubiquitous.

Digital media were a different story. Computer Art, after a promising debut, with exhibitions like *Computer-Generated Pictures*, staged in 1965 by the Howard Wise Gallery in New York, and *Cybernetic Serendipity*, held in 1968 at the ICA in London – retired to the labs it had come out of. The medium was still too complex and inaccessible for artists without particular technical skills, and digital artists carved out a comfortable niche for themselves, working in close contact with technicians, scientists and engineers. The decision to engage in art "with a prefix" became a survival strategy, with artists holed up in "peer" communities to continue experimenting, without running the risk of over-simplifying things. Companies and institutions started to offer lab facilities and awarded prizes, and the first international festivals and conferences came into being: Siggraph, Ars Electronica, etc. Even when digital media managed to put in an appearance at traditional art venues (like Documenta 6, or the 1986 Venice Biennale), those involved found it hard to view this as anything but an exceptional, one-off thing, and to envisage a confident encounter with contemporary art.

The world of New Media Art thus grew and firmed up, and when in the mid 90s, thanks to the advent of the web and the explosion of so-called consumer IT, the medium finally became accessible to all, this parallel art world was stronger and more solid than ever before.

In this context the phenomenon of net.art played a formidable role historically speaking, despite the fact that it perhaps never came to full fruition. What it brought to the world of "New Media" – up till that time dominated by buzzwords like "interactive" "multimedia" and "virtual" – was critical culture, the ironic eye of an avant-garde movement, political activism, conceptual play and a healthy disregard for pixel poisoning (the New Media version of Duchamp's "turpentine poisoning"). Net.art managed to bring digital media into the ring with contemporary art, and lay the basis for a dialogue. I have never viewed New Media Art as an avant-garde movement, but I have no doubt that net.art was. Not incidentally, the big museums – from Guggenheim to SFMoma - began courting net.art like never before; and not incidentally the encounter with "old school" New Media Art was often more of a clash, as in 1999 with the *Net.art Browser* created by Jeffrey Shaw for *Net_condition*.

In other words, net.art managed to bridge that great cultural divide between what Lev Manovich in a 1996 essay called "Duchamp Land" and "Turing Land" [1]. At the same time however, all the emphasis on the internet as the new ground for art, and the anti-establishment (and anti-market) stance of the first net.art led it to view the advances of the art world somewhat ironically, if not with open disdain.

As for the world of New Media Art, there is no doubt that it is now doing better than ever before. And this is a good thing. Digital media have not lost their potential for risk-taking, and there is still groundbreaking work being done that can only exist "at the edge of art", to quote the title of a great book by Joline Blais and Jon

Ippolito [2]. For this reason it is a good thing that there continues to be a kind of "no-man's land" for experimentation, inhabited by specialists, alien to market and product logic, stimulating production of and debate on a form of art that cannot or does not want to conform to these rules: an ecosystem in which digital media research can develop free of any kind of restriction. What I protest against, and what many artists, critics and curators have protested against before me, is that transfers from one world to the other are still so rare, and so difficult to achieve; that the audiences of the two spheres are still so different, even though the art itself is often culturally very similar; that those who write about contemporary art know nothing about New Media Art, while those who write about New Media Art hardly ever do so in a contemporary art journal, and that an artist with five Transmediale and four Ars Electronica appearances under his or her belt, as well as years of experience, but without at least one solo show in a private gallery, is viewed as a new arrival.

And that we talk about New Media Art, when we could simply talk about art. Because when all is said and done, this is the point: in the last fifteen years, New Media Art has lost its prefix. Even when it is highly self-referential and technical, the popularity of the medium makes its technical feats appreciable to even a lay public. Unfortunately – or fortunately – the computer has become almost a household appliance. We might not be able to identify the heating element, but we all know it needs protecting from limescale. What's more, the pervasive nature of the medium goes hand in hand with its ability to influence our present and condition our future; a present and future that few artists know how to decode as lucidly as new media artists.

As Inke Arns recently wrote: «The specific character of the media arts under post-medium conditions is today not the media, but their specific form of *contemporaneity*...». And she continues, intentionally provocative: «There is no area of contemporary art in which a comparably intensive engagement with the growing medial constitution of our world is taking place on both a substantive and conceptual plane». [3]

At this point the concept of *Holy Fire* starts to become clearer. *Holy Fire* sets out to bridge the gap between these two worlds, in the belief that there is no radical difference between the language they speak. Or, better still, *Holy Fire* wants to prove that there is already a bridge between these two worlds, which consists in the multitude of artists, critics, curators and professionals of various kinds and levels that work astride both. It wants to show the contemporary art world that there is loads of interesting stuff on the other side: works that talk about us, the machines we live with, the media, its political role and social impact, our relationship with the world, space, time and nature, and the fragmentation of the ego and its translation into information flows.

With regards to the world of New Media Art, *Holy Fire* wants to challenge some die-hard preconceptions, like its dismissive attitude towards the role played by the market and its reiterated assumption that New Media Art is "immaterial", "disseminated", "collaborative", and "open": difficult to preserve and therefore not preservable; difficult to collect and therefore not collectable; difficult to sell and therefore not saleable. Difficult to preserve? What about Leonardo's *Last Supper?* Difficult to collect? Christo! Immaterial? *Air de Paris* by Duchamp. Collaborative? The Fluxus boxes. All things that have found their own solid position in art history.

As for the market, its defects are common knowledge. The dynamics of the transformation of art into goods, and goods into fetish, are perverse under many aspects, and have undone hundreds of artists, after fêting them. But socially and culturally speaking there's not much we can about it: everything that has been recognized as art in the last hundred years or so has traveled that path. And when it functions as it should, the market plays a decisive role. It acts as a buffer between artists' freedom to experiment and the historicization of works. On one side there is complete freedom, on the other a series of prerequisites (material, economic and cultural) which are indispensable if a work is to survive over time. The outcome of this collision is called "work of art". The market is not the only entity that can play this role, anything but: it would be desirable for critics, curators and museums to look to other contexts as well. Occasionally this happens, and has happened in the past, but the results have not been up to much.

At the high point of the New Economy, the American museums devoted much attention to Media Art: shows, debates and collections all publicized with great hype. Without wishing to belittle the importance of that phase, the fallout is there for all to see. Nowadays the initiatives organized by mainstream museums in the digital media field are almost always perceived as low profile operations, and presented as a kind of sideline.

But where the Guggenheim, MoMA and Walker Art Center have failed, a small Spanish museum, MEIAC in Badajoz, has been successful. Thanks to the work of curator António Cerveira Pinto, in 2005 the museum purchased works by 26 "New Media" artists, including many net-based works. This was possible because it did not call for projects, but works. It challenged formalism and trusted in the fact that New Media Art does not necessarily have to be "immaterial", "ephemeral", or non-preservable, and that even when it is, it is the museum's job to look after it [4].

I am convinced that the fact that fifty years of New Media Art have even been touched on in *Art since 1900*, the establishment bible published by Foster-Krauss-Bois-Buchloh, is not an oversight (or maybe it is: some oversight!), nor does it demonstrate that the topic is uninteresting. In my opinion it is more a question of strategy, the strategy adopted in the New Media Art field. It is this strategy that has to be rewritten. Our beautiful city has turned into a ghetto: well it's time to tear down the walls. This is why works like the *Art Appliances* by John F. Simon, computers and screens turned into sculptures, are so important, as are Eddo Stern's installations and Carlo Zanni's *Altarboy* [5]: they make possible things that we critics declare to be impossible. When, in 2002, Eva and Franco Mattes began talking to gallery owner Fabio Paris, they had two Biennales to their credit, as well as various high profile operations, but their entire oeuvre lay on a network server and a partition of a hard disk. The path they chose – that of translating pieces of performance art that use the net as favoured medium or logistic support, into relatively "traditional" formats (prints, video, sculptures) – was adopted almost in parallel by other artists (such as the Austrian duo UBERMORGEN.COM). Now it is one of the most popular ways of adapting for exhibition space works conceived and created on a computer screen. The other approach, also well represented in the show, does not attempt to abandon the machine or surpass the software, but rather integrates it into the layout, in forms which are now known to be highly stable and collector-friendly. Without over-simplifying things, the first approach is used by artists of a "conceptual" nature, who view the machine as a theatre for a story that can also be subsequently told in ways which are more suited to exhibition space, using traditional media, while the second approach is used by artists whose works attribute considerable importance to the process-driven or interactive nature of the medium, or its time-based character. This does not prevent many artists from switching easily between approaches, according to the demands of the work in question: Olia Lialina & Dragan Espenschied chose a touch-screen for *Midnight*, and prints on aluminium for *With Elements of Web 2.0*; Casey Reas at times opts to print his "processes", and John F. Simon always teams the fluid vitality of software with drawings.

My Last New Media Art Exhibition

«Forget the new, drop the media, enjoy art.» Regine Debatty

When I began working on *Holy Fire*, I contacted Brody Condon, an artist I very much wished to feature in the exhibition. Not just because his recent work – which uses the graphic engines of videogames to create bizarrely syncretic animated altarpieces – would have shed new light on the title of the show, but also because his brief career is emblematic of many of the topics we have explored here: his well-defined poetics – that of a child of the 90s dealing with the big themes (death, violence and religion) by means of daily videogaming – are combined with a style that is able to pass, with a keen awareness of the internal needs of the work, from sculpture to direct intervention on the digital medium. This led to a lively debate, during the course of which Condon said:

> «every time you describe these artists by material, you are hurting, and not helping them [...] It's about ideas, not material. I don't give a shit about new media, it's just the material I understand intuitively from my youth. I've never been to one of these famous 'new media art festivals' you speak of. Many of these people listed have been participating in art fairs regularly, and are already doing fine in traditional art collections. What's new here? [...] It's time to step up the game. New media needs a PR campaign in the traditional arts demographic for sure, it's very marginalized, but is this it?»

I personally see Condon's refusal as a positive sign: proof that out there exists an avant-garde body of artists who have already surpassed the mediation-oriented perspective of *Holy Fire* – artists that have already moved on. For me his words have been a guide and a warning throughout my work on the exhibition.

Like Inke Arns and Jakob Lillemose [6], I believe that the days of "specialized" exhibitions are over. Like Condon, I believe that every time I describe these artists by material, I'm hurting, and not helping them. I can see that daily, and this is why I have decided that this will be my last time, albeit in a rather unusual way. *Holy Fire* sets out to be the swansong for New Media Art exhibitions. Its main flaw – the lack of cohesion between the works – is in fact its statement, one of the reasons for its existence. I want the audience, the audience of one of the main contemporary art fairs, ArtBrussels, to realize that there is no connection between the work of Casey Reas and that of Gazira Babeli, but that they are both outstanding works. And I want *Holy Fire* to be a push for change: so that the next time members of the public see a work by Casey Reas, it will be in an exhibition of late 20th century abstract art, alongside Sol LeWitt and Peter Halley (I think I only really *got* the work of Casey Reas when I saw one of his "processes" projected onto a big plasterboard wall beside one of Sol LeWitt's *Wall Drawings* [7]); and that the next time they see a Gazira Babeli it will be in a show exploring the human body and identity, alongside Cindy Sherman and Matthew Barney. I want to kill off my own specialization and move on to the next stage.

Naturally this is a personal stance, even though the group interview that follows [8] shows that it is common to more people than I would ever have imagined. It is evident that there exists a generation of artists and curators who see the separation between the two worlds as a gap to be bridged. There are various ways and forms of accomplishing this. Brody Condon, and many other artists, have chosen to stand directly on the other side, not acknowledging the existence of another world that might appreciate their work. Arns and Lillemose, in the essay quoted, feel that the world of "computer-based art" should open up to "non-computer-based" art, highlighting its dynamic nature, its contact with other cultures – to forge a dialogue which could not be more productive. They came up with the challenge of staging an exhibition of "computer-based art" without computers. These are all signs of a process of evolution, a process that *Holy Fire* desires to be a part of.

Conclusions

> «I hate to shatter your lovely mythos there, but if art can come out of a camera, it's got no problem crawling out of a support tank... I have the holy fire now. That's a silly name for it, I guess, but it's as real as dirt, so why should I care what you call it?» [9]

The holy fire we have borrowed from Bruce Sterling is, first and foremost, the holy fire of art, which without hyperbole we recognize in all the artists presented here. Their "novelty" lies not in their medium – as Sterling's collector Helene comments to the artist Mia/Maya, "any fool gets cheap novelty from a new medium" – but in "a different subjectivity", namely the ability to talk about our present as few others are able to. In their acknowledgement of something that many others leave by the wayside, these artists really do possess something special, something which they all have in common, and which is capable of breathing new life into the art world: the liquid, processual nature of software in the works of Reas and Mealey, Zanni and Boredomresearch; the exploration of identity, as hybrid, multiplied and fragmented, evolved or involved in the constant interferences between the biological and digital dimensions, in the works of Babeli, the Mattes, UBERMORGEN.COM and Stern; addressing a new conception of space and time, the dialogue between real landscape and information landscapes, between natural and artificial in the works of Staehle and Napier, Chatonsky and Bruno, Leandre, Lab[au] and Simon; tackling the media, in terms of culture, aesthetics and past and present conventions in the works of Arcangel and Jodi, Olia Lialina and Dragan Espenschied, Cosic, Slocum, Alexei Shulgin and Aristarkh Chernyshev; dealing with life and its evolution in Hope and Chevalier; and language, narration and its innovative potential in Sebti, Levin and Sandison.

But the holy fire of the title is also a reference and a tribute to the passion that drives all the people variously involved in this process of mediation between two so distant worlds: persevering gallery owners who present art which others have declared to be unsaleable and out of the market; persevering collectors who gather the fruits of an art which others have declared to be uncollectable; and the curators, critics, artists... *Holy Fire* is the result of a concerted effort, and the resulting chorus of voices, not necessarily in unison, is what the exhibition, and this book, pays homage to.

First published in D. Quaranta, Y. Bernard (eds.), *Holy Fire. Art of the Digital Age*, exhibition catalogue. FPEditions, Brescia 2008. Translated from Italian by Anna Rosemary Carruthers.

[1] Lev Manovich, "The Death of Computer Art", 1996 [revised 2001]. Available at www.manovich.net/TEXT/death.html.

[2] Joline Blais, Jon Ippolito, *At the Edge of Art*, Thames & Hudson, London – New York 2006.

[3] Inke Arns, "And it exists after all. On the contemporaneity of the medial arts", 2008, unpublished. Courtesy of the author.

[4] More information at www.meiac.es.

[5] *AltarBoy* is a sculpture and a platform to show and to sell net based artworks. It consists of a customized case equipped with a laptop cpu, a 15" tft touch screen and a built-in auto logging web server. The Hard Disk hosts all the netart work scripts and once AltarBoy is connected to the web the work becomes visible and available for Internet users. For more informations, see www.zanni.org/html/altarboyallinfo.htm.

[6] Inke Arns & Jacob Lillemose, "'It's contemporary art, stupid'. Curating computer based art out of the ghetto", August 2005. First Published in: Anke Buxmann, Frie Depraetere (eds), *Argos Festival*, argoseditions, Brussels 2005, pp. 136 - 145.

[7] In the exhibition *Feedback. Art Responsive to Instructions, Input or its Environment*, March 30 – June 30, 2007, LABoral Centro de Arte y Creación Industrial, Gijon, Spain. Curated by Christiane Paul, Jemima Rellie, Charlie Gere.

[8] Cf. the catalogue of the show. The group interview included: Inke Arns & Jacob Lillemose, Aristarkh Chernyshev, Roman Minaev & Alexei Shulgin, Vuk Cosic, Régine Debatty, Steve Dietz, Joan Leandre, Olia Lialina & Dragan Espenschied, Patrick Lichty, Wolf Lieser, Vicente Matallana, Eva & Franco Mattes aka 0100101110101101.org, Fabio Paris, Christiane Paul, Charles Sandison, Magdalena Sawon & Tamas Banovich, Paul Slocum, Bruce Sterling, Michele Thursz, Mark Tribe, UBERMORGEN.COM, Karen A. Verschooren.

[9] Bruce Sterling, *Holy Fire*, 1996. P. 338 of the Spectra - Bantam Mass Market Edition, 1997.

Lost in Translation. Or, Bringing Net Art to Another Place? Pardon, Context

The dramatic explosion of the internet around the mid 90s, and its diffusion as an artistic medium, has ignited the theoretical debate on curatorial practice, rarely livelier than in these last fifteen years. There are many reasons behind this, though it is beyond the scope of this essay to examine them all individually. On the one hand the Net makes the curator's job much simpler: it ensures faster, easier access to information, and email facilitates relations with artists and other members of the art system. Some assert that it makes the curator all the more necessary, because this vast sea of information calls for a filter, while others believe that the curatorial role has become somewhat redundant, as information is better filtered using the specific tools available – curatorial software – and because, in the era of links and tag aggregators, the filtering function attributed to the curator can be performed by virtually all users.

With regards to art on the Net, the debate has developed in two complementary directions. The first sees the web as a new context for curatorial practice, which can be summed up as "online curating", while the second tackles the concept of bringing works designed for the web into the "physical" arena, and how this process of translation might be effected. The concept of translation plays a key role for both: the first looks at translating curatorial practice into forms suitable for the Web, while the second regards translating works that exist on the Net into forms that are practicable in the real world. Lastly, both approaches have flaws of formulation, something which has inevitable repercussions on the debate itself, rendering it often tedious and stale, and forcing it to focus on seemingly false problems.

In the first case the main error, in my view, lies in viewing the operative arena of the online curator as Net Art. On the internet, art exists in many different ways, and draws life from a constant interchange with a wide range of practices, cultures and subcultures. In the first years of its existence, when the efforts of artists and critics were focused on identifying the specifics of this artistic practice, certain barriers made sense, but now we all know that it's one thing to put your work on the Web, and quite another to create Net Art; now we all know that there is a big difference between software and software art, between fan culture and game art, machinima and video art. Maintaining these barriers means, at the very least, contributing to the ghettoization of Net Art, isolating it artificially from its context, and cutting the very ties that make it vital, interesting and contemporary. Just as it is about time for Net Art to appear on the cultural horizons of contemporary art curators, it is time for online curators to start looking beyond Net Art, to explore its links with contemporary art, corporate software, film narration, vernacular practices and so forth [1].

In the second case, which brings us to the subject of this essay, the main error lies in considering the intangible nature of data and the presence of technology as the main obstacles that the curator must tackle in his or her mediation work; if you will, interpreting curatorial practice as a mediation between two spaces, rather than two radically different contexts. The curator's priorities are thus as follows: to transform the work into an object, whatever that might be; to bring technology into the exhibition venue and display it as if it were a key element of the work, and to be familiar with technology. As a consequence, curators do little more than complain about the fact that exhibition venues are not suitable containers for New Media Art; that New Media Art cannot be stored or commercialized; that people don't "get" it, and that the art system is not interested. Rarely, however, do they get round to thinking that this is largely due to their own inability. The scarce appeal of New Media Art, so powerfully exposed by Geert Lovink in *Zero Comments* [2], is due first and foremost, in my view, to the inexperience of curators, their inability to comprehend that the mediation they must implement is above all cultural in nature, and the way they have banalized the concept of translation, which deserves to be reinstated in all its complexity [3]. New Media Art is cooler than ever: we just have to make people able to appreciate its beauty.

Barbarisms

«Translation is the action of interpretation of the meaning of a text, and subsequent production of an equivalent text, also called a translation, that communicates the same message in another language. The text to be translated is called the source text, and the language it is to be translated into is called the target language; the final product is sometimes called the target text». [4]

The first thing we learn from the Wikipedia definition of the term "translation" is that translating means interpreting, seeking an equivalent for conveying a message in another language. If we try to import this statement into our argument, we can see that installing a computer in an exhibition space, and using it to display a website or work of software does not constitute an act of translation. This is more akin to a foreignism: a word taken from another language when there is no equivalent in one's own language. Foreignisms are generally looked down on by translators, as they represent a failed act of translation, and when they are unnecessary they are usually reviled as barbarisms.

The question we must address at this point is the following: when we are in the position of exhibiting an online work in a real space, are foreignisms necessary? Is there really no "equivalent" that would enable us to convey the same "message" in a totally different context from the work's original one (the Net, the computer screen, the "private" use of a work accessible to all)? In other words: are we looking at a foreignism – undesirable but necessary – or a barbarism?

When it comes to the first occasions where Net Art tackled the arena of real space, the records include shows like *PORT: Navigating Digital Culture* (1996) [5] and *Documenta X* (1997). Both started out from the assumption that the dimension of Net Art was the Web, and that organizing a "real" exhibition meant not a display of "works" but a sort of access portal to another context. Both shows saw this foreignism as necessary, but tackled it in very different ways. In *Port*, the curators

Robbin Murphy and Remo Campopiano created a lab-like space with technology exhibited as a cornerstone of the Net Art experience. This was at an early stage, where technology was still viewed as geeky, and where the exceptional nature of New Media Art lay in fact that it was "New Media" - very new, very media. At *Documenta X*, on the other hand, the French curator Simon Lamunière came up with an office-like space, with works accessible from various terminals not hooked up to the Net. It is significant that the main criticism of *Documenta X* concerned the office metaphor and this lack of connection: at that time no-one believed that these works could be "translated" into forms suitable for real space. Foreignisms were regarded as necessary not only by curators, but also by artists, critics and the public. What was challenged was the way in which it was incorporated into the target language: the frame, or, if you will, the notes in the margin.

Also in 1999, with the *Net.art Browser* designed by Jeffrey Shaw for *net_condition* [6], there was no debate over the fact that the works were accessible via a screen in the exhibition venue: the problem was the fact that they were overwhelmed by a high-tech frame that had little in common with the spirit of the works, and that was in fact an artistic installation in its own right.

So when did foreignisms cease to be inevitable? The answer is banal: when artists stopped viewing them as such, and began to work directly on new ways of translating their works. When they began to think that technology could be put aside without necessarily interfering with the integrity of the message, or be adapted to the needs of the exhibition space. And when the public and the curators began thinking in the same way. At that time, a whole new era in Net Art and New Media Art in general opened up, deriving from a freedom of interaction with its medium that video art never enjoyed, and that is actually comparable to performance art. Video art remains bound to its medium, something that to date, and in spite of its success, has rendered it entirely unsuitable for exhibition purposes, an inadequacy never resolved by television screens, video boxes or screenings, and which is basically to do with its temporality and need for isolation in terms of lighting and sound.

As for performance art, there was a time when artists did not conceive of any kind of translation, in view of the blatantly unique, unrepeatable character of events. Nowadays not only can performance art be staged on more than one occasion, but also using a series of alternative presentational approaches: objects, props transformed into installations, images and video documentaries, etc. [7] New Media Art, when curators get round to realizing it, can aspire to a similar freedom. For this reason, confining a work of Net Art to a horrible networked computer in a corner of the exhibition space is a crime, or worse, a barbarism. That any good translator should avoid like the plague.

Mind the context!

«Translation must take into account constraints that include context, the rules of grammar of the two languages, their writing conventions, and their idioms. A common misconception is that there exists a simple word-for-word correspondence between any two languages, and that translation is a straightforward mechanical process. A word-for-word translation does not take into account context, grammar, conventions, and idioms». [8]

«A good translator understands the source language well, has specific experience in the subject matter of the text, and is a good writer in the target language. Moreover, he is not only bilingual but bicultural». [9]

Another die-hard assumption, and the most fatal for any kind of translation attempt, is that the transition is just a question of state: from bits to atoms, from process to object, from the intangible world of the media to the material world of life. From this angle there are no real translations, only metaphrasis, literal translations, like those offered by the numerous translation programmes available on the Net, producing translations that sound wrong to anyone who speaks the target language. Translating a work of Net Art for "physical" space does not mean simply transforming it into an object or an installation: it means adapting it to fit the aesthetic, cultural and formal needs of an audience different to that of the net. It means knowing the context, the grammar, the conventions and the idioms of the target language. It means, for example, knowing that there are contexts like Ars Electronica and the Venice Biennale which have entirely different conventions and idioms.

In an essay written around ten years ago [10], Lev Manovich proposed distinguishing between two radically different territories, in terms of culture and needs: Duchamp Land, namely the contemporary art world (interested in ironic, self-referencing, content-oriented, sophisticated works) and Turing Land, namely the New Media Art world (interested in simple works with a technological orientation, which take technology seriously and where possible deploy it to the utmost of its potential). This distinction, albeit toned down by a decade of New Media Art of a Duchampian matrix, still exists. Toshio Iwai feels more at home at Ars Electronica than UBERMORGEN.COM. I would add a third category to the original two, which, following on from the Manovich model, could be called Baran Land. This is the world of the net, the people who vote for videos on Youtube, blog about their passions and give rise to 15-second crazes and celebrities. Those in question are often young, with a low attention span but high critical faculties, culturally voracious, technologically savvy, often nomadic and constantly moving between different worlds: Turing Land and Duchamp Land, naturally, but also fashion, design, videogames, film, subcultures of all kinds and degrees. The high end model could be Régine Debatty or Tom Moody, but the variations are endless. This is the Net Art public, an audience that does not look to art in search of a collectable item, or a novel application of a new technology, just a cultural stimulus.

But when we move away from that world, if we want to make a mark we need to fulfill other demands. Neglecting these out of ignorance, arrogance or a flawed idea of consistency means creating a translation which is unsuccessful, and therefore essentially unfaithful. It should of course be remembered that translation is not always necessary. If I feel that my text only has full meaning in its native language, I can oblige other readers to read it in this form only. Many net.art projects that challenged the concept of a work of art as a unique object, and questioned the other premises of the art system, never left the web: the art public sought them out in their own context, and loved them for their very radicalism. Zero compromise = avant-garde, which net.art indeed was. But if we choose to go down the translation route, we need to compromise. It is about identifying the essence of each work, and trying to translate that into another language. In general, in Duchamp Land, if the technological interface, the connectivity, the processual aspect, the accessibility, the openness and non-unique nature of the work are not essential, it is a good idea to put them aside. If this is not the case, it is as well to keep them: the art world is open enough to accept open, replicable, processual works, if these aspects are an essential part of the work in question, and if their value can be transferred onto something else. Tino Sehgal's performances are an effective example. What is fundamental is that the translator, whether artist or curator, be not only bilingual, but also bicultural: and if he or she works both in the new media sphere and the contemporary art world, tricultural.

Translation Approaches

What I have said so far should be enough to highlight, if need be, the fact that there are no rules for translating works of Net Art into forms suited to real space, other than respecting the work and its essence (*fidelity* [11]), and knowledge of the cultural contexts of origin and destination (*transparency* [12]). Without these two factors, the price to pay is incommunicability – in other words the death of the work. The translation must be calibrated case by case, by the artist or curator (if possible in constant contact with the artist). Based on how things have developed so far, we can identify at least three basic approaches:

1. documentation;

2. translation;

3. derivative works.

In the first case the work is not translated but recounted, documented using the remains of the production process or documentary materials created as needed. At the artist's discretion both of these kinds of artifacts can be transformed into fetish objects, namely works of art in their own right.

This is what happened with performance art, and it is no coincidence that this model fits particularly well with performative works of Net Art. The documentation approach inevitably entails a kind of "diminished" translation of the original, but this "dilution" is accepted as a necessary evil both by the translator and the public. One interesting example of documentation, a minor curatorial masterpiece, was the 2002 show *net.ephemera*, curated by Mark Tribe for the Moving Image Gallery in New York [13]. Invited to curate a low budget Net Art exhibition for a physical space, the curator asked the artists concerned to submit not actual works, but ephemeral material on paper, the remains of the production process (sketches, diagrams, notes) or derivative works: the *net ephemera* of the title.

Translation, in the proper sense, occurs when the curator selects a work of Net Art and works out how to adapt it to a real-life context, if possible together with the artist, usually in the form of an installation. The result aims not to be a "diminished" presentation, but another version of the work; if you like, another interface for the same contents, an option offered by the variability that characterizes new media. In 2006, invited to curate an exhibition on the relation between the Net and the art of weaving [14], I decided to present a work by Lisa Jevbratt, *Infome Imager* (2002-2005). This is an online application that «allows the user to create "crawlers" (software robots, which could be thought of as automated web browsers) that gather data from the web, and provides methods for visualizing the collected data». [15] I contacted the artist, who told me that the work could be presented using prints (derivative works) or as a "workshop", with the artist's high quality prints displayed alongside a user-accessible installation, with a worktable, a computer connected to the Net, a printer and drawing pins for pinning up the images produced by visitors. As I believed that the participation component was essential to understanding the project, I decided to go for the second option. This obviously meant bringing an unsightly computer into the exhibition space (in this case, a deconsecrated church), a defect remedied by the conceptual framework of the workshop, which prevented viewers from limiting the work to what appeared on the screen, and which recalled the familiar aesthetics of DIY. The result, also in view of the space (believe it or not, a deconsecrated church is not exactly the ideal venue for a workshop), was not entirely satisfactory from the point of view of the design of the installation, but nonetheless the work was appreciated, and more importantly, understood.

As we have seen, the same work could have been presented using derivative works, in this case a series of prints. Derivative works are not the same thing as the work itself, but are objects that recall, wholly or in part, the conceptual nucleus of the work, and transfer its meaning onto items that unlike the former (and thanks to it) may also acquire financial value. In the New Media Art world, it is rather fashionable to dismiss derivative works, often created in traditional media (prints, video, sculptures) as mere "concessions to the market". And this is true: they are concessions to the market. But these concessions, in turn, are translation stratagems for a context, the art world, where cultural value has to translate into economic value to ensure the success, circulation and museification of the work.

In many cases these solutions coexist, and are adopted in relation to the context in which the work is presented. A case in point, in this regard, is the work *Biennale.py* which was created in 2001, by the partnership between [epidemiC] and 0100101110101101.ORG. The original work was a virus written in Python which was circulated on the Net on occasion of the two groups' appearance at the 49th Venice Biennale. From the outset the work had a double edge, both formal and performative. The performance consisted in the dissemination of the virus by email but also in the form of t-shirts distributed at the Slovenian pavilion of the Biennale, and its detection by the main antivirus software in circulation. Formally-speaking, if read by a computer the code is a virus, while to the eyes of a human reader it resembles a love poem. Now, obviously, the work can no longer be presented in its original form. Like all performances, it was a one-off event. Both [epidemiC] and 0100101110101101.ORG widely documented the initiative on the Net, on their respective sites [16]. In a real exhibition space "documenting" the work would mean displaying the original t-shirts, presenting a video of the virus "spreading" through the Biennale on the bodies of visitors, along with a print-out of the virus, press response, and a diagram of its dissemination on the Net. 0100101110101101.ORG actually did create a panel of this kind for the show *Connessioni leggendarie*, which we will return to later. On that occasion the panel was accompanied with a framed, "annotated" version of the virus, an item of ephemera that documents the production process and easily becomes a work of art in its own right.

0100101110101101.ORG even went one step further, at the end of the project, producing a series of sculptures in the form of computers infected by the virus, entitled *Perpetual Self Dis/Infecting Machine* (2001-2003). These works, which can be considered as derivative works, are also independent works of art in their own right. The computer, reassembled and placed inside a plexiglass case, has its own aesthetic and presents as a work to be observed and pondered, with its eternal process of infection and disinfection. It does more than just document the work *Biennale.py*, offering further original reflections on the virus that generated the former. At the same time it allowed a virus, the most intangible entity imaginable, to be brought into exhibition space. And, why not, sold.

Among the projects I have worked on myself, *Connessioni leggendarie* and *Holy Fire* could be seen as meta-projects on the significance that curatorial practice acquires when tackling a Net Art problem. *Connessioni leggendarie. Net.art 1995-2005* [17], a joint project with Luca Lampo, 0100101110101101.ORG and Marco Deseriis, was, overall, a documentation exhibition, though it did include a few "originals" (in the Software Art section) and a number of "derivative works" (like Alexei Shulgin's *386dx* and the *Management Leisure Suit* by the Yes Men). The idea was to tell the story of net.art as a movement, to draw out its relational, experimental nature, its ability to generate stories and make History, and, if need be, Legend. The first thing we realized was that to tell the story of net.art, computers were not needed, except in a few rare instances. Although we contacted the artists, we gave ourselves free rein when it came to presenting the projects: telling a story is different from exhibiting works, and we wanted to exploit the freedom of interpretation and subjectivity that the narrative angle afforded. The section dedicated to plagiarism, for example, was largely composed of graphic panels presenting images of the various projects (from the splash page of *Documenta Done* to that of *Hell.com* copied by 0100101110101101.ORG), accompanied with lengthy explanatory notes. In the code poetry section the panels – designed to "copy" the visual poetry aesthetic – were accompanied with videos of various recitals. The most "narrative" section – the section dedicated to media hacktivism – featured a combination of documentary videos and illustrative panels, with the idea of using images to portray hallmark projects such as *Digital Hijack* and *Toywar*, *Female Extension*, *Vote Auction* and *Nikeground*.

Holy Fire. Art of the Digital Age [18] could be viewed as the cynical alter ego of *Connessioni leggendarie*, and in a way it is. The concept was intentionally simple: to present the recent history of New Media Art as it is filtered by the market and enters private collections. As for *Connessioni leggendarie*, the stance was both affirmative and provocative. In the first case we wanted to affirm the avant-garde nature of net.art, and its significance in the history of contemporary art, taking a stand against those with a tendency to belittle its importance. In the second case it was about asserting that, despite the skepticism on both sides (both the contemporary art world and the new media world), in the context of New Media Art collecting is not only possible, but also necessary, if we want new media culture to make its mark on contemporary art, and gain some of the recognition that is still denied it; and pointing out that many of the leading artists are indeed working in this direction.

From the curatorial point of view, *Holy Fire* did not present particular problems: there was nothing to translate, as everything had already been translated by the artists. The main task lay in identifying the most effective translation approaches, those that gallerists and collectors had opted for. Two basic strands emerged: the translation of projects into "traditional" artifacts (prints, video and video installations, sculptures and installations), a strategy favored for content-based works; and the development of "art appliances", "screen-based" artifacts customized in such a way as to personalize, display or conceal the technological infrastructure. This approach was favored for software and generative works, or works where processual or interactive aspects were prominent [19].

In this essay I have tried to analyze the work of the curator by adopting an operative model based on "translation": a time-honored craft, but one which many curators tend to adopt in its most simplistic, naïve version. The translation model lends itself very well to illustrating the issues that the curator interested in Net Art must tackle. Net Art, but not only that: digital data is just one of the components of a babel of old and new languages that need to be translated into the esperanto of contemporary art. Which means that the contemporary art world will increasingly be in need of multilingual operators, and above all, good translators.

First published in *Vague Terrain*, Issue 11, September 2008, online at http://vagueterrain.net/journal11/. Translation from Italian by Anna Rosemary Carruthers.

[1] This paragraph obviously oversimplifies the issue, as my focus is more on "translating net art for the physical space". My aim was to comment on online exhibitions and their usually limited target, when the Net offers much greater possibilities. And there is certainly nostalgia for the period of events such as *Refresh, Desktop IS* or W*WW Art Award,* all organized by Alexei Shulgin (check www.easylife.org), or *1000 $ Page Context*, by Olia Lialina (http://art.teleportacia.org/1000$).
[2] Geert Lovink, *Zero Comments: Blogging and Critical Internet Culture*, New York, Routledge 2007.
[3] The marginality of New Media Art in the contemporary art world and discourse is another hot issue, difficult to sum up in a few lines. According to Lovink, New Media Art never managed to find its "cool obscure". My point is

that this is just a problem of bad translation – therefore, first and foremost, of bad translators.

[4] From *Wikipedia*, http://en.wikipedia.org/wiki/Translation.

[5] *PORT: Navigating Digital Culture*, organized by artnetweb for the MIT List Visual Arts Center, Cambridge, MA. January 25 through March 29, 1997. Online at http://artnetweb.com/port/index.html.

[6] *net_condition*, curated by Peter Weibel, Walter van der Cruijsen, Johannes Goebel, Golo Föllmer, Hans-Peter Schwarz, Jeffrey Shaw, Benjamin Weil. Center for Art and Media Technology (ZKM), Karlsruhe, Germany, 1999.

[7] See Marina Abramovic's considerations in M. Abramovic, *7 Easy Pieces*, Charta, Milan 2007.

[8] From *Wikipedia*, http://en.wikipedia.org/wiki/Translation.

[9] Ibid.

[10] Lev Manovich, "The Death of Computer Art", 1996. Available online at www.manovich.net/TEXT/death.html.

[11] «Fidelity pertains to the extent to which a translation accurately renders the meaning of the source text, without adding to or subtracting from it, without intensifying or weakening any part of the meaning, and otherwise without distorting it». From *Wikipedia*, quoted.

[12] «Transparency pertains to the extent to which a translation appears to a native speaker of the target language to have originally been written in that language, and conforms to the language's grammatical, syntactic and idiomatic conventions». Ibid.

[13] *net.ephemera*, curated by Mark Tribe, Moving Image Gallery, New York, NY, May 3 - May 31, 2002.

[14] *in_rete*, curated by Luciano Caramel and Domenico Quaranta, Miniartextil 2006, Como (IT), October 7 – November 12, 2006.

[15] Lisa Jevbratt, "Infome Imager Description", online at http://128.111.69.4/~jevbratt/infome_imager/lite/description.html.

[16] See www.0100101110101101.org/home/biennale_py/ and www.epidemic.ws/biannual.html respectively.

[17] The exhibition site is no longer online. For a photographic record of the event, see http://ilribaltatore.net/connessionileggendarie/OpeningANDpeople/.

[18] *Holy Fire. Art of the Digital Age*, curated by D. Quaranta and Yves Bernard, iMAL Center for Digital Culture and Technologies, Brussels, April 18 – 30, 2008. Online at www.imal.org/HolyFire/.

[19] Another over-simplification. For a deeper analysis of the ways artists "translate" their work for the art world, see the two intro texts featured in the *Holy Fire* catalogue. Besides that, we also have to notice that, even if this essay focuses on translation, this concept may not work so well for the most recent developments of New Media Art. An artist, or a curator, has to translate something that exists only in another context, or cultural space. Today, what we are seeing more and more is that formerly known "net artists" don't just work online, but approach the same problem from different points of view, and with different media, at the same time. Patrick Lichty has a name for that: he calls this attitude "multivalence". *Holy Fire* displayed some examples of multivalent works: UBERMORGEN.COM's *Psych|OS* project, or Joan Leandre's *In the Name of Kernel*, to name but a few.

Interview with Jon Ippolito

In 2003, I was reviewing my thesis in order to make a book out of it. The book was later published by my university press with the title "Net Art 1994 – 1998. La vicenda di äda'web" (2004). As the title shows, it was all about äda'web, a "digital foundry" launched in 1994 in New York by the curator Benjamin Weil and the entrepreneur John Borthwick that commissioned many online projects between 1994 and 1998, when it was shut down for lack of funding.

Äda'web was lucky enough to see three of the major American media art curators actively involved in its process of production and, later, preservation and archiving: Benjamin Weil, Steve Dietz and Jon Ippolito. While Weil was äda'web's chief curator, Steve Dietz was the Director of the New Media Initiatives at the Walker Art Center in Minneapolis when Weil failed to put the website on auction at Christie's, and decided to donate it to a museum. äda'web entered the collection of the WAC, that still takes care of it. Dietz decided not only to store the website on the WAC servers and make it permanently available to web surfers, but also commissioned a "parasite" project from Janet Cohen, Keith Frank and Jon Ippolito, providing a different take on archiving. An occasional artist, Ippolito had been working at the Guggenheim Museum in New York since the mid-nineties, and was later one of the founders of the Variable Media Initiative, a project that is still perceived as one of the best approaches to archiving and preserving "variable" media.

While for the book I relied purely on existing online or offline materials, when the book was done I felt the urge to ask them some questions. I contacted them all and emailed my questions. My interviews with Weil and Dietz saw the light in 2003, and are still available in the archives of the online magazine Noemalab. Ippolito took his time to reply, and I only got his email two years later, in 2005.

WHAT DO YOU THINK ABOUT ÄDA'WEB? DOES IT STILL HAVE SOMETHING TO TEACH TO ARTISTS APPROACHING THE INTERNET?

äda'web's role in the history of Internet art is unmistakable [1]. There were certainly works of Internet art that preceded äda'web and / or reached beyond its cultural and geographic bias – most notably the classic European "net.art" works of the early 90s. Nevertheless, äda'web was the first and foremost platform for Internet art in the mid-1990s, and remains relevant to this day. That said, my artistic collaborators Janet Cohen, Keith Frank, and I didn't like everything on äda'web – which is why we set out to "improve" it [2].

WHAT ABOUT THE WAY ÄDA'WEB HAS BEEN COLLECTED BY THE WALKER ART CENTER?

While other curators wrung their hands about the nightmare of archiving digital media, Steve Dietz, the architect of the *Walker's Digital Study Collection*, leapt into the abyss and resurfaced with a pearl. Of course it would have been great for him to do variable media interviews with all the artists first, but you have to remember that one of the inspirations for the Variable Media Network was Steve's daring leap. In new media, we learn by doing, and Steve was the first to do it in a thoughtful way.

HOW DID THE UNRELIABLE ARCHIVIST SEE THE LIGHT?

Janet and Keith and I often joked about our Force Majeure resume – Force Majeure being the clause that lets parties break a contract thanks to an "act of God" like a war or hurricane. This resume was full of exhibitions and publications cancelled at the last minute because of ceilings declared unsafe and so on.

When äda'web curator Benjamin Weil offered to let us make the next featured work for äda'web, we were very excited – until we heard that AOL dropped äda'web's funding, at which point we thought, OK there's another line for our Force Majeure resume. Then Steve heard about our proposal and the light turned green again.

As an aside, I've worked with and alongside curators who simply shuffle commissions in and out of their exhibitions to coincide with prevailing fashions. Steve was a provocative and engaged interlocutor in our collaboration, both in refining and contextualizing the project. He probably deserves credit as one of our artistic collaborators.

WHY "UNRELIABLE"? DO YOU THINK THERE'S A RELIABLE WAY TO ARCHIVE A PIECE OF NET ART?

Ha! No, you're right. The word "archive" derives from the Greek word for "house of government" - the same root as monarchy – and their centralized, controlling nature is proving increasingly unreliable for the preservation of digital culture. That said, I'm working with some collaborators on a completely distributed model for documenting digital art and criticism. I should also say that I think archiving and collecting are two different things; the former implies fixed documentation, while the latter requires a more variable approach to preservation.

HOW MUCH OF THE CURATOR JON IPPOLITO CAN WE FIND IN THE UNRELIABLE ARCHIVIST?

Hopefully none. A curator's job is to nourish artists and safeguard their work. In *The Unreliable Archivist*, my job was to knock them off their pedestals.

IN AN INTERVIEW YOU HAD WITH LIISA OGBURN IN APRIL 2000, YOU ASKED YOURSELF A QUESTION: «WHAT WOULD IT MEAN TO ADAPT MUSEUM CULTURE TO NET CULTURE?» CAN I ASK YOU THE SAME QUESTION? [3]

It would mean complementing archivists with animateurs. Animateurs are those loony folks who re-enact historical moments, whether medieval jousting tournaments or the Wright brothers' first flight. One of internet art's first "historians", Robbin Murphy, once suggested that thinking about animateurs might help us understand what's missing in new media preservation, and I think he was right. We need this kind of person – for their anachronistic skills (whether it's wielding a crossbow or Commodore), their interpretive fidelity (how do you cast Hamlet in a chat room?), and their enthusiasm for the process of re-creation.

AS NEW MEDIA CURATOR AT THE GUGGENHEIM MUSEUM, NEW YORK, YOU CONCEIVED THE VARIABLE MEDIA INITIATIVE. WHAT'S THE CURRENT STATUS OF THE PROJECT?

I was never alone in working on the idea; collaborators like Keith Frank and Rick Rinehart have contributed more to the idea of variable media, while folks at the Guggenheim and Langlois Foundation have done most of the heavy lifting. One of the most ambitious projects we've accomplished to date is a test of emulation, which is one of the most important tools in the animateur toolbox. In 2004 Caitlin Jones, Carol Stringari, Alain Depocas, and I organized *Seeing Double* [4], a Guggenheim exhibition that paired works still running on their original hardware – such as Grahame Weinbren and Roberta Friedman's *Erl King* from 1982 – with emulated versions running on completely different hardware. We did audience surveys and held a symposium to gauge the reaction of viewers to the digital doppelgangers we built in the gallery.

Along with innovations like *Seeing Double*, we continue to refine the variable media questionnaire, a tool for allowing artists and others to articulate their visions of how a work may – or may not – be re-created in a new medium once its current medium becomes obsolete. Although anyone can currently download the prototype just by requesting it, our latest thought is to get a Web version up so a broader audience can play with it.

HOW DID ARTISTS REACT TO THE VMI?

Almost without exception in our case studies to date, artists have reacted to the questionnaire with serious and sustained imagining of how their work might unfold over time. Some had already devoted some thought to the future of their work; for others the experience was a revelation. In every case, as far as I can remember, there was at least one question the artist had never considered before.

I did get criticism from a few artists who had no direct knowledge of the variable media paradigm. They had heard that we asked artists to give the museum permission to re-create works, and these critics figured it was just a way for museums to wrest control of the work away from the artist. Whereas in fact it is precisely the opposite - as the market's influence on the ultimate fate of Dan Flavin's light installations has made painfully clear.

THE VMI STARTED AS AN ATTEMPT TO PRESERVE NET ART AND DIGITAL MEDIA, BUT PROVED TO WORK WELL WITH OLDER MEDIA AND MORE TRADITIONAL PRACTICES. IN THIS SENSE, CAN WE SAY THAT NET ART CAN HAVE AN INVALUABLE ROLE IN UPDATING THE MUSEUM ENGINE?

Absolutely. The hardest innovation for the museum to swallow is the network, for museums have historically been defined in the exact opposite terms (centrality, stasis, rarity, disconnection).

> IN 1998 YOU WROTE: «THE MOST EXTREME DEPARTURES FROM THE MATERIAL OBJECT, DIGITAL OR OTHERWISE, ARE ULTIMATELY THE ONES WHOSE FUTURE DEPENDS ON THE VERY INSTITUTION THEY WERE DESIGNED TO RENDER OBSOLETE.» [5] DOES NET ART NEED MUSEUMS TO SURVIVE? DO YOU SEE OTHER POSSIBLE SOLUTIONS?

Net art doesn't need today's museums – it needs what museums will morph into if they take up the challenge of adapting to the needs of an increasingly networked culture. To be sure, my colleagues in the Variable Media Network and I have been exploring more distributed alternatives to documenting and preserving Internet creativity. But even the most net-native scheme requires someone somewhere who dedicates herself to keeping culture alive. More than technical knowledge, that person needs interpretive skills and a passion for preserving history, undaunted by the many challenges in her way. Right now that person is most likely to be found in a museum.

> THE VMI RUNS THE RISK OF TURNING INTO AN AGGRESSIVE THERAPY. LOOKING AT THE QUESTIONNAIRE, AND THINKING ABOUT STRATEGIES LIKE EMULATION, I CAN'T REJECT THE IDEA THAT THEY ARE BASED ON A QUESTION LIKE: «HOW WOULD YOU LIKE TO LIVE WHEN YOU'LL BE DEAD?» WHAT DO YOU THINK?

New media artworks die and are reborn constantly, with or without the variable media paradigm. *Apartment*, a networked piece by Martin Wattenberg, Marek Walczak, and Jonathan Feinberg, went through some 30-odd variations from 2000 to 2002 alone; it has been incarnated variously as a net-native piece, a single-user installation, and a dual-user installation.

While the artists are still alive and kicking, they can direct the life cycles of their artworks. But before the artists themselves kick the bucket, they should have the option of entrusting others to supervise future re-incarnations of their work.

Your question implies that the Variable Media Network could explore the possibility of resuscitating dead artists as well as artworks – definitely an option I hadn't considered! Researchers like Hans Moravec and Ray Kurzweil have proposed that we download our consciousnesses into hard drives for use with new bodies once our present ones disintegrate. The reason I find that suggestion so revolting is that I feel very much part of my body. Partly this is because all my experience is mediated by it; I might be writing different words now if I were a woman penning a manuscript in a monastery rather than a guy typing on a laptop in an airport. But the other reason I've grown attached to my body is that I've never been separated from it. This is not the case for digital artworks, whose bodies are swapped out for new parts all the time.

> TODAY, THE 'LOVE AFFAIR' BETWEEN CONTEMPORARY ART MUSEUMS AND NET ART SEEMS TO BE IN TROUBLE. WHAT DO YOU THINK ABOUT THE FUTURE OF THIS RELATIONSHIP?

Sure, the relationship is on the rocks now. But there's a groundswell of interest in internet art on the part of graduate students in art history and museum studies departments. Things may change once this new generation gets a foothold in the museum world. But even then, these folks will bring a perspective on networked culture that's different from geezers like me.

WHAT ARE YOU DOING NOW?

I'm about to publish a book with Joline Blais called *At the Edge of Art*, which proposes a functional definition for art in the age of the Internet [6]. We argue that the most creative work these days is coming out of scientific labs and online activism, and conversely that a lot of works in galleries – paintings, sculptures, installations – aren't up to the new tasks that art must fulfill in the 21st century. The book is sure to piss off curators who assume Duchamp granted the power to define art to the white cube's gatekeepers. But if Duchamp could be reincarnated as you suggest, I like to think he would have a good laugh at their expense.

First published in the online magazine *Noemalab* (www.noemalab.org) in October 2005 with the title "Leaping into the abyss and resurfacing with a pearl. Interview with Jon Ippolito".

[1] äda'web can still be visited at the address www.adaweb.com.
[2] Janet Cohen, Keith Frank and Jon Ippolito's improvement was called "The Unreliable Archivist", and was launched in November 1998 for the website of the Walker Art Center. As I write (January 2010), the work (previously available at www.three.org/z/UA/) is no longer online, but the WAC still provides full documentation about it. Check it out at
www.walkerart.org/archive/9/9C73F1E2F09A04F96179.htm.
[3] Cf. Liisa Ogburn, "What's Your Story: Jon Ippolito," *Eatthesewords.com*, October 2, 2001. Available online at
www.three.org/ippolito/writing/ippolito_ogburn_interview.pdf.
[4] Documentation on the exhibition can be found on the website of the VMI, at the address www.variablemedia.net/e/seeingdouble/.
The website variablemedia.net provides access to various materials produced by the VMI, including symposium transcripts, the questionnaire and the publication by Alain Depocas, Jon Ippolito, and Caitlin Jones (eds), *Permanence Through Change: The Variable media Approach*, The Solomon R. Guggenheim Museum, New York, and the Daniel Langlois Foundation, Montreal 2003.
[5] Cf. Jon Ippolito, "The Museum of the Future: A Contradiction in Terms?", in *Artbyte* (New York) 1, no. 2 (June-July 1998), pp. 18 – 19. Available online at www.three.org/ippolito/writing/wri_cross_museum.html.
[6] Cf. Joline Blais, Jon Ippolito, *At the Edge of Art*, Thames & Hudson, London 2006.

Don't Say New Media!

«Don't say new media – Say art!» Gazira Babeli

«Forget the new, drop the media, enjoy art». Régine Debatty [1]

These two quotations, both very recent, are emblematic for several reasons. The first constitutes the warning that Gazira Babeli, an artist living in the synthetic world of Second Life, uses to accompany the spectacular punishment she inflicts on anyone who dares to pronounce the words "New Media" in front of any of her works: a tornado that hurls our digital alter ego, or avatar, into the air until the latter corrects itself and the word "art" is heard. Régine Debatty is, on the other hand, an art critic of Belgian origin who became famous for her blog called *We Make Money Not Art*, before shocking – and in some cases thwarting – her readers by shifting her focus from technology to art without prefixes. The two comments most significantly reveal that there is an area, ambiguously dubbed "New Media" or "New Media Art", that both Régine and Gazira are associated with, in spite of themselves; a term and an area with which perhaps, at one time, they did indeed identify themselves, but which no longer satisfies them.

This type of dissatisfaction is anything but rare. Andreas Broeckmann, a German curator who has been the artistic director of the Transmediale festival for many years, recently curated an exhibition for the Stedelijk Museum in Amsterdam. There, he programatically abandoned the "New Media" paradigm to reflect in full on the consequences of the digital revolution on contemporary art [2]. As early as 2005, Steve Dietz, the former director of the New Media Initiatives at the Walker Art Center in Minneapolis, organized an exhibition entitled *The Art Formerly Known as New Media*; and the American artist Brody Condon recently declared: «It's about ideas, not material […] I don't give a shit about new media, it's just the material I understand intuitively from my youth». [3] This disclosure seems to echo the practically concurrent one made by the German curator Inke Arns: «The specific character of media arts under post-medium conditions is today not the media, but their specific form of contemporaneity». [4]

The average reader, extraneous to the debate underway, will probably observe two concepts in these words: the controversy around a label that stresses the medium, and the desire to reposition New Media Art, describing it as an important chapter in contemporary art. The same reader might wonder: hasn't it always been this way? No, it hasn't always been this way. And, unfortunately, the answer to the problem is not a simple one.

An Ambiguous Term

The expression New Media Art is one of the most ambiguous terms that recent art criticism has bestowed upon us. Firstly, the previous quotations reveal how it rather indifferently alternates between its two forms: "New Media" and "Media Art". Needless to say, this terminological ambiguity hides something that goes much deeper. The term "Media Art", used by Inke Arns and preferred by criticism of German origin [5], has a longer history, and refers to art that carries on a dialogue with, and occasionally makes use of, the communication media that emerged during the twentieth century: from photography to video, from cinema to satellite communication to the internet. In other words, the term Media Art defines a territory that ranges from Cindy Sherman to Matthew Barney, by way of kinetic and optical art and the closed-circuit video installations of the seventies. New Media is an even vaguer expression. As many have observed, from the collage onwards, any new medium available to artists is a "new medium". Nonetheless, during the eighties and the nineties the equation "New Media = digital media" gradually came to the fore. The equivalence caught on in everyday language first of all, and was then ratified in academic studies and by several influential figures. In the United States and Central Europe universities and art schools began to offer courses in New Media, and set up New Media departments. In 2001, the American scholar Lev Manovich published *The Language of New Media* [6], which quickly became one of the sacred texts of the nascent discipline of New Media Studies, whose ultimate affirmation was determined by the publication of *The New Media Reader* in 2003 [7].

An indirect consequence of this process was the victory of the expression New Media Art over other varyingly suited labels that had come to the fore in previous decades. Terms such as Computer Art, Digital Art, Cyber Art, Multimedia, Hypermedia, Electronic Art etc. quickly disappeared from circulation, or were redefined to apply to specific periods in the history of New Media Art.

Turing Land

If we want a better understanding of New Media Art, a look at its history is a good place to start. The first attempts to use computer technology for artistic purposes hark back to the marvelous sixties, and the experimental explosion that followed the crisis of Abstract Expressionism. Video Art and Kinetic Art originated during the same period as what was then known as "Computer Art". Both had some difficulty finding a path in an art world that they challenged at different levels, but both, in some way, managed to make it. That of the computer is another story. On one hand, access to the means was complicated, economically (twenty years would have to go by for the first "home computers" to appear), and technically. Without a background in engineering it was difficult to own and use such a device. Moreover, the device itself was something very different. Based on digital calculation, the computer did not just carry out a single operation, but rather it redefined all previous operations. It was a medium in the making, and creativity and art could actively contribute to this process. Life had to be breathed into interfaces, forms of interaction between the human being and the machine designed, new ways of organizing contents imagined. This brought about an absolutely new relationship between artistic research and the medium – a relationship that was destined to have a long-lasting impact on New Media Art itself. As Manovich points out in his introduction to *The New Media Reader*, the two stories (that of the actual construction of the medium and that of New Media Art) were intertwined to the point that it is possible to describe the digital media themselves as the best result of artistic research with computers: thus, for example, the Apple Macintosh and its human-computer interface is probably the best result of the creative research on interactivity; and the World Wide Web is probably the crowning achievement of creative research on hyper-textual literature.

These elective affinities lent New Media Art an entirely new role – and one that has yet to be explored – within the cultural history of the twentieth century. Yet, on the other hand, they made it an "anomalous" art, in terms of content and from a formal point of view, and a "marginal" one, if viewed in relation to the realm simply known as art. Anomalous, because it responded to requests that were very different from those usual in contemporary art; and marginal, because it had originated, and was exhibited and discussed, outside the realm of art itself. In other words, New Media Art gave rise to a real, autonomous "art world", with its own needs and a public that rarely, and only minimally, overlapped with that of contemporary art. It was a territory defined by festivals such as Ars Electronica, meetings like ISEA, museums like ZKM in Karlsruhe, or the ICC in Tokyo, reviews such as *Leonardo*, and publishers like the MIT Press. Manovich himself, in a text written in 1996 [8], called this world "Turing Land", as a tribute to Alan Turing (the father of the computer) and in opposition to what he called "Duchamp Land", that is the contemporary art world.

According to Manovich, the latter requires works that are "content-oriented", "sophisticated", "ironic", "self-referential", usually addressing their medium in a destructive way; while on the other hand, Turing Land requires works that are technophilic, simple and without irony, that take technology very seriously and explore the creative potential of the medium. There, the attention to "craft" which has disappeared from the value system of contemporary art, resurfaces, while the traditional separation between art, design and industrial creativity fades.

The date for Manovich's text is not coincidental. 1996 was a crucial year for New Media Art, and for insight into its recent developments. The advent of the internet and the mass diffusion of personal computers delivered a hard blow to forty years of experimentation "at the margins". net.art, which made its appearance during those years, had nothing in common with the Turing Land as described by Manovich: it was ironic, deconstructive and technologically playful, and it concentrated more on contents than on technology. It had an ambivalent relationship with the latter, a love-hate relationship: it focused of the medium, exalting some of its potential and criticizing the rest. It looked to Duchamp and Nam June Paik, and it was very critical of the cumbersome interactive installations of the previous decade. net.art heralded a new way of relating to technology: it was an approach that was destined to spread virally, irreversibly transforming New Media Art, and ending up making its own definition, and any presumed distinction between the two worlds, obsolete. It is at this point that we have come full circle.

A New Phase

Is a convergence between the two worlds thus imminent? In 1996, Manovich answered "no" to this question. Ten years later his answer is the same, but much less emphatically. At a time when, as Germano Celant [9] also noted, the computer has become an indispensable element for each and every creative process, among artists that use photography without considering themselves photographers and artists that use video without calling themselves video artists, there are artists that use new media without calling themselves new media artists. Some have quickly conquered the highest peaks of the art world : I am thinking of Olafur Eliasson, Carsten Holler, Carsten Nicolai, Pierre Huyghe, "new media artists" who were lucky enough never to have anything to do with this label.

At the same time, a festival like Ars Electronica in Linz has turned into a strange combination of art exhibition, industrial fair and amusement park, where works of art find themselves cohabiting with industrial prototypes, design objects and all sorts of gadgets. Here works which assign foremost importance to contents are read and evaluated in relation to their use of the medium. In the past edition, for example, in a section devoted to the very topical theme of virtual worlds, the re-enactments by Eva and Franco Mattes, staging some of the most celebrated performance art of the seventies in Second Life with the purpose of investigating the meaning of concepts such as "body", "violence" and "sexuality" in a synthetic world, could be measured against *Stiff People League*: a prototype invented by the Sociable Media Group of the MIT Media Lab that allows the "real" public to play soccer on a "virtual" field. And in the selection devoted to digital animation, video artists cohabit (and compete) with the colossal Hollywood epic *Pirates of the Caribbean*.

Thanks to consistent public and private investments, the world of New Media Art has grown, and it has proven dynamic enough to incorporate tendencies and research that have very little to do with its ideological assumptions and history. To adapt to it means building a career in a dynamic and mutable context, one that is meritocratic and open to innovation, inside a community characterized by a strong sense of belonging; but it also means remaining external to a critical discourse on contemporary art, and to the mechanisms that contemporary art uses to attribute value.

The result is that, as we were saying, critics, curators, and artists are increasingly intolerant of this context and consequently of the New Media Art label itself.

Getting rid of this label is the first step along the difficult path towards the meaning system of contemporary art, undertaken by an ever-growing number of artists. But it is no easy task: it often means breaking away from one's own history, rebuilding a career within a context – that of contemporary art – that may even be more mature, but that is also less adaptable, certainly more conservative. As observed by Joline Blais and Jon Ippolito [10], the contemporary art world has transformed Duchamp 's game – the contextual definition of art as what takes place in the art world – into a form of intellectual laziness, characterized by the inability to elaborate new definitions for art. And yet, this path has indeed been undertaken, and there is no turning back. New Media Art has emerged from its heaven on earth, and must come to terms with a much more complex reality. To change this reality, importing what has made New Media Art one of the most relevant phenomena of the last sixty years, is the challenge. Learning its rules is the necessity.

Let it be clear, however, that this does not in any way eliminate Turing Land. The challenge is to continue being an incubator and stop being a prison. To cultivate the hybridization of languages, to reflect on and determine the evolution of the media. To operate virtuously on the edge. New Media Art is dead! Long live New Media Art!

First published in *FMR Bianca*, n° 5, Franco Maria Ricci, Bologna, December 2008. Originally translated from Italian by Sylvia Adrian Notini.

[1] Régine Debatty, in D. Quaranta, Yves Bernard (eds.), *Holy Fire. Art of the Digital Age*, FPEditions, Brescia 2008.
[2] Cf. Andreas Broeckmann, "Deep Screen. Art in Digital Culture. An Introduction", in A. Broeckmann (ed.), *Deep Screen. Art in Digital Culture*, exhibition catalogue, Amsterdam, Stedelijk Museum 2008.
[3] Brody Condon, in D. Quaranta., Y. Bernard (eds.), Op. Cit.
[4] Inke Arms, "And It Exists After All. On the contemporaneity of medial arts", 2008. Unpublished, courtesy of the author.
[5] Cf., for example, Oliver Grau (ed.), *Media Art Histories*, Cambridge (Mass.), MIT Press, 2007; and the online resource *Media Art Net*, edited by Dieter Daniels, available online at www.medienkunstnetz.de.
[6] Lev Manovich, *The Language of New Media*, Cambridge (Mass.), MIT Press 2001.
[7] Noah Wardrip-Fruin, Nick Monfort (eds.), *The New Media Reader*, Cambridge (Mass.), MIT Press 2003.
[8] Lev Manovich, "The Death of Computer Art", 1996 [revised 2001]. Available at www.manovich.net/TEXT/death.html.
[9] In his recent book *Artmix*, Milan, Feltrinelli 2008.
[10] Joline Blais, Jon Ippolito, "Looking for Art in All the Wrong Places", 2001. Available at www.three.org/ippolito/writing/looking_for_art.html.

Interview with Oron Catts

Australian artist Oron Catts is the founder of The Tissue Culture & Art Project (TC&A), an ongoing research and development project that explores issues of partial life and semi-living beings. Catts founded the TC&A in 1996, and was joined by Ionat Zurr shortly after. Guy Ben Ary was also a member from 1999 to 2003, and the collective sometimes work in collaboration with other artists.

After a four year residency at the University of Perth for the TC&A, Catts co-founded SymbioticA, a research laboratory dedicated to the exploration of scientific knowledge and biological technologies. In 2008 SymbioticA became the Centre of Excellence in Biological Arts.

LET'S START FROM THE USUAL QUESTION: WHAT DO YOU THINK YOU'RE DOING, PLAYING GOD?

There are two ways to answer this question – one is that the concept of God is a human construct so actually the question can be read as "what do you think you're doing, playing human?"

The second way of responding to such a question is that following its internal logic any form of manipulation of living systems is a form of playing God, therefore this question can be directed at farmers, gardeners, chefs, people who are doing flower arrangement etc. In both cases you can see that this is not going to take us anywhere.

I believe that this type of response to our work stems from exactly the point that we are trying to raise through the work – that there is a immense discrepancy between our cultural perceptions of life and what can be done with life with the knowledge of modern biology and it's application through biotechnology and biomedical research. This question can be relevant only as a starting point in the discussion in regard to the limits of manipulation of living systems by humans. However, using God as "a side" in this discussion is quite futile as no one seems to agree about who/what is his/her/its real representative down here.

BIOTECHNOLOGIES SEEM TO MAKE THE DREAM OF PYGMALION FINALLY COME TRUE: BRINGING WORKS OF ART TO LIFE. IS EVERY TISSUE ENGINEER THEREFORE AN ARTIST?

To be specific, tissue engineering is not about creating new life. It does, however, transform life. Tissue engineering in the context of our work is about maintaining and prolonging the life of parts (i.e. fragments of the body), while removing them from their original context and transplanting them into the context of the semi-living. So unlike Pygmalion life is the starting point for our work.

It was the intention of the Tissue Culture & Art Project to grow semi-living sculptures, that do not necessarily conform to the original "natural" design of the body, and to keep them alive for as long as possible outside and independent of the body (with the assistance of the techno-scientific body).

DO YOU ENGAGE WITH BIOTECHNOLOGIES AS A TOOL OR AS A MEDIUM? HOW DO THEY INFLUENCE THE CONTENT OF YOUR WORK?

We are using tissue technologies both as a medium and as a subject matter. In general, the TC&A was set up to explore the use of tissue technologies as a medium for artistic expression. We are investigating our relationships with the different gradients of life through the construction/growth of a new class of object/being – that of the Semi-Living. These evocative objects are a tangible example that brings into question deep rooted perceptions of life and identity, concept of self, and the position of the human in regard to other living beings and the environment. We are interested in the new discourses and new ethics / epistemologies that surround issues of partial life and the contestable future scenarios they are offering us.

We will be concerned about what might happen when the use of the medium of living tissue becomes less critical and self referential and will become a force of domesticating of the technology rather then a resisting force.

WHAT EXHIBITION CRITERIA DO YOU ADOPT WHEN SHOWING YOUR PROJECTS TO THE PUBLIC? TO WHAT EXTENT ARE THEY CONDITIONED BY THE CONTEXT WHERE YOU SHOW THEM?

As the presentation of living tissue sculptures is somewhat of a precedent we are experimenting with the aesthetic strategies we employ. We usually produce site specific installations based around the research projects we are working on and the context of the show. Whenever possible we try to maintain the semi-living sculptures alive for as long as we can. For that we construct a laboratory in the space. The laboratory fulfills two main conceptual purposes in addition to be the practical way to keep the semi-living. The conceptual purposes are to emphasis that our work is process based and to demonstrate the care that is needed to keep the semi-living. We make a point to tend to the needs of our semi-livings during gallery opening hours so the audience could witness the responsibilities we have once we transform life in such a way.

We try to strike a balance between presenting the technology needed to care for the semi-livings and the story we try to tell. The elements of the different installations contain many references to the history of partial life, as well as references to popular culture and art. We like our installations to be ambiguous, but in all projects we try to confront the viewer with an evocative experience that challenges his/her perception of life.

We are exhibiting in a wide variety of contexts, from exhibitions with a focus on the biotech era to exhibitions about textiles. We also presented our work in artistic, scientific, and other conferences. It is important for us to speak to a large and varied audience (rather than strictly artists or scientists).

We try to avoid falling into a trap of exhibitions that celebrates biotechnology, though we believe that the content of our work and the ambiguity and subtlety of our message can be interpreted in many ways.

ALL YOUR PROJECTS CAN BE READ IN VARIOUS WAYS: AS SCIENTIFIC EXPERIMENTS AND COMPLEX NARRATIVES, AS A PROCESS OR AS A PRACTICE THAT PRODUCES SCULPTURAL OBJECTS. WHICH OF THESE LAYERS DO YOU FEEL AS YOURS?

All of the above and more, we also deal with narratives surrounding species, eugenics and the treatment of the other, but more than anything else our work is about life and its complexity. When we present our work as an installation, the work should be experienced (rather than just read). We use different methods and techniques as times goes by and we are gaining more experience, though the bottom line is to have the multiplicity of narratives and discourses that are subtle and ambiguous. We would like the audience to form their own opinions (and love when they share it with us). We believe in complexity and look at "life" and/or "biotech" in a wider social / economical / political context that have many grades of shade rather than a black and white explanation. Our written publications are more "revealing" in an ideological and political sense.

WHAT ABOUT THE "KILLING RITUAL" THAT ENDS ALL YOUR PROJECTS? WHAT ROLE DOES IT PLAY IN SHAPING THE MEANING OF THE WORK?

During the exhibition of the Semi-Living sculptures we are performing routinely the "Feeding Ritual" in which the audience can view when we feed and care for our sculptures. The most pronounced act of violence in the work of TC&A is that of the public release of the semi-living from the techno-scientific body by the end of the exhibition. This act results in the death of the tissue and is known as the killing ritual. TC&A durational installations usually culminate with that public action in which the organizers of the event as well as the wider community are invited to touch the exposed semi-living and by that hasten their death. The killing only takes place when we reach a point when no one can take care of the semi-living any longer, either because we could not stay around for the rest of the exhibition or when the exhibition ends and we can not take the semi-living with us. The killing ritual can be seen as either the ultimate pitiless act, as an essential show of compassion; euthanasia of a living being that has no one to care for it, or just returning it to the cultural accepted state of "a sticky mess of lifeless bits of meat". It is important for us to be transparent in regard to the fate of the living art work in the end of the exhibition. It's also interesting to note that in some occasions members of the public came to us after participating in the killing ritual and told us that only by killing the semi-living they believed that the work was actually alive.

SYMBIOTICA IS A WONDERFUL EXAMPLE OF WHAT HAPPENS WHEN ARTISTS AND SCIENTISTS START PLAYING TOGETHER. HOW DID IT COME ABOUT? WHY IN AUSTRALIA?

SymbioticA is a research laboratory dedicated to the exploration of scientific knowledge in general and biological technologies in particular, from an artistic perspective. It is located in The School of Anatomy & Human Biology at The University of Western Australia. SymbioticA is the first research laboratory of its kind, in that it enables artists to engage in wet biology practices in a biological science department.

The decision to set up SymbioticA was made after four years of residency of The Tissue Culture & Art Project (Ionat Zurr and Oron Catts) at the School of Anatomy & Human Biology in UWA. When we realized that our project was ongoing and that it seemed that other artists were starting to get interested in similar practices, we decided to formalize the relationship with the university to be able to provide other artists access to the facilities in the school without going through the hassles that we had as artists in residence. The Tissue Culture and Art Project is now hosted by SymbioticA alongside the other core research group – The SymbioticA Research Group and individual artists in residence.

A very important point in establishing SymbioticA was that it is an actual physical space that the visiting artists can call "home" and not be in the position of a guest.

When we were looking for support for the establishment of SymbioticA we received much more positive reaction from the science community than from the art community here in Perth. Now things are a bit different and it seems that a major part of the art community here is becoming very supportive while some of scientists that originally supported us seem to realize that their expectations of what SymbioticA will do were based on archaic and sometimes exploitative views of the role of contemporary arts.

SymbioticA was founded by Prof. Miranda D. Grounds, Dr. Stuart Bunt and myself – Oron Catts – in 2000. The physical space called SymbioticA was completed in April 2000. It resulted from at least two years of trying to generate funds and to establish a framework in regard to SymbioticA's role and mode of operation. The beginning was quite humble, with SymbioticA acting for its first year as a "studio" for two artists in residence and almost nothing else. During this year Ionat and I were in Boston so we could not play an active role in SymbioticA. It gave us the opportunity to reflect on the needs of future residents in SymbioticA and to develop more ambitious plans for the kind of activities SymbioticA should pursue.

When Ionat and I came back in April 2001 we started to implement our plans. We formed the SymbioticA Research Group as a fluid and dynamic trans-disciplinary group of core researchers in SymbioticA and other interested people. We also started to develop the academic part of SymbioticA and together with Adam Zaretsky (who was our first international resident) we offered a unit in Art and Biology for undergraduate students. Since then we have developed two more undergraduate elective courses and had a number of postgraduate students conducting their research in SymbioticA.

A growing number of artists (locally, nationally and internationally) have taken residencies here, from short and occasional visits to long term projects.

Just recently the Australia Council for the Arts announced their plan to establish ongoing support for our residency program by offering funds (on a yearly basis) for Australian artists to have a six month residency in SymbioticA. In addition the amount of requests for residencies from international artists has being steadily growing.

All of these developments show that there is growing and genuine interest in this kind of art and science collaborations and in particular in the area of life sciences. SymbioticA has proven that critical artistic engagement with scientific knowledge and technological applications is possible in an environment of collaborative research and within scientific institutions.

WHAT DOES IT MEAN, FOR AN ARTIST, TO WORK WITH A TEAM OF HIGHLY QUALIFIED SCIENTISTS?

SymbioticA's model for art and science collaboration is based on mutual respect of the differences between these two modes of practice, while acknowledging areas of common interest. The resident artists are encouraged to critically engage with the new sets of knowledge and their application, while getting involved hands-on with the processes and techniques of science. The relationship between the new residents and the scientists they work with is initially that of mentorship. The residents develop the framework for their projects with consultation with SymbioticA staff and collaborating scientists and then go to learn the techniques needed for the fulfillment of their project. In no case the scientists are producing the work for the artists, and similarly, the artists do not work for the scientists. The long term residents (six months and longer) are appointed as honorary research fellows in the school of Anatomy & Human Biology, which makes them equal in their position to the post Doc research fellows in the other research laboratories within the school.

Many of the artists are interested in problematizing the knowledge and technologies they are engaged with, questioning the motivations, agendas and possible impact of these new developments. In most cases the research develops into the production of evocative cultural objects that brings the ethical, philosophical and cultural ramifications of scientific discovery and technological application into a wider context.

Due to the fact that SymbioticA was a bottom-up initiative that evolved organically, artists seem to have much more freedom and independence in the ways they choose to critique and present their findings. SymbioticA seems to operate very differently from most art and science initiatives in that it is not about creating public acceptance of new technologies and sets of knowledge but rather bringing them into question.

Who the author is is not a simple question when people are working together in a creative team. SymbioticA is encouraging collaborative work (with all its associated difficulties) with the belief that different people from different disciplines and indoctrinations who are open to each other's differences and ethical sensitivities can create a meaningful project. However, we are aware of the limitations of such cross fertilization, that might cause some cross contamination and in many cases we welcome that. We are not hiding the differences among the fields of Art and Science. We are also aware that in some instances these differences are important and should be emphasized. What I find interesting in many of the projects coming out of SymbioticA is multiple narratives and concerns expressed through the one artistic object. This is true not only of the different scientific and artistic practitioners but even among artists working on the same project.

This interview was originally done for the Italian magazine *Cluster. On Innovation*, and published in issue 4, 2004 (Biotech), pp. 158 – 163. The full version was later published (2005) in *Noemalab* (www.noemalab.org).

It Isn't Immaterial, Stupid! The Unbearable Materiality of the Digital

I have always had problems with the presumed "immateriality" of the digital. First of all because, in the years of the "new media" hype, it has always been sold as a novelty, and as a problem. Second, because it is not true. Hey guys, immateriality in art is all but new: I'm glad to inform you that Yves Klein's *Zones of immaterial pictorial sensibility* belong to the Sixties, and that Lucy Lippard wrote about it in the same years (1973). And it's not a problem. If we are talking about market and saleability, well… Tino Sehgal's works are immaterial, and they sell quite well; and if we are talking about preservation, when a museum curator has to preserve a video, a neon sculpture or an installation by, let's say, Mario Merz, all he needs is a couple of tips and tricks to preserve digital art. As Christiane Paul pointed out for new media art [1], digital code may be computable, process-oriented, time-based, dynamic, real-time, participatory, collaborative, performative, modular, variable, generative, customizable. But not immaterial.

"That's ok", you might say. "But why do you say that a software piece, or a net-based artwork, is not immaterial? We can't touch it." You are right: we can't touch a software. But a digital code needs a machine in order to be processed, and some kind of interface in order to be seen. The most "immaterial" piece of digital code I've ever seen is called *unix shell forkbomb* and was written in 2002 by the free software programmer and hacktivist Jaromil. It looks like this:

```
:(){ :|:& };:
```

It is a series of 13 ascii characters that, if typed on any UNIX terminal, makes it crash without any stirring of emotion. For Jaromil, «viruses are spontaneous compositions which are like lyrical poems in causing imperfections in machines 'made to work' and in representing the rebellion of our digital serfs». [2] Apparently, it's difficult to find something more "immaterial" than a computer virus. More often than not, it is even invisible, hiding in some forgotten part of the machine. Yet, if executed, it crashes the machine, causing real physical damage. As a "lyrical poem", it can be written in a Web page or a txt file, and thus be seen through a screen; or it can be printed. For the *I Love You* [3] exhibition in Frankfurt (2002), for example, the ascii forkbomb was printed on a square panel, like some kind of visual poetry from the Sixties. With a similar attitude, the *Biennale.py* [4] virus, released by [epidemiC] and 0100101110101101.ORG at the Venice Biennale in 2001, was circulated on the net, recorded on a limited edition run of golden cd-roms, printed on t-shirts, shown on a computer. Some years later, 0100101110101101.ORG created a series of re-assembled computers infected with the virus and intent on an eternal process of infection and disinfection, of hunting, killing and resurrection.

Of course, digital code can refuse any kind of visualization. During the Nineties, another Italian artist, Maurizio Bolognini [5], tried to do this in the most undervalued piece of new media art ever made, *Programmed Machines* (since

1992). He basically programmed about 200 computers to make them generate a never-ending flow of images, ad infinitum; and then he sealed them, making it impossible for anyone to see what the machines were programmed for. The computers are usually shown on the floor, working; hiding the output, the artist makes us think about the process and the (not so) silent life of a computer, rather than the result. The core of the work is immaterial, but the installations are on the heavy side.

Examples such as 0100101110101101.0RG's *Perpetual Self Dis/Infecting Machines* (2001 – 2003) and Bolognini's *Programmed Machines* may lead us to talk about the so-called "rematerialization" of media art, but I'm not that interested in the subject – or, maybe I have written about it too much. Yet, before exploring another issue, I would like to offer another example, something I like a lot. *Alerting Infrastructure!* was made in 2003 by Jonah Brucker-Cohen [6], who has since moved from place to place. *Alerting Infrastructure!* is a physical hit counter – actually a drill – that translates hits to the web site of an organization into interior damage of the physical building that website or organization represents. In other words: the virtual is replacing the physical, but it's doing it… physically.

Concrete Digits

But if saying that new media art is immaterial can create a lot of misunderstandings, which can be dangerous for the work of the artists, then saying that the increasing presence of software, networks and interfaces in our relationship with culture is making the latter more and more intangible and fluid is absolutely true. Today it's almost commonplace that works of art (digital or not) are not closed, finished objects, but are constantly changing according to the kind of interface we adopt. And even if copyright laws still apply, objects (and artworks) are no longer something that should be respected, but something that can be manipulated, appropriated, customized.

Yet, if digital culture is changing our relationship with physical objects, the opposite is also true. What I'm trying to say is that the recent evolution of the digital medium is increasingly bringing reality and physical laws into the machine. In the last part of this article, I would like to focus on two works that show how two important issues such as identity construction and the representation of time have changed in the last few years.

«I'm always at home. I don't go to exhibitions, I don't make conferences – but, look: I will have two solo and three group exhibitions in a bunch of months». In a way, Gazira Babeli [7] was able to live the dream of any hardcore net artist: to exist purely on a computer screen. If you want to really know her, go to East of Odyssey – a land in the virtual world of Second Life – one of these days. At some point, your digital alter ego will start to be kicked around, more and more violently, by some mysterious meteoroids falling from the sky. Gazira became known in Second Life for works like this: storms of question marks, bananas and Super Marios; earthquakes and tornados activated by saying the wrong word; giant Campbell's

Soup cans persecuting visitors; falling marble towers, a Greek temple playing Pong with you in place of the ball, and scripts stretching your avatar like an used towel. Gazira Babeli is a constructed identity that we perceive as real: she has a body, she hurts our bodies, and she treats the world we both live in like a real world, with physical laws that she systematically violates. If we compare her with Netochka Nezvanova [8], the mythical cyber-identity who appeared on the net in the late Nineties, we can see that something has changed in the construction of a virtual persona.

Recently Gazira started "exporting" her works from Second Life, in the shape of a standalone software that, when launched, opens up a micro-virtual world inhabited just by the work. The visitor can go through it controlling Gazira's body with the help of a joystick or a touch screen. *Gaz' of the Desert – Locusolus Lands* (2009), for example, collects some narrative elements from the artist's movie *Gaz' of the Desert* (2007), but translates them into a completely new, absurdist, hallucinatory playground. You can walk through the desert, fall into an office/jail, sit on a column as a bizarre, latex-clad stylite and listen to the dialogue between the Boss and the President, two other characters lost in the desert and talking about art. The feeling is that of being suddenly hurled into a surreal dream, or in the Little Prince's desert. Time passes slowly, and nothing happens.

Something similar can be experienced in front of John Gerrard's realtime 3D landscapes, such as *Sentry (Kit Carson, Colorado)* or *Grow Finish Unit (Elkhart, Kansas)*, both made in 2008 [9]. Gerrard reconstructs real places with a 3D engine, and makes them live in real time while a camera tracks slowly around them, showing all angles. The works focus on the American landscape, and on its unmistakeable mix of nature and civilization, peace and activity, freedom and control. The photorealism of videogames references with the American painting tradition, from Hopper to Sheeler [10]. Nothing happens, besides some repetitive, minimal actions. In *Sentry*, a red oil derrick continuously pumps oil. In *Grow Finish Unit* we see a large pig farming facility with a lake of excrement all around it; every six-eight months, a fleet of trucks arrives at some point to silently remove and replace the occupants. Time moves on slowly, day after day, according to the timezone of the original place. Even more interesting is *Oil Stick Work (Angelo Martinez, Richfield, Kansas)*, where Angelo Martinez, a tiny virtual character, works from dawn to dusk, seven days a week, on a lifelong project: painting a barn black using just stick oil. In 2038, he will finish his task and leave the scene.

Though very different, both Babeli's and Gerrard's virtual scenarios explore a new level in the representation of time. In this case, a comparison with an early piece of software art tackling the issue of time offers key insight. With *Every Icon* (1997), American artist John F. Simon Jr. [11] activated a process destined to work virtually ad infinitum (or at least 5.85 billion years). The application (a 32 x 32 grid programmed to display every possible combination of black and white squares) looks very abstract, but is not that different from Babeli's and Gerrard's works: in both cases, software controls an environment, making some strange things happen through time. But while Simon's grid just displays a process, Babeli and Gerrard build immersive environments, places we can enter and get lost in, characters we can love or hate. Intangible but real.

Commissioned by and first published in the Spanish art magazine *Artecontexto*, Issue 2, 2009.

[1] Cfr. Christiane Paul, "The Myth of Immateriality: Presenting and Preserving New Media", in Oliver Grau (ed), *Media Art Histories*, The MIT Press, Cambridge (Massachusetts) – London (England) 2007, pp. 251 – 274.
[2] Cfr. Jaromil, ":(){ :|:& };:", in *Digitalcraft.org*, 2002, available online at www.digitalcraft.org/?artikel_id=292.
[3] *I love you – computer_viruses_hacker_culture*, Museum of Applied Arts Frankfurt, May 23 – June 23 2002. Documented online at www.digitalcraft.org/?artikel_id=244.
[4] Cfr. www.0100101110101101.org/home/biennale_py/.
[5] Cfr. www.bolognini.org.
[6] Cfr.www.mee.tcd.ie/~bruckerj/projects/alertinginfrastructure.html.
[7] Cfr. www.gazirababeli.com.
[8] Cfr. http://en.wikipedia.org/wiki/Netochka_Nezvanova.
[9] Cfr. www.johngerrard.net.
[10] Cfr. Roberta Smith, "John Gerrard", in *New York Times*, February 19, 2009, online at www.nytimes.com/2009/02/20/arts/design/20gall.html?_r=2.
[11] Cfr. www.numeral.com.

Re:akt! Things that Happen Twice

During recent years the term re-enactment and the practices it refers to have enjoyed increasing success in the artistic context. On one hand this success is due to the advent, and success, of a new generation of performance artists interested in staging seminal performances of the past, while on the other hand a series of events, shows and conferences have had a hand in drawing attention to the practice. A list, albeit provisional, could include *A Little Bit of History Repeated* (Berlin, KunstWerke 2001), in which contemporary artists staged performances of the sixties and seventies; *A Short History of Performance* (London, Whitechapel Art Gallery 2003), where the original artists re-staged their own performances; *Experience, Memory, Reenactment* (Piet Zwart Institute, Rotterdam 2004), a series of lectures and screenings involving, among others, Rod Dickinson, Steve Rushton and Pierre Huyghe; *Life, Once More - Forms of Reenactment in Contemporary Art* (Witte de With, Rotterdam 2005), featuring a number of pieces which have become part of the canons of historic re-enactment, from *The Milgram Reenactment* by Rod Dickinson to *Spielberg's List* by Omer Fast; *7 Easy Pieces* (Guggenheim Museum, New York 2005), an outstanding personal exhibition by Marina Abramović, during which the artist re-staged seven performances of her own and others, attempting at the same time to offer a model for re-staging performances of the past; and the recent *History Will Repeat Itself. Strategies of reenactment in contemporary (media) art and performance* (HMKV at Phoenix Halle, Dortmund 2007), which provided a relatively exhaustive overview of re-enactment inspired by past events, both historical and topical.

Despite the rather summary mention we have room for here, the aforementioned events reveal some of the key aspects of the re-enactment phenomenon, and call for a reflection on its complexity. On one hand, indeed, the success of re-enactment appears to be connected to a parallel, vigorous return to performance art, both as a genre practiced by the new generations, and as an artistic practice with its own historicization. On the other hand the term re-enactment accompanies two phenomena that at least at first glance have very little in common: restaging artistic performances of the past, and revisiting, in performance form, "real" events – be they linked to history or current affairs, past or present. Both of these aspects deserve attention, not least for the fact that they reveal the complexity of the phenomenon, and the motivations and operative approaches that are gathered under the umbrella term of re-enactment.

The Return of Performance Art

The advent of re-enactment in the artistic context appears to lie at the point where two parallel, only seemingly conflictual processes converge: the predominance of 'mediatized' (or mediated) experience over direct experience, and the resurfacing of performance art.

The mass media (newspapers, radio and television) has long been our main interface with current affairs, but only in recent years, with the second Gulf War and 9-11, has it become the principal "destiny" of historic events, the witness for whom history is played out and experienced. But it is not just history – events which in one way or another belong to the upper register of our collective existence – that mainly occurs by means of the media: our daily lives are now increasingly "mediated". Digital cameras and videocameras painstakingly document our daily existences, filling our computers and the internet with an unprecedented quantity of amateur media material. E-mail, mobile phones, chat rooms, social networks and virtual worlds are the means that we delegate a growing portion of our social relations to, and in the 3D arenas of videogames some of us experience what we reckon is the best version of our lives.

In spite of this, performance art, which became established in the late sixties and throughout the seventies, then was cast aside in the eighties when the market recovered and more traditional genres re-emerged, before being feebly relaunched in the nineties, now appears to be experiencing a second life. And this is a highly apt turn of phrase, when we consider the numerous reinterpretations of historic performances, that in the microeconomy of contemporary art appear to have acquired the clout of musical cover versions. A second life it is, but not a second youth. The performance art of today seems much more mature, conciliating and reasonable, and less pure and radical compared to its first season. Back then, documenting performances in photos and videos, when not expressly forbidden, was done in a lowly, 'for the record' way, and these documents were openly anti-aesthetic. Now, on the other hand, performance art does not exist without media-based documentation; so much so that Tino Sehgal's request not to publish images of his performances looks more like a celebrity whim than a groundbreaking stance.

Performance art came into being as an anti-establishment practice, a radical rejection of the commercialization of art – I use my body because it is the only thing that no-one can ever sell – and then gradually changed, with props becoming fetish objects, and its documentation (now carried out by professional photographers and cameramen) becoming a series of works in their own right. In this way performance art has ended up being the protégé of a spectacular system that demands experiences rather than products, events rather than objects. Or as Jennifer Allen writes:

> «In retrospect, performance art – from expanded cinema to happenings - seems to have anticipated an economy beyond the traditional material commodity, where spectacles, adventures, experiences and services could be packaged and sold.» [1]

So it was that performance art came to an agreement with the media, which on one hand guarantees its survival over time, and reconciles it to the market, and on the other offers it new scope for action, from live broadcasts to the use of virtual platforms for performance purposes. Which means that performance art no longer necessarily involves the body, and that increasingly, the rapport with the media is no longer one of subordination, but on equal terms: the media no longer simply "documents" events, but participates in them and becomes a part of them.

All of this is central to the question of re-enactment, which is linked to the issue of mediation for various reasons: firstly because reconstructing the past often relies on media documentation, rather than direct knowledge, if not narrative or fictional accounts [2]; secondly because the very *raison d'être* of re-enactment is often its photographic or video documentation [3]; and lastly because re-enactment occasionally comes into being in an entirely mediatized form [4].

Performance, Remediation, Citation

It is not easy to identify the route by which re-enactment entered the history of performance art. One thing for sure is that the concept is a vague one, linked as it is to two practices which are fundamentally different in terms of origins and motivations: restaging performances and reproducing historic events.

The first form lies entirely within the realm of art, and the particular history of performance. In the sixties and seventies, when performance art came into being as a contemporary art practice, the main aim of the artists was to distinguish what they were doing from theatre. Vito Acconci has said: «We hated the word 'performance' [...] performance had a place, and that place by definition was theatre, a place you went to like a museum.» [5] The theatre was rejected as an institution, and also as the canonical arena for representation, in terms of theatrical make-believe, for being non-authentic. Performance art, on the other hand, was about authenticity, the here and now, endurance. "No rehearsal, no repetition, no predicted end", to quote the conditions of Marina Abramović [6]. Who, it has to be said, refused to keep or display props, and refused to attribute work of art, fetish-like status to the documentation of her performances, which she did however keep. Many other artists also did so, both then and now. The repetition of performances was another widespread practice, and in Fluxus events was even part of the DNA, based as they were on an instruction, a repeatable script. But the fact that a rule is disregarded does not prevent it from conditioning the context that generated it. It is only when this rule is cancelled from the canons of performance that repetition becomes re-enactment. In Abramović's career this happened when, after splitting up with Ulay, the artist felt the need to take her distance from her life and works, and she discovered that the best way of doing this was to "restage it" in the language of the theatre, which she had avoided like the plague till that moment. The result was *Biography* (from 2002), a "show" in which Abramović constructs her biography out of some of her historic performances interpreted according to the language and conventions of the theatre. She later gradually abandoned acting in the show herself, getting her pupils and collaborators to stage it. *7 Easy Pieces* (2005) was the next step, springing from a need and a duty, as the artist explains:

> «I feel the need not just to personally re-experience some performances from the past, but also to think about how they can be re-performed today in front of a public that never saw them. [...] After thirty years of performing, I feel like it is my duty to retell the story of

performance art in a way that respects the past and also leaves space for reinterpretation.» [7]

On one hand then, there is a personal need to 're-experience' some of her own and others' performances, while on the other the artist feels the duty to commit these experiences to history, at the same time detaching them from the mystification created by poor documentation:

> «Due to the dire conditions of performance art documentation, these substitutable media never did justice to the actual performances. The only real way to document a performance art piece is to re-perform the piece itself.» [8]

But apart from Abramović's personal motivations, it is clear that reenacting performance art is only possible in the context of a renewed, extended conception of this art form. In the catalogue of the touring exhibition [9] *No lo llames performance / Don't Call it Performance* (2003), Paco Barragan lists eight points that he believes characterize performance art today. Some of these are especially relevant to the practice of re-enactment:

> «2. The action is of a 'portable' character, able to be reproduced in different environments and before different audiences. [...] 4. Loss of hierarchy: live action is not automatically valued above its recording. [...] 6. The 'remake' of given historical performances is not seen as a mere reproduction of the original action, it has become a new art form.»

This new art form, while it often uses mediation (during both preparation and staging), therefore springs from a dynamic which is the exact opposite of mediation, namely the desire to recover the original in all its immediacy, and therefore in the only possible way: by experiencing it. It is a highly self-referential art form, in view of the fact that it takes place entirely within the art world, whether motivated by historicization, tribute or celebration, or by a desire to verify the validity of a given performance when set in another era, another arena, and with other actors. The idea of repetition implicit in the "re" prefix tends to make us forget that the heart of every re-enactment lies not in its fidelity to the original model, but in the differences between the original and the 'remake'. These differences may be actively pursued (for example by changing the sex, age or nationality of the actors) or avoided, but are inevitable.

The concept of self-referencing, in particular, is fundamental to understanding this form of re-enactment. It is in fact more of a "citation" or act of appropriation, rather than the restaging of an event or a theatrical reproduction. This happens because art is always a linguistic act, even when it becomes an event; and because this event, in the meantime, has in turn become a fetish object that can be plucked out of the sea of confusion that is our cultural panorama. The motivations mentioned by Abramović, the reasons she gives for embracing the practice of re-enactment, include an advertising campaign that appeared in *Vogue Italia*. Without her authorization the magazine had appropriated one of her performances, and the event, transformed into an image, became an icon, therefore able to be appropriated, recycled, repeated, relived [10]. This does not mean that re-enactment is appropriation, citation, plagiarism or the like, but only that it relates to and dialogues with these artistic languages. In its respect for the original event, and its attempt to bring it to life in a different context, re-enactment is the way that performance art survives and makes its mark in the age of post-production.

History as an Act

When it comes to re-enactments of events outside the art world – be they historical events, distant or recent news items, experiments, literary excerpts, and so on, we enter a completely different conceptual arena. The forms that this can take are in fact so different that at times gathering them all under a single term (re-enactment) and confining them to a single operative arena (performance art) might seem specious and arbitrary. Another limiting factor, that many critics have lingered over, is the comparison between historic re-enactments (reliving a past event, in virtue of its being in the past) and the artistic version (which relives a past event in view of the meaning this holds for the present) [11]. It might make more sense to talk about "reactivating" an event, or a sign: a term which is also legitimized by the verb "enact": this not only means "to act out (a role or play) on stage", but also, "to put into practice", often used with reference to a law coming into force. From this point of view re-enactment is not so much, or not only, the restaging of an event, but its translation into an act: an act which may be, but is not necessarily, performance-based.

Re-enactments of historic events are inevitably obliged to take account of other practices of reactivation belonging to popular culture, of which it sometimes takes on the approaches and forms. These practices include re-evocations, role-playing and cosplaying. Reevocations, which are particularly popular in English-speaking countries, often regard village fairs and the restaging of historical events belonging to a particular local context, which they stand out from for their aspirations to authenticity and historic accuracy [12]. Re-enactors, who often appear in the crowd scenes of historic films, carefully study the costumes, lifestyles and language of the era they want to reenact, and rather than restaging it, they actually relive it. Role-playing and cosplaying are only apparently less faithful to historic fact: in actual fact they often involve the same level of philological precision as historic re-enactments, but with reference to a literary theme, usually linked to the fantasy genre, as seen in the first role-playing games, and later videogames. The level of identification with the game character is often so complete that it would put the top students at Actor's Studio to shame [13].

Among the other practices that re-enactment occasionally takes on, we should not forget historical fakes, media hoaxes and film, in so far as it is make-believe based on reality. There are numerous examples of this, from the previously mentioned video-installation by Pierre Huyghe *The Third Memory*, where the actual event is constantly filtered by its cinematographic alter ego, to *Greenwich Degree Zero* (2006) by Rod Dickinson and Tom McCarthy: an installation that presents the documentation of an event which never actually happened. In short, Dickinson and McCarthy take up the story of a failed terrorist attack at Greenwich Observatory in

1894 by a French anarchist, and document it as if it really did take place, by manipulating the media of the day. Works like these demonstrate that in the practice of re-enactment, references to events of the past resuscitated for the meaning they can acquire in the present is only one of the many possibilities [14].

While it is therefore evident that in re-enactment the original event or "text" is not necessarily expressed in performance form, it is true that it always translates into a script or narrative, and that when this is staged as a performance it inevitably begs a comparison with theatre and its "suspension of disbelief" aspect. Performance-based re-enactments use actors who know their parts to perfection, sophisticated scripts and painstakingly reconstructed sets, so why not talk about theatre rather than performance art? The reason is that re-enactment, while replicating a past event, is not about representation, but action: it does not want to be viewed as fiction, but as an authentic fact, something happening in the here and now. Performance-based re-enactments do not take place in theatres or sets (arenas for representation) but in real-life venues, and by the same token the spectators are never an audience, but witnesses. Lastly, we could assert that re-enactment does not tackle history and the original event in terms of creating an account or reproduction, but more in terms of taking a sample. The event itself is viewed as a ready-made that can be isolated, sampled, decontextualized and reproposed.

The Topical Nature of Re-enactment

We have yet to address the question of why the two lines of re-enactment, apparently so mutually independent, took root in more or less the same period, and appear to capture the *zeitgeist* so aptly. In actual fact there are a few pointers: the renewed topicality of performance art, which has become one of the pillars of the spectacular system of art and its peculiar economy; the fact that our experience of history is by and large mediated, which on one hand increases our desire for "real events", and on the other has got us accustomed to reliving the same events over and over, simply by pressing "replay". Then there is life itself, which on one hand is increasingly based on mediated experiences, and on the other is often based on nothing other than the remediation of a media model. The videos of the Palestinian kamikazes are all pretty much alike, and have now become a model on which teen psychopaths without a cause base their messages, uploading them to Youtube before dashing into school, gun in hand. The Columbine massacre remediated a shoot-up in a videogame, and in *Elephant* Gus Van Sant restaged the images from the school's security cameras. Peggy Phelan offers a highly interesting analysis of the attempted shooting of Reagan as the remediation of a series of narrative events, films (*Taxi Driver*), and real events obsessively regurgitated by the media, like the Kennedy assassination – connections which gain even more significance when you think of the role the media began to play in American democracy precisely as of the Reagan administration – under a president who was a former film star [15].

In other words re-enactment is actually the art form *par excellence* in a society where mediation has triumphed completely over direct experience, and has stealthily taken over everyday life. The appeal of re-enactment lies in its very ambiguity, in how it manages to be both a confirmation of the power of the media and an illusory *revanche* of direct experience.

Lastly the concept of history as readymade introduced in the previous paragraph, leads us to consider re-enactment as one of the many forms assumed by what Nicolas Bourriaud has identified as the predominant form of contemporary art in the information age: post-production. In this sense re-enactment could be seen as one of the products of that new form of culture that Bourriaud calls the "culture of use or culture of activity", in which:

> «[...] the artwork functions as the temporary terminal of a network of interconnected elements, like a narrative that extends and reinterprets preceding narratives. [...] Going beyond its traditional role as a receptacle of the artist's vision, it now functions as an active agent, a musical score, an unfolding scenario [...]. In generating behaviors and potential reuses, art challenges passive culture, composed of merchandise and consumers.» [16]

Isolating the "re-": the Mount Triglav Series

Connecting the phenomenon of re-enactment with the more generic concept of postproduction means opening our eyes to a broader horizon than that indicated by this term: a horizon defined not as before, by the concept of 'updating' something, but by the semantic arena evoked by that short prefix at the start of the word. This is the context of the work developed in the *Re:akt!* platform. The idea of repetition is just one of the concepts implied by this particle. There are other interesting ideas which run alongside it, such as "response", and "reaction". All of the works in the *Re:akt!* platform bring 'up to date' an event (artistic or otherwise), and also respond or react to that event. And lastly, they offer a wider meta-reflection on the idea of action (Re-garding act). More than just re-enactment, then: rather, as Duchamp described art, "a game among men of all eras".

It wouldn't be easy to find a better description for the Mount Triglav series, in which three groups of men from different decades are playing among them and with the same symbol. To understand this body of work, created in different periods by different artists, we should distinguish between two different levels right from the start: the history of the symbol in the context of the collective perception and memory of a population; and the history of repeated attempts to appropriate this symbol, against the background of an artistic history as particular as that of Slovenia.

The symbol in question is Mount Triglav, which, standing at 2,864 meters, is the highest mountain in Slovenia and the Julian Alps. The name ("tri", three and "glave", heads) would appear to derive from its characteristic three-pointed shape, though some link it to a three-headed divinity from Slavic mythology. Traditionally the mountain is one of the symbols of Slovenia, though it took some time to become an official icon. Mentioned in one of the most popular patriotic songs (*Oj, Triglav, moj dom* by Jakob Aljaž), Triglav only appeared on the Slovenian flag in 1991 [17], in place of the red socialist star, when the country left the Socialist Federal Republic of Yugoslavia. It did, however, appear in military insignia as of the post war period. Around 2003 the design of the flag, too similar to the Slovakian flag, was called into question; nothing was done, but it is significant that the winning sketch was based entirely on the stylized outline of the mountain. In January 2007, Mount Triglav put in an appearance on Slovenia's 50 euro cents coin.

We are therefore dealing with a national symbol, but that of a nation whose recent history is considerably tormented. One of the first provinces of the Austro-Hungarian Empire to have its flag recognized, after the First World War Slovenia became part of the newly-formed Kingdom of Serbs, Croats and Slovenes. During the Second World War parts of the country were variously occupied by Italy, Germany and Hungary, then in the post-war period it became part of the Socialist Federal Republic of Yugoslavia. On 25 June 1991 Slovenia declared independence from Yugoslavia, obtaining it after a brief conflict known as the "Ten-Day War". The stability it subsequently achieved, both politically and economically, led to it being the first Balkan nation to enter the European Union, in 2004.

On 30 December 1968, at the Zvezda Park in Ljubljana, three members of the group OHO (Milenko Matanović, David Nez, and Drago Dellabernardina) donned a heavy black sheet which reached down to their feet, leaving only their faces visible. The performance – in actual fact little more than a tableau-vivant – was entitled *Mount Triglav*. The newly-founded group was set to become one of the most interesting players in the brief season of the Slovenian artistic neo-avantgarde. Having started life with an open artistic identity, as an interdisciplinary context hosting different practices, in 1969 OHO set about forming a genuine artistic collective, working on the confines between conceptual art, performance and process art. An anti-art stance soon began to predominate, and between 1970 and 1971 OHO evolved into a kind of hippy commune, in an attempt to take the fusion of art and life to extremes. The OHO story is emblematic of a very particular phase in Slovenian art, in which protests against the art market and the work of art as object, and the anarchist, libertarian stance of the international neo-avantgarde movements, were expressed in a particularly extreme way, something that enabled the art scene in Slovenia, unlike in other contexts, to avoid being integrated into the system. *Mount Triglav* is emblematic of this attitude: OHO takes on the task of "embodying" a national symbol, at a time in which the nation's dream of self-determination appears painfully subjugated to a utopia under threat. And even though the long hippy hair of the performers does introduce a note of parody, the members of OHO are careful not to give their performance any specific ideological connotations. *Mount Triglav* still appears as impenetrable as the rock face of the symbol it incarnates. As Katie Kitamura writes, "OHO's performance seemed both to inhabit the national symbol and to claim it for itself, replacing the anonymous peaks of the mountain with the faces of 1960s' counterculture." [18]

Beyond other more historic connotations, like their conceptual aptitude for working with language, as noted by Miško Šuvaković [19], and the "objectification of the human", highlighted by Kitamura, what strikes us about this work, and justifies the subsequent re-enactments, is the deconstruction and reconstruction of the symbol. The performance interferes with a symbol, and creates another: the tiny blurred photos of the event are an emblem of performance art in the sixties and seventies – more interested in the process than the object – and in the construction of an event more than its duration over time; they are also artistic fetish objects. Precisely in view of their neglected, anti-aesthetic feel and non-mediated character, these objects are ideal witnesses to the authenticity of an event that, at a distance, has acquired an almost sacred status. These images, like many others which document early performances, are like the relics of saints: their aura is not self-made, but acquired, independently of the intentions of those who produced them.

This latter aspect is decisive for the comprehension of *Like to Like* (2003-2004), a project by the group Irwin, which takes the form of six large format prints of some of the historic works by OHO, including *Mount Triglav*. On one level, the entire operation can be interpreted as a reflection on performance art and its ability to give rise to iconic images. In *Like to Like*, Irwin appropriates some projects (performance art, but also installations, environmental art, etc.), and transforms them into images. The performance aspect of the various projects is lost, and what is highlighted is their ability to give rise to images that lodge in the memory, both individually and collectively, withstanding the test of time, becoming part of history and manipulating an identity. The painstaking philology with which Irwin stages the OHO performance is at odds with its betrayal of the initial premise of the original work: performance as bringing an end to the artistic object. This basically means two things: on one hand Irwin operates in an entirely different artistic context, where performance art exists in virtue of the media it generates; while on the other hand, the group is performing an operation of historiography. This operation resembles that implemented, in a different way, in *East Art Map*, the volume that reconstructs "the missing history of contemporary art, art networks, and art conditions in Eastern Europe from the East European perspective" [20]: in *Like to Like* Irwin manipulates memory, and writes the history of Slovenian art. To quote the statement that introduces the "texts" section of their website: "There is Greek art; there is German art and there is French art. But there is no art as such. The more Slovene our art is, the better. "

At this point we should consider the artistic intentions of the Irwin group. Founded in 1984, Irwin represents the "visual arts" division of the Neue Slowenische Kunst, an ambitious collective project that consists in reliving the trauma experienced by the avant-garde movements when they witnessed totalitarian regimes appropriating their utopian impetus. As Eda Kufer and Irwin write: "Retro avant-garde is the basic artistic procedure of Neue Slowenische Kunst, based on the premise that traumas from the past affecting the present and the future can be healed only by returning to the initial conflicts. Modern art has not yet overcome the conflict brought about by the rapid and efficient assimilation of historical avant-garde movements in the systems of totalitarian states." [21] In other words, NSK could be described as the most colossal re-enactment in the history of contemporary art: that of the avant-garde and its trauma.

In Irwin's artistic program, this concept is declined into three main principles: the "retro-principle", based on decoding and re-coding the art of the past; emphatic eclecticism, and asserting the Slovenian nationality and national culture [22]. This can be seen, for example, in their famous *Icons*, paintings that use collage to mingle avant-garde art with totalitarian propaganda, sacred iconography and the formal characteristics of tradition. The symbols of totalitarian power are demolished not through criticism or parody, but by means of a much more subtle process of over-identification, also termed "subversive affirmation" [23]. The ideology of the NSK oeuvre is not explicitly stated, and this very semantic ambiguity was its strong point in the eighties and nineties. Avant-garde art is not challenged or glorified: it is rewritten.

Nowadays, after the collapse of the totalitarian regimes, and in a context that Vladimir P. Štefanec, playing with the language of government propaganda, has dubbed "relaxed capitalism" [24], it is not clear whether the avant-garde trauma has been overcome or not. One thing for sure is that Irwin has become a definitive point of reference for the new generation of artists, Slovenian and otherwise; and that the relationship between art and the political establishment is a lot more ambiguous and stratified than it was in the days of the avant-garde movements.

In this context Janez Janša, Janez Janša and Janez Janša appear. On 6 August 2007 they staged a performance entitled *Mount Triglav on Mount Triglav*, which provisionally closes this matrioska-style story initiated by OHO in 1968. Slovenia has found itself a place in the new world order, and Mount Triglav has survived the transition intact, taking pride of place on one of the coins that symbolizes the victory of capitalism. In recent years cracks have begun to show in the latter, but capitalist democracy seems to be the only available model, the model which countries recovering from the collapse of the great narrations attempt to evolve towards. The powers that be have developed such a strong resistance to criticism, that not only parody, but also over-identification, appear weak strategies.

When they staged *Mount Triglav on Mount Triglav*, the three Janšas had just completed a long bureaucratic procedure enabling them all to take the same name: a name that also happened to belong to the then Prime Minister of Slovenia. While the three artists have always attempted not to reduce this operation to its purely political significance, claiming "personal reasons" for the change of identity, it becomes very difficult to exclude the political element when we see *Mount Triglav on Mount Triglav*. When "Janez Janša" tackles the ascent of Mount Triglav (a sort of rite for Slovenians, something like Muslims going to Mecca) to re-stage the work of a hippy collective in the sixties, they create a kind of short circuit that nothing and no-one seems to come out of unscathed. With Janez Janša we are beyond over-identification as a performance strategy and resistance tactic; what we have here is an oblique attack which functions by annihilating the identity of the symbol: this affirms on one hand the power of the symbol itself, and on the other our resistance to its magnetism.

Davide Grassi, Žiga Kariž and Emil Hrvatin have cancelled themselves out to become Janez Janša, a living, transitory symbol of political power; and Janez Janša nullifies himself in Triglav, the eternal symbol of a nation. The work on the name of the mountain continues, and the "three heads" of OHO become one: that of Janez Janša, which is both single and trinity. This does not however imply that each renounces his own artistic [25] and national individuality. Like the three members of OHO who staged the original performance, the three Janezs are of different nationalities. In *Mount Triglav on Mount Triglav*, this fact is ironically underlined by the position of the three heads and the direction of their gazes: the artist formerly known as Davide Grassi looks towards Italy, and the Croat Hrvatin towards Croatia, while the Slovenian Janez appears to look generally around.

The troubled relationship with a symbol that stands the test of time thanks to a series of adaptations and variations, which at times are imperceptible, is evident in the numerous anniversaries that occasion the performance, according to the statement given by the three Janšas: "Janez Janša, Janez Janša and Janez Janša performed the action entitled *Mount Triglav on Mount Triglav*, in order to commemorate the 80th anniversary of the death of Jakob Aljaž; the 33rd anniversary of the Footpath from Vrhnika to Mount Triglav; the 5th anniversary of the Footpath from the Wörthersee Lake across Mount Triglav to the Bohinj Lake; the 25th anniversary of the publication of Nova Revija magazine and the 20th anniversary of the 57th issue of Nova Revija, the premiere publication of the Slovenian Spring; and the 16th anniversary of the independent state of Slovenia."

It would almost appear that Janez Janša, Janez Janša and Janez Janša are celebrating a country full of anniversaries yet without an identity, unable to comprehend the meaning of its own festivities. Yet, like in the two previous cases, the ambiguity persists: are we sure they are striking a blow on the symbolic meaning of Mount Triglav, or are they actually trying to rid it of all its accumulated dross in an attempt to restore its original identity?

As for formal strategies, it is significant that Janez Janša, Janez Janša and Janez Janša, who asked Irwin to loan them the canvas used three years previously in *Like to Like*, abandon the vertical format used by both OHO and Irwin, which was clearly inspired by the stylized outline of the mountain (as it appears on the flag and coat of arms). They chose to adopt a horizontal angle, which is less recognizable but more similar to the real shape of the mountain. Here once again there appears to be an attempt to return to the origins, aware of all the symbolic encrustations, but at the same time determined to do away with them.

Triglav, the national symbol of Slovenia, which thanks to OHO and Irwin, has also become an emblem of Slovenian art, has completed its process of monumentalization: from object to symbol, from symbol to reinterpreted, subverted icon, to image, to monument. In the golden sculpture entitled *Monument to the National Contemporary Art (Golden Triglav)* created by Janez Janša, Janez Janša and Janez Janša, the mountain is once more an object, not merely a linguistic construct. In *Mount Triglav on Mount Triglav*, the symbols explode due to their very accumulation. But what emerges at the end, under all the layers, is not a meaningless fetish object, but the hard rock of the mountain.

Beyond Re-enactment

Other projects featured in the Re:akt! platform address the notion of re-enactment in a similar way. More then actual re-enactments, they could better be described as a critical re-action to the very notion of re-enactment. In *Ich Lubbe*

Berlin! (2005), the Slovenian artistic collective SilentCell Network re-enacts the Reichstag fire in a "symbolic", playful, ironic way. No-one notices the performer but the neutral eye of the camera that follows him from the start of his journey, while he throws little cardboard flames into the bins around the Reichstag. His gesture is minimal and silent, but this is precisely where its power lies: he moves away from the choice between black or white, in search of a third way, a less significant but effective third way. His action takes the form of a minimal comment, a note in the margin of a system of control which gets progressively more ambiguous the more it hides behind the pretext of an alleged "state of emergency".

In *Das Kapital* (2006), Janez Janša works in a similar way, re-enacting the Prague Spring and Jan Palach's protest in a street artist style, using remote controlled toy tanks, a fan, a map and fabric flames, and playing with the double meaning of the word "kapital". *Das Kapital* is the German title of Karl Marx's *Capital,* held to be the founding work of Marxism. In the performance logo, the name takes the form of a tank, and the red star of Communism symbolizes a shot being fired. The symbolism is evident, almost scholastic: both the Soviet troops and the Czechoslovakian student are fighting to defend their own interpretation of the same utopia. From this point of view, *Das Kapital* could be viewed as a metaphorical translation of Palach's gesture, rather than a simple re-interpretation. But there is more to it than that. The tank does not enter the map of Czechoslovakia as it was in 1968, but that of the geopolitical form the country assumed in 1993, when after the fall of Communism Czechoslovakia split into two separate countries - the Czech Republic and Slovakia. And it was then that Prague suffered yet another invasion, that of Western capital – which was heavily invested in post-Communist countries, with many businesses moving there – and liberal capitalism.

In *C'était un rendez-vous (déjà vu)*, Janez Janša and Quentin Drouet pay an homage to Claude Lelouch's cult movie *C'était un rendez-vous* (1976), a 9 minutes long film featuring a breakneck spin through Paris, filmed from a subjective angle by a camera mounted on the front of the car, which we never see. Doing the same mounting a camera on the shell of a "Golden Greek" tortoise, Janša and Drouet are "reverse-engineering" the film itself, turning speed into slowness, "cinéma-vérité" into parody, lie and postproduction: the footage is compressed to 9 minutes, and like in the original, "red lights are ignored, one-way streets are violated and centre lines are crossed." Furthermore, the artists turned what was a simple movie into a complex media object, a plexiglass case containing the video playing, synchronized with a list of the streets covered by the lead character and a satellite map of the route, and with a tortoise shell with a red "blobject" on it (a camera designed in a Ferrari-like style). But what can be seen as a simple, postmodern parody if we look at the object, becomes a real re-enactment if we look at the process. The reinterpretation does not view *C'était un rendez-vous* as a finished artifact, but as an *open* work, which includes the production process – which was substantially different from what was declared in the beginning – and the legends it has generated, and skillfully managed, for more than 30 years – between the first release of the movie in 1976 and the DVD version in 2003.

VD as VB (2000 – ongoing), by Vaginal Davis, and *Synthetic Performances* (2007 – ongoing) by Eva and Franco Mattes aka 0100101110101101.ORG are both dealing with performances of the past. Vaginal Davis, a giant, charismatic Afro-American drag queen, since 2000 is organizing performances inspired by those that changed Vanessa Beecroft into an art system celebrity. In actual fact, Vaginal Davis does more than just tackle individual performances, but reworks (and subverts) the entire VB phenomenon: the artist as celebrity and the subject of gossip, fully integrated not only into the art world, but also the realm of communications and advertising; the ritual nature of the performances, from the selection mechanism to the rules for the models (detachment, silence, endurance, etc.), and the cold, refined aesthetic of the images.

Eva and Franco Mattes' *Synthetic Performances* are a series of (by now) six re-enactments of historic performances of the 60s and 70s, staged by the artists' virtual alter-egos in the synthetic world of Second Life. As they have stated, the series arose out of their polemical stance with regard to the concept of performance art and the very works that they "pay tribute" to. This leads them on the one hand to breach the classic rules of performance art, and on the other to present these works – the efficacy of which was based on the radical way they explored the issues of the body, violence (Chris Burden), sexuality (Valie Export, Vito Acconci, Marina Abramović), identity (Gilbert & George), and the environment and public space (Joseph Beuys) – in a context where these issues acquire a completely different meaning, and as a consequence the original energy of the performance, and its power to provoke, dissipates, or turns into something completely different. In the words of the Mattes: "We chose actions that were particularly paradoxical if performed in a virtual world." Thus, these "re-enactments" could be described more effectively as "displacements"; or, since the space where these performances take place is actually a medium, as "remediations".

Three other "chapters" of Re:akt! are dealing, on the contrary, with historical events of the past. *Slovene National Theatre* (2007), by Janez Janša, is a theatre performance commenting on something happened in Slovenia right one year before, in Winter 2006, but almost immediately removed from the collective memory. On 28 October 2006 the Strojans, a gipsy family, were forced to leave the Slovenian village of Ambrus under police escort, and taken to a refugee centre in Postojna, 30 miles away. They had been under siege for two days, trapped by a crowd of fellow townspeople who were demanding they leave the town, under threat of death. The disturbing story of the family soon became a political case which brought forth the xenophobia of an entire nation, which until then had been viewed as a haven of peace and prosperity in the troubled Balkans.

In Janez Janša's work, the original event is not represented, as you would expect with a piece of theatre, or reconstructed, as you would expect with a re-enactment. The only thing about the Ambrus episode that is presented, with total fidelity, is the linguistic aspect, as it was conveyed in the media. But the form that this "re-invoicement" takes, with the actors mechanically repeating what they hear in their headphones, strips the original media documentation of any vestige of drama. Or rather, it strips the word of the rhetoric and anesthetizing slant of the media, and offers it to the spectator bare, without inflection, and as a result, laden with a different kind of drama. At the same time, by detaching these utterances from the media and lending them the immediacy of a live experience, having them spoken by people right there in front of us, Janez Janša brings these words out of oblivion and consigns them to memory.

In *The Day São Paulo Stopped* (2009), Brazilian artist Lucas Bambozzi is dealing similarly with something happened quite recently, that he himself experienced first hand, both directly and via the media. In May 2006, some members of the Primeiro Comando da Capital, or PCC, an anti-establishment Brazilian prison gang and criminal organization, were able to coordinate from the prison – using their mobile phone – a rebellion which was intended to spread to the entire state of São Paulo. After three days of riots, the final outcome was horrific: 141 dead (according to the most cautious estimates) and 53 injured, among police, criminals and civilians; 299 attacks against police stations, courts, banks and buses, and the largest city in Latin America brought to a standstill, with residential areas resembling ghost towns and the big highways gridlocked by the most spectacular jams of the year. Attracted by the role played by the media in the entire episode, Bambozzi realized a series of videos, meant to be displayed as a multi-screen video installation. Mixing "original" material, conveyed by the mass media or produced by those involved in the events, and material "reconstructed" by the artist for the occasion, he produced a media flow which roll out different versions of the events, and which, when taken together, form a complex, fragmented, multi-faceted mockumentary.

A far more unusual approach to re-enactment is used by Janez Janša in *Il porto dell'amore* (2009), dealing with the short-lived Repubblica del Carnaro, founded by the Italian poet Gabriele d'Annunzio in the Istrian town of Fiume in 1919, and held for almost sixteen months. The Fiume episode has long been blighted by the shadow of Fascism, and only in recent years Fiume has begun to be treated with an attitude that differs from "irreverent underestimation" or "acritical apologia". For example, the anarchist thinker Hakim Bey, in his legendary essay *T.A.Z.* (1985), on temporary autonomous zones, describes Fiume as "the last of the pirate utopias (or the only modern example)" and "the first modern TAZ", comparing it with the Paris uprising of 1968.

Even if, from a narrative point of view, it is based on these recent historiographical approaches, *Il porto dell'amore* doesn't want to rewrite history, being more interested in persuading a local community to conceal with its own history (and with its own ghosts). In fact, *Il porto dell'amore* is an architectural project based around a re-branding of the city of Fiume, including initiatives like the construction of a monumental interactive lighthouse in the port, the renaming of streets and squares and the introduction of various references to the lost history of Fiume. Far from being an act of historic revisionism in dubious taste, *Il porto dell'amore* actually is an act of love towards a place, that, at a certain point in its history, was hit by a wave of energy and poetry that no other place can lay claim to, and that its current guise of provincial town in a former Socialist country would never lead you to imagine. Fiume: Port of Love, City of Life, Universal Meeting Place, Great Opportunity, Fifth Season of the World, Rainbow City, Holocaust City... What other city in the world has ever merited such an avalanche of epithets?

Janša again is responsible for the most un-orthodox work of the Re:akt!

platform: *SS-XXX | Die Frau Helga. The Borghild Project Reconstruction* (2007). The project is based on a story news item which did the rounds in 2005, and was reported on as authentic by various esteemed newspapers, from the Spanish *Clarin* to the German *Der Spiegel* to the Italian *Corriere della Sera*. The story, which appeared on the German site borghild.de, with many details, (most of) which can be verified, regards the work carried out by a team of Nazi scientists, from 1941 onwards, on the creation of the first sex doll in the history of humanity. This was designed to satisfy the comprehensible sexual urges of German soldiers at war, while avoiding the unpleasant health risks connected to frequenting brothels. It quickly transpired that the story was a hoax, artfully created by a (still anonymous) author.

Yet, regardless of its authenticity, the modern day success of the *Borghild Project*, and the very fact that someone decided to dig it up (or, more probably, invent it from scratch), reveals the lasting appeal of Nazi history, and the problems that Germany – and the rest of the world – has in coming to terms with it. How much of our current technology is indebted to research performed by German industry between 1933 and 1945? As an erotic model has the "Nordic type" disappeared altogether, or is it still present in the fantasies of millions of internauts, attracted by the proliferation of porn from North East Europe, and the model of the current silicone sex dolls? Have we overcome the trauma of Nazism, or does it actually still return to haunt many contemporary issues?

Janez Janša's reconstruction appears to be principally interested in these aspects of the project. The work appears to explore three parallel strands: "updating" the project using objects found or created as needed; "verifying its authenticity" by means of historic research and documentary proof, and "implementing" it by means of new details. It is significant that all of these approaches have been explored by those – journalists or enthusiasts – who picked up on the story.

Janša works with the ambiguities of re-enactments, reconstructions, re-appropriations and the like, playing on the common Latin root of the words tradition and betrayal (*tradere*, meaning to hand over, pass on, transmit). The story hinges on this ambiguity, due to the fact that the original event, though well documented, has been lost for ever. Isn't this, in the end, the motivation beyond any re-enactment?

In its present form, this text was first published in autumn 2009 in the Croatian magazine *frakcija / Performing Arts Journal* (Issue 51 – 52, pp. 87 – 107) in Croatian and English. The text was originally written for the book *RE:akt! Reconstruction, Re-enactment, Re-reporting* (edited by A. Caronia, J. Janša, D. Quaranta, FPEditions, Brescia 2009), printed as a companion of the traveling show of the same name that I curated.

[1] Jennifer Allen, ""Einmal ist keinmal"". Observations on Re-enactment", in A. Caronia, J. Janša, D. Quaranta (eds), *RE:akt! Reconstruction, Re-enactment,*

Re-reporting, FPEditions, Brescia 2009, p. 30.

[2] One classic example is *The Third Memory* (1999), the video-installation by Pierre Huyghe in which John Woytowiczs' hold-up in the Chase Manhattan Bank in New York in August 1972 is restaged by the same protagonist, with constant references to the film of the story, *Dog Day Afternoon* (1975) by Sidney Lumet, starring Al Pacino.

[3] Here there are numerous examples. Naturally, if events of the past only exist for us in mediated form, we should not be surprised if what is restaged is not the actual event but the media artifact that conveys it.

[4] Take the videogame *Waco Resurrection*, for example, which was produced in 2004 by the American team c-level (Eddo Stern, Peter Brinson, Brody Condon, Michael Wilson, Mark Allen and Jessica Hutchins). The game is a classic shoot 'em up which enables the player to relive first hand the massacre of the Branch Davidians by the FBI, in the role of the leader of the sect David Koresh. Thanks to the immersive nature of videogames, each session of play consists in a re-enactment of the actual events, rendered particularly realistic by the faces of the characters, based on the real people involved, and the soundtrack which plays through the headphones.

[5] Quoted in Michael Rush, *New Media in Late 20-th Century Art*, 1999, Thames & Hudson Ltd, London, p. 52.

[6] In AAVV, *Marina Abramović. 7 Easy Pieces*, exhibition catalogue, Charta, Milan 2007, p. 15.

[7] Ibid., p. 10.

[8] Ibid., p. 11.

[9] Organized by the Audiovisuals Department of the Centro de Arte Reina Sofía Nacional (Madrid, Spain), and presented there in 2003, the show travelled to Centro Andaluz de Arte Contemporáneo (Seville, Spain), Centro Párraga (Murcia, Spain) and El Museo del Barrio (New York, USA). See Paco Barragan, *No Lo Llames Performance, Don't Call It Performance*, El Museo del Barrio, New York 2004.

[10] The campaign, by Steven Meisel, was inspired by *Relation in Space* (1976) and published in issue 579 of *Vogue Italia*, in November 1998. See AAVV, *Marina Abramović. 7 Easy Pieces*, quoted, pag. 8.

[11] See Inke Arns, "History Will Repeat Itself", in Inke Arns, Gabriele Horn (eds), *History Will Repeat Itself. Strategies of reenactment in contemporary (media) art and performance*, exhibition catalogue, Hartware MedienKunstVerein, Dortmund and KW Institute for Contemporary Art, Berlin 2007.

[12] Historic re-enactment is explored at length by Sven Lütticken in his essay "An Arena in Which To Reenact", in Sven Lütticken (ed), *Life, Once More. Forms of Reenactment in Contemporary Art*, exhibition catalogue, Witte de With, Rotterdam 2005, pp. 17 – 60. Lütticken traces a line between the phenomenon of the "pageant" – the Medieval religious representations on floats – and the battle re-enactments which became popular in the 1960s, first in the US and then in Britain, underlining their historicist nature: "Reenactments are happenings. At a time when pop art, Fluxus and minimalism celebrated the now, reenactments tried to create an experience of the past as present, or as much present as possible" (ibid, p. 27).

[13] This extraordinary immersive capacity, which leaves us in no doubt over how real role-players perceive their fantasy worlds to be, greatly struck the American artist Brody Condon, who in summer 2008, on occasion of Sonsbeek 2008: Grandeur International public sculpture exhibition, orchestrated *Twentyfivefold Manifestation*, a massive performance involving around 80 actors, based on a series of ritual type "games". For more information see www.sonsbeeklive.org.

[14] In the *Re:Akt!* platform, re-enactment as the progression of a media hoax is the fulcrum of the project *SS-XXX | Die Frau Helga. The Borghild Project Reconstruction*, while the reference to cinematographic narration returns in *C'était un rendez-vous (déjà vu)*, both by Janez Janša.

[15] See Peggy Phelan, "Hinkley and Ronald Reagan: Reenactment and the Ethics of the Real", in Sven Lütticken (ed), *Life, Once More. Forms of Reenactment in Contemporary Art*, quoted.

[16] See Nicolas Bourriaud, *Postproduction. Culture as screenplay: how art reprograms the world*, 2002.

[17] On this occasion, the symbol on the flag was redesigned by Marko Pogačnik, none other than a member of the OHO group: a curious intersection between the collective history and artistic history of the symbol, which acquires further meaning in the light of what follows.

[18] Katie Kitamura, "Triglav", in *Frieze Magazine*, Issue 113, March 2008.

[19] "The artistic work, which models a mountain, showed the relationship between 'mountain as material' and 'name as label'. Three real human hippie heads were similar to the three peaks of the mountain." In Miško Šuvaković, "3 x Triglav: controversies and problems regarding Mount Triglav", in Janez Janša, Janez Janša, Janez Janša (eds), *NAME Readymade*, Moderna galerija / Museum of Modern Art, Ljubljana 2008, p. 70.

[20] Irwin (eds), *East Art Map: Contemporary Art and Eastern Europe*, Afterall Books 2006.

[21] Eda Cufer & Irwin, "NSK State in Time", 1993. Available online at www.nskstate.com/irwin/texts/nsk-state-in-time.php.

[22] From "The Program of Irwin Group", April 1984, www.nskstate.com/irwin/texts/irwin-pro-uk.php.

[23] In this regard see the special edition of the journal *Maska* edited by Inke Arns and Sylvia Sasse (*Maska*, vol. XXI, n° 98-99, Spring 2006).

[24] Vladimir P. Štefanec, "Evolucija motiva", in *DELO*, October 20, 2007. Štefanec uses the word "sproščen" which means "relaxed": a key term in the right-wing political propaganda used by Janša to emphasize how idyllic, easy and tension-free everything is.

[25] For an analysis of the continuity between the work of the three artists before their name change, and their joint work as Janez Janša, see Zdenka Badovinac, "What is the importance of being Janez?", in Janez Janša, Janez Janša, Janez Janša (eds), *NAME Readymade*, Moderna galerija / Museum of Modern Art, Ljubljana 2008, pp. 51 – 65.

Art and Videogames. Enclosures and Border Crossings

This text was written in spring 2009 for the catalogue of a show of "concept art", a term used in the world of videogames to describe the sketches and illustrations developed by talented artisans in the making of games. The editors wanted to broaden the viewpoint of the show, and asked me to write a text about other uses of the word "art" in relation to games. I took the opportunity to try to bring some order into the mess that usually develops around the rise of a new cultural genre, and its acceptance into the broader world of culture. Warhol's work felt like a good starting point...

1949: Andrew Warhola, the son of a factory worker of Rusyn origin in Pittsburgh, arrives in New York. He had studied art, and his blotted line drawings, which made an uncertain, wavering line on the paper, attracted the attention of the art director of *Glamour*, who commissioned a series of drawings of shoes for the magazine. In the space of a few years Andrew became "the most sought-after illustrator of women's accessories in New York", as Calvin Tomkins wrote [1]. He changed his name to Andy Warhol, met Truman Capote, had his nose redone, founded a company and started making a lot of money, yet he was not satisfied. The art world kept him on the margin, despite his various attempts to make inroads. Paradoxically, his refined blotted line drawings of food, shoes and other consumer items looked too personal, too subtle and too nonchalant to carve a niche in the avant-garde art scene of the day – divided as it was between the macho heroism of Abstract Expressionism, and the impersonality of Pop Art [2]. It was attending Leo Castelli's gallery, where he saw the work of Jasper Johns and Roy Lichtenstein, that Andy found the path that would lead him to success: instead of depicting consumer goods, he began serial reproductions, first using a cold, impersonal style of painting, then a mechanical process (silkscreen printing). From elegant shoes decorated with gold-leaf he passed to giant, brutal cans of Campbell's soup. In 1963 he confessed: "[When I was doing advertising] I'd have to invent and now I don't; those commercial drawings would have feelings, they would have a style... the attitude had feeling to it."

What he did from that moment on changed the course of contemporary art. As for the drawings, they remained at the bottom of a drawer for years before being discovered. We now see them as engaging works of art: our idea of art has changed, making room for something that was not admitted in the past.

Enclosures and Border Crossings

In July 1962 Warhol exhibited his *Campbell's Soup Cans* for the first time in

Los Angeles. Four months previously, an unknown programmer at the Massachusetts Institute of Technology released the first version of *Spacewar!*, the first videogame in history. Two clusters of white dots move around a dark space shooting at each other. Half a century later not only have we learned to appreciate Warhol's shoes: the offspring of *Spacewar!* have become the biggest cultural industry in the world, with revenues overtaking those of the film industry. The white dots have been supplanted by 3D figures, realistic settings, sophisticated storylines, gameplay that often requires weeks of training. Every game is worked on by teams of experts in graphics, writing, programming and interaction – who work on the same project for months, often even years. Several generations have grown up with them, and characters like Super Mario and Lara Croft are an indelible part of our cultural baggage, alongside *The Catcher in the Rye* and Obi-Wan Kenobi.

Pondering the relationships between art and videogames means opening a vast Pandora's box that lets loose a flood of responses, often unpredictable. In the first part of this essay I will present some of them, hopefully without boring you. In the second part I will try to explain what Warhol's example has to teach the artists featured in *The Art of Games*, and its spellbound spectators.

Even just the phrase "art and videogames" is somewhat ambiguous, with that 'and' presuming some kind of relationship – but what kind? I imagine there are at least three different possible interpretations:

> that videogames are art;

> that videogames are inspired by art;

> that art is inspired by videogames.

The first of the three might make many gamers – for whom videogames are decidedly better than art – jump out of their chairs, as well as art lovers, who regard videogames as vulgar form of entertainment, but this type of resistance highlights only a few aspects of a complex question. First and foremost, the time is ripe for videogames to be recognised as an "art form" in their own right, just as happened with photography and film. Some games, like *Rez* (Dreamcast 2001) and *Spore* (Electronic Arts 2008), are already held by some to be works of art. This does not mean that all videogames can be considered works of art, merely a number of them which satisfy certain criteria [3]. The example of film and photography is instructive. Diane Arbus is an artist, but most fashion photographers are not. An Alfred Hitchcock film is a work of art, but most thrillers are, at best, good examples of the genre.

Secondly, for a number of years now some visual artists have taken to developing videogames that see themselves as works of art – "art games" – appropriating the videogame medium just as Man Ray did with photography in his day, Salvador Dalì did with cinema, and Nam June Paik did with video. Their works belong both to the history of "videogames as an art form" and "videogames as a language of contemporary art". They are borderline works capable of appealing to both gaming fanatics and compulsive gallery-goers.

The second interpretation is the one that creates the fewest problems. Like all forms of cultural entertainment, videogames tap into our cultural traditions, often manipulating the most tried and tested strategies for their own ends. Renaissance perspective, Romantic landscapes, film noir lighting, the *topos* of science fiction, characters from the epic genre, fairytale narrative mechanisms... All of this and much more besides goes into the blender, material for the construction of a good game. Remediations [4] of forms and aesthetics from other media, postmodern citationism, etc., are all familiar ploys for the creators of videogames, as they are for all good professionals of the culture industry.

The third interpretation, on the other hand, is so complex that even the formula I have used to convey it, ("art is inspired by videogames"), appears on closer inspection to be ineffective and incomplete. The ambiguity, first and foremost, lies in the subject. Just what do we mean by the term "art"? In the first place it can be useful to distinguish by genre. By now there are at least as many films inspired by videogames as there are videogames inspired by films, but it is even more interesting to explore the traces that videogames leave in the construction of a film, independently of any direct inspiration. A similar argument could be made for fiction, which has produced various novels inspired by the world of videogames, some of which are high quality works: take *Skill* (2004), by Alessandra C, and *A Big Boy Did It and Ran Away* (2001), by Christopher Brookmyre. Then there are the visual arts, a context that introduces a new distinction, this time to do with level. In the first place there is a grassroots level, belonging to pop culture, which includes fan art and all the subcultures linked to the world of videogames. Fan art, according to *Wikipedia*, "is artwork that is based on a character, costume, item, or story that was created by someone other than the artist. The term, while it can apply to art done by fans of characters from books, is usually used to refer to art derived from visual media such as comics, movies or video games. Usually, it refers to artworks by amateur artists, or artists who are unpaid for their fan creations." [5] Fan art, which until recently was a low-profile niche phenomenon, has literally exploded with the advent of social network sites and Web 2.0 applications like flickr and Youtube. But videogames have done more than just construct a paratextual aura of pencil drawings, photoshopped images, oil paintings, little sculptures and so on. Cosplaying and role-playing, for example, are performance phenomena that bring storylines and characters from videogames alive. Moreover, the evolution of videogames into productive platforms that not only allow users to play but also elicit creative contributions from them has paved the way for an infinite series of practices. In the early 90s the introduction of level editors "normalised" and legitimised a series of intrusive practices (game hacking) already in use in the previous decade, enabling users to adapt games to suit their needs. In a similar process, the trend for gamers to film themselves in action has evolved into a genuine cinematographic sub-genre (known as *machinima*), with the introduction into videogames of integrated directing tools. Lastly, the birth of virtual worlds like Second Life, in which the game-playing component gives way to user creativity (without which the virtual world would not be much to write home about), has given rise to genuine creative communities that operate within the 3D scenarios of a game.

In most cases these practices are not qualified, and have no desire to qualify themselves, as art. They are creative practices which take place within a community, and which often follow rules that have nothing to do with those of the world of "high" art, which they generally disparage. Yet in the last decade each of these practices has been adopted by artists and introduced into the high circuits of contemporary art and New Media Art. This phenomenon, usually dubbed "Game Art", has been explored in a countless number of exhibitions and publications [6], which is why here I will merely offer an overview of it – enough to see that art does much more than just take "inspiration" from videogames. Art takes up the storylines, characters, imagery and aesthetics of videogames: see Miltos Manetas' paintings, Eva and Franco Mattes' prints, and many of the works of Eddo Stern and Brody Condon. It penetrates, subverts and modifies the videogame and its technology, turning it into something else: Jodi, Joan Leandre and Cory Arcangel are some of the most prominent examples of this. It appropriates the form of the videogame and gameplay for artistic purposes (giving rise to the aforementioned art games, but also gaming installations such as those of Julian Oliver and Eddo Stern). It mixes the language of role-playing with that of performance (Brody Condon once more), or uses videogames themselves as a performance platform (Joseph Delappe, Gazira Babeli). It creates *machinima* that are art videos (Eddo Stern once more) or explores videogame culture in documentary fashion. All of these names are well worth exploring.

Among all these practices and levels, the barriers constructed by those who engage in them, by the nascent field of videogame criticism, and the worlds of sociology and art criticism might seem insurmountable. In a way, it is a good thing that these barriers exist: ever since the human race began applying reasoning to its world, it has needed to create groups, subgroups and taxonomies in order to comprehend a given phenomenon. At the same time, however, the dynamism, potential for evolution and future survival of a practice all lie in border-crossing, hybridisation, cross-breeds. Which is why these barriers should always be erected with the greatest respect for what is on the other side, and openings should always be left. The art of the future springs from things which are not considered art today, or that correspond to different ideas of art. *flOw* (2006), for example, is an "art game" that circulated on the web and featured in various exhibitions before being developed for the Playstation platform and forging a keen following among traditional players too [7]. Its serene, anti-competitive, contemplative gameplay not only represents a development in the world of videogames, but also extends our idea of art. Cory Arcangel, who recently (March 2009) made it onto the cover of *Artforum*, is an artist who has managed to earn the respect of the art world, the hacking community and the fans of the old 8bit games. In an era in which art is seen by most as self-referencing and elite, this is undoubtedly an achievement.

Concept Art and Beyond

But the question is far from resolved. The attentive reader will have realised that we have not yet identified a category for the works in this catalogue. Never fear: this is not an oversight. The fact is that a videogame, like a film, is the result of the convergence of various different activities, creative and not. "Concept art" is one of these. As Wikipedia explains: "Concept art is a form of illustration where the main goal is to convey a visual representation of a design, idea, and/or mood for use in movies, video games, animation, or comic books before it is put into the final product. Concept art is also referred to as visual development and/or concept design." [8] Concept art is a very important part of the life of a videogame. It is not just about studying the look of the characters or creating the settings they operate in; and it is not just something that goes on behind the scenes, something that the public never sees. Concept art "opens" the life of a videogame, announcing it in trade magazines and on websites, generating expectations and introducing the story and characters; it accompanies the game in books and manuals, and it guarantees continuity between different versions of a game, which can often be rather dissimilar, due to various technological limits being overcome between versions.

Lara Croft's look has changed considerably since her first appearance in 1996, but concept art offers an imprinting that guarantees the continuity of the character. When videogames were anything but photorealistic, concept art gave the gamer's imagination the input to fill in the missing links in the technology. In a "holographic approach" to videogames (Laurie Taylor [9]), concept art plays a role that is anything but secondary, and lastly, it is an indispensable basis for fan art, with which it often forges a dialectical relationship.

All the artists in this book work as "concept artists" for companies that produce videogames. Concept art is both a "service" art and a paratext. As a service art it contributes to the development of a series of tools of mass entertainment that will probably be recognised, in a not too distant future, as "art forms". It plays the same function that storyboards and sets play in the film world, and it is based on internal criteria and value judgements. As a paratext it is related to the illustrations that enrich popular fiction, from fantasy to sci-fi, and to the art of the film poster and the imagery developed for role-playing games, which are a direct forerunner of many videogames. And, like all these pop iconography phenomena, it is capable of eliciting a following, a field of criticism, and the interest of collectors.

It is not only the fact that concept art is art "with a function" that keeps it locked out of contemporary art. Many of these artists occasionally produce works for their own sake, not connected to any videogame in particular. By way of example, on Jason Felix's website [10], alongside the channel "concept art" there is a channel he calls "fine art". The problem (if we want to call it a problem) is that the works in that section are based on the same value criteria and judgments as concept art: criteria - beauty as a measure of judgment, technical ability as a value, the virtuoso use of a certain tool – that have little in common with those we use to define a work of contemporary art as "art". In other words, even the so-called "fine art" of the concept artists remains bound to a vernacular level, as "popular culture", rather than making the grade as contemporary art. It remains on the level of "craft", rather than high brow art.

With this statement I am diligently performing my role of "gatekeeper", policing the border between high and low art. At the same time, however, it is important to leave an opening: in the first place because this "service" art is often capable of generating unpredictable brushstrokes, where this distinction does not apply: consider two outstanding examples like Saul Bass and Milton Glaser; and secondly, because the fusions between high and low, as the example of so-called "Game Art" shows, are infinitely more complex than traditional criticism enables us to see. And lastly, because art critics should never forget the example of the young Andrew Warhola, an adman who wanted to be an artist and who only posthumously gained recognition for the extraordinary value of the work he produced for the world of advertising.

These reflections are what lead me to attribute great importance to a project like *The Art of Games*, the first high profile exhibition to explore the as yet uncharted terrain of concept art. For keen gamers and fans, the exhibition will be a kind of seventh heaven, a chance to linger over their objects of desire and gain insight into the techniques of their idols. For those interested in the impact of digital culture on the contemporary horizon, *The Art of Games* will be a great eye-opener. As for gallery goers, I would recommend they look with interest, restraining the urge to scoff if they feel that the term "art" is being used irrelevantly. For all three groups, the exhibition will be a great opportunity to interface and interact. And a much needed opportunity to cross cultural and social borders.

First published in Debora Ferrari, Luca Traini (eds), *The Art of Games. Nuove frontiere tra gioco e bellezza*, TraRari TIPI, Aosta 2009.

[1] "Raggedy Andy", in Calvin Tomkins, *The Scene: Reports on Post-Modern Art*, Viking Press, New York 1976.

[2] With regard to Warhol's "pre-pop" work see, at least AA.VV., *Andy Warhol. Una retrospettiva*, cat., Milan 1990.

[3] With regard to these criteria, I strongly recommend reading Ernest W. Adams' contribution to *Videogames and Art* (2007): Ernest W. Adams, "Will Computer Games Ever Be a Legitimate Art Form?", in Andy Clarke, Grethe Mitchell (eds), *Videogames and Art*, Intellect Books, Bristol (UK) – Chicago (USA) 2007, pp. 254 – 264. The book as a whole makes an excellent introduction to the issues discussed on the forthcoming pages.

[4] Cf. Jay David Bolter, Richard Grusin, *Remediation. Understanding New Media*, The MIT Press, Cambridge (MASS) 1999.

[5] In *Wikipedia*, http://en.wikipedia.org/wiki/Fan_art.

[6] Apart from the book edited by Clarke and Mitchell, we should mention at least: M. Bittanti, D. Quaranta (eds), *GameScenes. Art in the Age of Videogames*, Milan, Johan & Levi 2006. As for exhibitions, a list which is anything but exhaustive should include: *Serious Games: Art Interaction Technology* (curated by Beryl Graham, Laing Art Gallery, Newcastle / Barbican Art Gallery, London, 1996 - 1997); *Cracking the Maze: Game Plug-ins and Patches as Hacker Art* (curated by Anne-Marie Schleiner, 1999, online: http://switch.sjsu.edu/CrackingtheMaze); *Shift Control* (curated by Antoinette LaFarge and Robert Nideffer, University of California ad Irvine, 2000); *Game Show*, (MASS MoCA, Massachusetts, 2001 - 2002); *L'oading* (curated by Valentina Tanni, Siracusa, Galleria Civica d'Arte Contemporanea 2003); *games. Computergames by artists* (curated by Tilman Baumgaertel, Hans D. Christ, Iris Dressler, Hartware MedienKunstverein, Dortmund 2003); *GameScenes* (curated by D. Quaranta, Turin, Piemonte Share Festival 2005); *Pong Mithos* (curated by Andreas Lange, Kornhausforum Bern - Communication Museum Frankfurt - Games Convention, Leipzig, 2006 - 2007); *GameScapes* (curated by Rosanna Pavoni, Monza, Galleria Civica 2006); *Playback: Simulated Realities* (Edith Russ Site for Media Art, Oldenburg, 2006); *GameWorld* (curated by Carl Goodman, Laboral Centro de Arte y Creación Industrial, Gijón 2007); *PlayWare* (Laboral Centro de Arte y Creación Industrial, Gijón 2007 - 2008); *Try Again* (curated by Juan Antonio Alvarez Reyes, La Casa Encendida, Madrid 2008); *Homo Ludens Ludens* (curated by Erich Berger, Laura Baigorri, Daphne Dragona, Laboral Centro de Arte y Creación Industrial, Gijón 2008); *Audience & Avatar* (curated by Don Fuller, University of South Florida Contemporary Art Museum, Tampa 2008); *BITMAP: as good as new* (curated by Marcin Ramocki, Vertexlist, New York - The Leonard Pearlstein Gallery, Philadelphia 2008).

[7] Cf. www.thatgamecompany.com/games/flow

[8] In *Wikipedia*, http://en.wikipedia.org/wiki/Concept_art.

[9] Laurie Taylor, "Networking Power. Videogame Structure from Concept Art", in A. Clarke, G. Mitchell (eds), *Videogames and Art*, cit., pp. 226 – 237.

[10] Cf. www.jasonfelix.com.

Cory Arcangel

The most striking thing about Cory Arcangel's work is its eclecticism and the way it totally eschews order. He himself confessed in an interview: «I am a classic multi-tasker. When I was younger, I used to do my homework while watching TV. Now when I watch TV, I surf the web.» [1] He has a website, or rather a blog, or rather two blogs; but these are not necessarily the best place to start for an understanding of his work. He describes himself as a programmer; but that is only one of his identities. He is also a teacher, musician, artist, performer, exhibition curator, and occasionally an art critic. Some of these activities he carries out as Cory Arcangel, others as a part of one of the many collectives of which he is either a member or occasional collaborator: Beige, Contagious Media Group, The 8-bit Construction Set, Gay Beatles, RSG, Paperrad. Often works are even presented as both individual and collective.

But once one gets over the confusion generated by defunct links, multiple identities and works classified in various ways, one discovers a rare coherence which is no less solid for being subterranean. There is a connecting thread. It may be traced by a dirty and tremulous mouse – befitting the "dirty style" he is so fond of – but it is unmistakable.

One of the bases for the coherence to be seen in his work is his love of "old systems". One might here speak of nostalgia: there is no doubt that the retro-chic fascination of his work – together with his irresistible gifts as a performer – have made him the darling of the New York scene, courted by the likes of Jeffrey Deitch and other private individuals and institutional bodies. However, I would say that the correct term to describe Cory Arcangel's attachment to old systems is economy. As he himself revealed in an interview with John Bruneau: «I like these systems not cause of nostalgia, but because they are cheap and easy to work. Also they are the perfect middle ground between analogue and digital video.» [2] There is an economy of means and knowledge: it is much easier and simpler to learn how to modify an old Nintendo cartridge than something more recent. And there is also economy of space, codes and bits: in this era of broadband, Arcangel produces remarkably light works, often of less than 32k. This is even an economy of intellectual reference: Cory himself has commented that «I would love to say there was some contemporary artist who's work really got me thinking, but lately I have just been trying to sort out twenty years of garbage TV culture that is filling my brain.» [3] He is someone who strives for maximum effect with minimum effort, considering it a positive thing "to do as little as possible". As Alexander Galloway wrote about *Data Diaries* (2002):

> «What did Cory Arcangel do in this piece? Next to nothing. The computer did the work, and he just gave it a form. His discovery was this: take a huge data file—in this case his computer's memory file—and fool Quicktime into thinking it's a video file. Then press play. Your computer's memory is now video art. Quicktime plays right through, not knowing that the squiggles and shards on the screen are actually the bits and bytes

of the computer's own brain. The data was always right in front of your nose. Now you can watch it.» [4]

Well – asked by John Bruneau about the presumed poverty of this work, Arcangel replied: «Simplicity is an asset, not a weakness...look at something like the cloud work. that is very simple. The smaller the idea the happier I am.» [5]

For Arcangel, lightness also involves a sort of Pop superficiality; hence his denial of any artistic influence that is not contemporary, and not the result of friendship; and hence his immense, passionate love of television and the internet. «I am a pop artist and all pop culture to me is fair game! I love it all. I don't have a TV now, cause if I did I would watch it all the TIME!!!» [6] As in Pop Art, there is a certain ostentation in this proclamation of superficiality; but the fact remains that all of his work arises from his own delight in creating it, from a conception of art as enjoyment, amusement, pleasure.

The way he tells Hanne Mugaas about his childhood in Buffalo, where he starts making his first videos with his sister, is very funny, but also reveals the roots of this approach:

> «First of all there was never ANYTHING to do, so I had to make my own fun, and this is how I ended up making videos with my sister when we were young. This I guess it quite common, but more specifically Buffalo, has this really strange video art culture. In the 70's all these insane video art people from New York moved there to teach at the University. These people included Stan and Woody Vasulka [...] and Tony Conrad [...] So the work of these artists really shaped the artistic identity of the city. I remember watching TV when I was younger and seeing these weirdo minimal color field videos late at night. It is hard to put into words, but by growing up there I never thought it was weird to make a 15 minute slow motion video. No one ever told me this was strange, ...I would see such strange stuff on the public TV all the time, that it wasn't until I moved away that I learned that these were 'art videos'.» [7]

After Buffalo, Cory moved to New York, where he studied classical guitar at the Oberlin. The Beige group was formed around 1997, when he was at music school, and is the "collective" background for all his subsequent artistic activities. Founded by Cory Arcangel, Joe Beuckman, Joe Bonn, and Paul B. Davis, this group of programmers was also a musical band and a small record label:

> «After a few records we all started to make some really weird stuff and eventually wandered off the map into hardware hacking, video art, and bead work [we do not really see any difference between audio and visual work] so we just went with the name BEIGE as an umbrella to describe everything we were doing.» [8]

Their first project of a certain scale was the *8-bit Construction Set* (1998-2000), which was the name of their band and of the record they released on the Beige Records label. In fact, it was a "battle record" comprising music, software and video; one side was recorded – and can be read – using a Commodore 64, the other using an Atari platform. The *8-bit Construction Set* reflects the predilection for low-tech and lo-fi aesthetics that is characteristic of a lot of European Net Art; but it also echoes the advent of 8-bit music, which was then emerging in both the US and Europe, with old platforms being used as musical instruments. It is no coincidences that, after the *8-bit Construction Set*, Beige experimented with the use of the Nintendo Entertainment System (NES) as an instrument for making music as well as video. These experiments led to *Fat Bits*, the group's first installation, which was presented in 2001 at the Chicago Deadtech. For Arcangel, NES cartridges were the perfect tool for making videos by working on minimal graphics and old platforms whilst remaining true to the nebulous resolution of the television image (which he finds much more fascinating than the precision of new pixel technology).

This fascination for old systems and lo-fi aesthetics explains his interest in old videogames better than any presumed nostalgia for an infancy spent on the Nintendo console:

> «I never really liked or played the game. At this point most of my interest in the game is in the 16 * 16 sidescrolling graphical limitations [...] I think there are a lot of people who missed that particular game, but no one who missed the aesthetic of the early computer and video game movement. [...] I don't love the games so much, but I really love the systems. I love the look that the old Systems have. For one, the NES directly accesses the TV's colors. So you tend to get these really bright colors on older TV's, much brighter than cable, or VHS tapes. This kinda thing also looks good even as a glow cast on a room. Like my cloud cartridge was really made for a TV I have in the corner of my apt, so at night it makes my living room glow that slurpy blue of the sky in the game. Second, I really like the idea of scrolling. Even more than movies, games tend to frame narratives in such a way that people really believe that the game world extends beyond the borders of the screen. All you have to do is move the joypad left or right to see it. And I really like the yucky stuff that the TV signal adds to the pixel perfect style. People forget that the pixel design style that is really popular is kinda like a mirage. That aesthetic only exists in the heads of designers because back on the day pixel graphics were all displayed on TV's which of course make everything blurry.» [9]

The "cloud cartridge" is *Super Mario Clouds* (2002), perhaps Arcangel's best-known work. It is a Super Mario Bros cartridge from which he erased everything except the clouds, which flow uninterruptedly left to right across the screen. It might look like video, but it isn't, particularly as it is much lighter – only 32k to be exact. In an entertaining tutorial written to illustrate the code of the work line by line, Arcangel explains that in the NES images are constructed with quadrants of 8x8 pixels, for a total graphics load of 8k. «These two hardware limitations defined the aesthetic of most early eighties videogames on the Nintendo, and making "art" for this system is a study of these limitations.» [10] By playing upon the limits of the machine and the programming code, Arcangel creates a hypnotic icon that is immediately recognizable. Its very lightness, which almost verges upon the idiotic, makes it into a delicate metaphor for his work as a whole.

Cory Arcangel would return to the Mario cartridges a number of times. Coming almost a year before the clouds, his *Super Abstract Brothers* substitutes all the characters and backgrounds with abstract forms and figures, transforming Mario Bros into a strange Tetris, undermining our memories from a world that, due to our absorption in the game, we tend to perceive as real. In *Fantasy Cutscenes # 2* (2004), on the other hand, Arcangel adds to the same cartridge captions that evoke both silent cinema and strip cartoons, thus causing a "collision" of various narrative genres. *Naptime*, for its part, is a hypnotic video in which a sleeping Mario dreams a constant flow of psychedelic code to the accompaniment of an 8-bit soundtrack composed by Arcangel's friend, Paul B. Davis. But it was with *Super Mario Movie*, the fruit of collaboration with Paperrad, that Arcangel once more achieved the success (and fascination) of *Super Mario Clouds*. Shown by Deitch Projects in January 2005, this is again a modified cartridge, with two pages (32k) of code producing a fifteen minute flow of sound and image. In the proposal he e-mailed to the gallery, Arcangel presents the work in this way:

> «The movie is gonna be about how Mario's world is falling apart. Like mad max, but in 8bits. Picture title screens, messed up fantasy worlds, castles floating on rainbow colored 8-bit clouds, waterfalls, underwater dungeon nightmare rave scapes, dance parties, floating/mushrooms level scenes, Mario alone on a cloud crying, fireball flicker patterns, and video synth knitted 60 frames per second seizure vidz. Each scene will also have music. & All being generated by this one 32k 1984 cartridge!!!!!!!!!!!» [11]

This is an almost epic work in which our hero surfs through a digital world that is breaking down, which is at times recognizable, at times completely abstract. The alternation of half-legible captions and fragments reveals the difficulties of communication which are caused by the imminent collapse of the system. In the exhibition venue the work was projected alongside the source code, which created a wallpaper effect, and the original cartridge modified and repainted by Paperrad was put on display as a work of art.

To date the act of transforming the cartridge into a sculpture, and therefore an artistic object in its own right, in some way independent of its contents, has been carried out with the minimum of intervention, because Arcangel considers larger scale changes less in line with a genuine "hack". However there is a precedent for this, in the work of the hackers who created cracks for Commodore 64 games and went so far as to sign them proudly with their own "tag", namely a brief video at the start of the game. Arcangel came across these tags while he was working, as BEIGE, on *Low Level All Stars* (2003), a research project made for the show "Kingdom of Piracy", in collaboration with Alexander Galloway [12]. The two artists examined more than 1,000 tags and selected ten of them to put on a DVD. To all intents and purposes the project represents a form of digital graffiti, saved by RSG from an underground scene where it risked being lost, with the aim of demonstrating its high level of self-awareness and offering an interesting comparison with "highbrow" culture.

All Arcangel's work, in a way, has some relationship with the graffiti art movement, and the people he hangs out with – from the rapper Rammellzee to Paperrad – can prove it. The defacement of pop culture myths is something that we can find in many of his works: *Sans Simon* (2004) is the video of a concert by Simon & Garfunkel where the silhouette of Simon is hidden – I would say censored – by the artist's hands; while *Beach Boys / Geto Boys* (2004) is a mash-up where the video of "Little Surfer Girl" – an icon of the surf culture of the Sixties – is played side by side with the video of an hip-hop song by the Geto Boys. The two songs, synchronized, become a single song, a weird harmony in which the differences between these two cultures collapse. Finally, the classic *I Shot Andy Warhol* (2002) combines hacker intrusion with graffiti defacement. The victim is the cartridge of "Holigan's Halley", another old game for NES. Our victim, on the other hand, is Andy Warhol, whose silvery wig and dark-rimmed glasses make him unmistakeable even in 8bit graphics, alongside the Pope and other pop icons. What we have to do is repeat ad infinitum the act of feminist Valerie Solanas in June 1968, with the difference that here Andy is set up as a target, flat and abstract like his numerous self portraits, until he actually turns invisible in the third level, where we are invited to throw the notorious Campbell's soup tins at him. Oh, and I was forgetting, the target is presented on a TV screen, and the joystick is a toy pistol.

In *Nipod* (2004) the subject of the defacement is a contemporary icon: the iPod, designed to become a cult object, is emulated in a way that can be either interpreted as a tribute or as a mockery. Indeed *Nipod* celebrates the retro, lo-fi, primitive, text-based aesthetics that is exactly the opposite of that sleek, lily-white "blogject", proudly showing off its gigabytes. Arcangel opposes what he found out in garbage and second-hand stores to the design object that can be found in an hi-tech store, modifying a Nintendo cartridge and turning it into a music platform that plays pop hits – from Eminem to Van Halen and 50 cents – in an 8bit style, projecting the simplified image of an iPod over the wall. He wrote: «I like the idea of making things out of trash [one can easily find an NES in a dumpster these days], and I like the idea of actually having to break into something that I find in the trash even better.» [13]

In other cartridges – from *Space Invader* (note the disappearance of the plural "s") to *F1 Racer Mod* and *Slow Tetris* (all produced in 2004) – what is defaced is the game itself, which becomes boring and unplayable. However, these works also reveal a more constructive aim, which was already to be glimpsed in *Super Mario Clouds*. True, the game can no longer be used as such; but it has been transformed into landscape, into a picture to be looked at. There is no action but that of sitting and observing, letting oneself be hypnotized by the flow of images, be bombarded by the cathode ray tube of the television. GameBoy Killed the Video Stars; but the videogame heroes must return to television if they are to have their fifteen minutes of fame, to become icons.

Slowed down, "Tetris" becomes an abstract picture, to be contemplated as one contemplates a Mondrian; separated from all his friends, the fearsome alien invader becomes an innocuous little spider we can annihilate whenever we want. As for the road in "Car Racer", when stripped of the roaring engines it becomes a poetic metaphor of travel and new frontiers, an American highway with mountains in the background, immobile clouds in the sky and a Nintendo advertising hoarding on the horizon. It is no coincidence that Arcangel has based a series of posters on this landscape, bringing out the full iconic power of the image.

He has said: «I have [...] grown used to programming only because it is the mechanism that seems to make most of the world move. Believe me, if I could order pizzas [...] by painting, I definitely would paint.» [14] And if, with his modified cartridges, he becomes a painter, he doesn't give up with pizza. *Pizza Party* (2004) is a UNIX command-line program with a GPL license that can be used to order pizza via the internet, and organize improvised pizza parties. The work is a hack of the Dominos Pizza ordering system, in which Arcangel mixes all the ingredients we get used to without ever getting bored of them: lightness, lo-fi aesthetics, a sense of humor, uselessness, apparent insanity. Almost unknown in the contemporary art world, Pizza Party became a cult project among hackers and geeks: an audience Arcangel never dumped for the gallery-goers.

First published in Spanish in *aminima*, issue 16, 2005. A partial English translation (by Jeremy Scott & Anna Carruthers) was published in the book *Gamescenes. Art in the Age of Videogames* (Milan 2006) with the title "Cory Arcangel – NES Landscapes".

[1] Hanne Mugaas, "Hanne Mugaas + Cory Arcangel = a Talk", 2005, online at www.hanne-mugaas.com/texts/hanne_mugaas_cory_arcangel_a_t/.
[2] John Bruneau, "Interview with Cory Arcangel", in *Switch 19*, Summer 2004, online at http://switch.sjsu.edu/v19/00000c.
[3] Eryk Salvaggio, "Cory Arcangel Doesn't Even Like Super Mario Brothers", in *Turbulence*, April 2003, online at www.turbulence.org/curators/salvaggio/arcangel.html.
[4] Alexander Galloway, "Data Diaries", 2002, online at www.turbulence.org/Works/arcangel/alex.php.
[5] In John Bruneau, op. cit.
[6] In Hanne Mugaas, op. cit.
[7] Ivi.
[8] In Erik Salvaggio, op. cit.
[9] Ivi.
[10] The tutorial is no longer available at the original address. Cory's current homepage features a shorter tutorial on the project's page, online at www.coryarcangel.com/things-i-made/supermarioclouds/. The quoted text can still be found through the *Web Archive*, at the address http://web.archive.org/web/20071231143259/www.beigerecords.com/cory/tags/artwork/.
[11] Cory Arcangel, "Idea", 12 June 2004, online at www.deitch.com/projects/sub.php?projId=153.
[12] The project was released as a collaboration between BEIGE and RSG (Radical Software Group), Alexander Galloway's collective identity (cf. http://r-s-g.org/). The project is not available online anymore, but is available for purchase via the Electronic Arts Intermix (EAI). Cf. www.eai.org/title.htm?id=7694.
[13] Cf. footnote n. 10.
[14] Cf. footnote n. 10.

Eddo Stern

In the beginning, there is life. Or, better, another level of life. It's the kind of life you can live on a screen, where your face and body change from time to time, according to the adventure you are playing at the time. It's a kind of life that implies gestures such as pressing furiously the buttons of a keyboard, speaking into a microphone, teaching all your muscles how to behave in order to make the movement of a joystick more fluent and responsive; and in which these gestures are translated into shots, curses, jumps, fights, runs. It's a kind of life that usually has a soundtrack. It's a kind of life that can be very similar to our daily life, or slightly different; but that, in both cases, mixes with the latter in a way that our brain, programmed for one life at a time, has some difficulties in making a clear distinction between the two. For example, if you are a soldier, it may be difficult for you to distinguish between your last mission in Afghanistan or Iraq and your last session of America's Army.

Mixing two levels of life does not mean that, as an avid player of GTA, you would feel a irrepressible need to take a bat and walk down 5th Avenue smashing up everything you find on your way; nor that you are going to experience performance anxiety because your Second Life avatar has a bigger penis, or your virtual partner seems more excited than your real one. It just means that, chatting to a friend, you will probably sum up your last adventure in World of Warcraft with the same words and the same enthusiasm you would use for a real event; and that feelings, anxieties, fears and passions related with your real life experience will probably change the way you live your life on the screen.

I don't know what Eddo Stern, who served in the Israeli army before moving to the States, feels when he plays a war game. What I know is that *Sheik Attack* (1999), Eddo Stern's first machinima film, is probably the best take on Israel's bloody history I have ever seen. One of the very first art videos using game footage to build up a narrative, *Sheik Attack* shows up an extraordinary maturity compared with the novelty of its genre. The narrative of the Zionist utopia, from the dream of rebuilding the state of Israel up to the current tragic situation, is told through a soundtrack of traditional Israeli songs and the editing of a series of scenes shot in games such as Sim City, Delta Force, and Command & Conquer. The low-resolution footage is in stark contrast to the strong emotional impact of the soundtrack. Stern manages to transform the expressive limitations of the tool – the repetitive nature of the gestures, the lack of dialogue – into a powerful medium in itself. This transformation can be understood if we look at the way Stern uses the cinematics of the first person shooter: the main character's point of view, used with some caution in traditional filmmaking, here is chosen to make the spectator identify simultaneously with the player and the narrative's main character, making him co-responsible for their atrocious actions. So, when the tragically polygonal sheik's wife, resting on her knees, is assassinated without blinking an eye, we are the ones holding the gun.

Machine Animation

Machinima is just a medium, as neutral as any other medium. Yet, as any other "remix" practice, it has an enormous potential that emerges when the existing material is used to convey a meaning that conflicts with its own source. The video becomes a kind of prosthetic narrative, which extends the game's narrative in an unpredictable direction. And that, sometimes, rejects the body it was designed for. From cut-up theory to culture jamming to Nicholas Bourriaud's "postproduction" model, many great theorists have discussed this potential: what is interesting to me is that, when it comes to games, your appropriation is not only dealing with "existing cultural material", or with a medium, but with your own life, the life you lived inside the game. In other words, making *Sheik Attack* is different from, let's say, shooting October or a masterpiece of plagiarism such as Negativland's *Gimme the Mermaid* (2002). The main difference is that Eddo Stern is, in the same time, the soldier who shot the helpless sheik's wife and the documentarian who reports the crime.

Both *Vietnam Romance* (2003) and *Deathstar* (2004) display this kind of potential. In Vietnam Romance Stern forces us to take part in a war that we know very well, but just from one single point of view: the one adopted by Hollywood in a steady stream of movies, from *Apocalypse Now* to *Platoon*, from *The Thin Red Line* to *Full Metal Jacket*, from *The Deer Hunter* to *Forrest Gump*. American movies that, even when critical towards the war and the way the US conducted it, share a similar atmosphere and articulate a common imaginary, that has become, through these movies the imaginary we all have come to share. Videogames remediate this kind of imaginary; but at the same time, force us to see the war through the eyes of the American military, and remove the critical filter that cinematic narrative provides. In videogames, the Vietnam War becomes, in Stern's words, "as clear cut as World War II". The story is simple: you are the good (American) guy who has to kill all those dirty (Vietnamese) rats. With the complicity of a soundtrack that resamples the famous hits of the Sixties and Seventies into electronic MIDI tracks, Stern re-appropriates this material and uses it to create a melancholic "romance", full of nostalgia for an age and a cinematographic genre that seems irremediably lost. The opening scene is phenomenal, with a prostitute parading through desolated outskirts on the notes of Nancy Sinatra's *These Boots are Made for Walking*.

Deathstar (2004) is a video in which the violence enacted against a single body, Osama Bin Laden's, is so up and close as to seem abstract. The work edits a series of sequences shot in different games devoted to the assassination of the public enemy number one, together with Mel Gibson's *The Passion of the Christ* soundtrack, as if trying to compare two different – yet strangely similar – versions of the iconography of violence and pain.

If appropriating game footage can be subversive, appropriating the game engine in order to force it to tell other stories can be even stronger (though it usually isn't). Again, a feature of more recent videogames is turned into a powerful instrument of criticism by the very way it is used. *Landlord Vigilante* (2006) is a video that uses the engine of such games as GTA San Andreas and The Sims in order to do what games seem completely unfit for: design a character, give her a credible psychology and tell her story. The story of Leslie Shirley, inspired by the artist's former landlady, has been translated into a script in collaboration with the artist and writer Jessica Z. Hutchins. Ms. Shirley is a cynical and strong woman who, driving a cab in Los Angeles, has been saving a good sum of money in order to buy some real estate to rent. Persuaded that tenants are "defective human beings", Leslie Shirley – the name chosen for her reassuring landlady's mask – capitalizes on their "dirty habits", trying to get the most from her investment. Stern and Hutchins use different games in order to exploit their peculiar aesthetics for the construction of the character and her environment: The Sims is used to design Leslie's "kind old lady" mask and her comfortable, traditional, tidy "country cottage"; while GTA San Andreas puts the "real" Leslie – an old witch hardened by life – in her natural environment – Los Angeles' slums. In the chapter "Mirrors", Leslie describes her complex relationship with her own body – that is, her interface with the world – in front of a mirror, while holding a camera as if it was a gun and shooting a picture of herself. Referencing the iconography of first person shooters, Stern and Hutchins illustrate the psychological process of identity deconstruction and construction, using the game to talk about real life.

The same strategy is adopted in Stern's more recent "machine animations", *Best...Flamewar...Ever: Leegattenby King of Bards v. Squire Rex* (2007) and *Level sounds like Devil: Baby in Christ vs. His Father* (2007). The first of which is a two channel 3D computer animation diptych recreating an online flame war about degrees of expertise around the computer fantasy game Everquest. If in this case the contention focuses on the "shifting codes of masculinity", in *Level sounds like Devil...* the discussion involves a teenager and his father, who believes that World of Warcraft is evil and tries to make him stop playing. Being himself a Christian, BabyInChrist contacts an online Christian forum for guidance in understanding if his father is right or not, and the community tries to help him, sometimes pointing to the differences between virtual and real, sometimes quoting the Holy Bible, and sometimes suggesting him to lie to his father. The faces of the characters are mapped with fan art and textures coming from online fantasy games such as Everquest and WoW, and become something in between an Arcimboldo allegory and a medieval standard. In this way, the characters become hybrid identities, summing up a way of life in which the two levels we described are no more separated – as, probably, they have never been.

Animated Machines

I call these videos "machine animations" because this expression, more than its portmanteau "machinima", makes clear what is at stake. If videogames, through photorealism and immersion, employ considerate effort to make the player forget the machine, Stern returns the machine to the forefront. This could be unpleasant for both gamers and non-gamers, but it's the only way to escape the magic of so-called virtual worlds and start making works that are critical or self. As Eddo Stern, who spent 2,000 hours in World of Warcraft, knows quite well, the machine is the only frame between you and the game reality, and the only way to break the illusion is to make it more visible, in your face. So, if his videos can be described as prosthetic narratives, his installations can be described as prosthetic machines; both of them introduce a feeling of alienation, the first using the games in ways they a not meant for and inserting reality into them, the latter bring the games to reality, in a way that makes their fictional constructs apparent.

This alienating element can be seen in action even in *Waco Resurrection* (2004), a game designed by Eddo Stern together with the c-level team (Peter Brinson, Brody Condon, Michael Wilson, Mark Allen, Jessica Hutchins). *Waco Resurrection* is a "classical" first person shooter, at least in the way it is designed: immersive, violent, photorealistic. The main novelty lies in the narrative, evoking the Waco siege, and the point of view, that of the Branch Davidians' leader David Koresh. While, in-game, a sense of alienation is created by the non player characters, which have the names and faces of the real individuals involved in the siege, it becomes stronger when the game is played in its installation version, wearing the voice activated, surround sound enabled, hard plastic 3D skin reproducing David Koresh. The player, through the Koresh skin, can hear Koresh's voice singing or delivering a sermon. This device brings the player back to reality, and forces him to think back to the real event, with all its complex political implications.

In a similar way, works such as *Runners* (1999 – 2000), *Tekken Torture Tournament* (2001), *Cockfight Arena* (2001) and *Dark Game* (2006) provide the player with such "heavy" interfaces that one can not ignore and ever forget "reality": head-gears, costumes, shocking arm straps, a triple mouse.

But it is in Stern's self-standing installations that this alienating factor becomes more patent. In the *God's Eye* series, Stern refers to a practice, quite common among avid gamers, of customizing their computer console, changing it into a unique piece of furniture – revealing something about their taste and personality. Here, computers are visible, yet integrated into huge sculptures that can be seen as monuments to the neo-medievalism so common in most fantasy games. *Crusade* (2002) transforms a computer 'tower' into a windmill. Alongside is a monitor on which we see, advancing towards us, five knights and a dragon (all to the accompaniment of a midi version of Led Zeppelin's Kashmir). The aggressive nature of western civilization is here cut down to size by the irony of these five strange avatars and a clear reference to Cervantes' Don Quixote. This irony returns even more powerfully in *Carnivore's Cathedral: Whose Child Is This?* (2003); "a neo-Christian Karaoke machine", as Stern calls it. This time the customized PC becomes a cathedral, complete with gargoyle waterspouts which move to the rhythm of an imperial motif. *USS Dragoon. One God to Rule them All ... And in the Darkness Bind Them* (2003) is an imposing installation of a modern warship guided by a computer that stands proudly at the helm. Along the bridge, crowded with knights in battle-dress, runs a text in Gothic Elven script, whilst the prow is adorned with two majestic dragons. Finally, *Fort Paladin: America's Army* (2003) is a computer in the guise of a medieval castle complete with hexagonal towers, crenellation, banners and even openings from which to pour down boiling oil onto enemies. In the façade of the castle, the space that would normally be occupied by the drawbridge is taken by a computer monitor, which introduces us to the authorized violence of America's Army, the videogame freely distributed on the American Army's website for training cum propaganda purposes. The game is played by the machine itself, which sends a series of messages to a system of pistons that press down directly onto keys on the keyboard.

According to Stern, neo-medievalism is the last incarnation of what he calls "An American pathology": that unceasing search for a glorious past, which in the United States goes hand-in-hand with the nation's increasingly imperialistic aims. And again, this criticism is developed by leaving the game, bringing its aesthetics and iconography to the real world and building up monumental, heavy, aggressive interfaces that can't be forgotten. When you hear Fort Paladin's pistons banging and watch them control the virtual soldiers of America's Army, looking at a game's reality as a separate "level of life" becomes more and more difficult.

Difficult, but not impossible. Eddo Stern is, and probably will always be, an avid gamer. His criticism doesn't prevent him, nor us, from enjoying and playing the game, and is not articulated towards this end. Stern's work is meant to explore the complex dynamics between reality and media, and to improve our understanding of both – not to explain to us why we should not play America's Army or World of Warcraft. So, his last series of "animated machines", as described in the press release written for their first public presentation, mine "the online gaming world at its paradoxical extremes: on one hand, an untenable perversion of everyday life spent slaying an endless stream of virtual monsters, on the other, an ultimate mirroring of the most familiar social dynamics. The struggles with masculinity, honor, aggression, faith, love and self worth are embroiled with the game world's vernacular aesthetics." In works such as *Narnia, Again* (2007), *Lotusman* (2007), *Man, Woman, Dragon (After World of Warcraft)* (2007) and *Tsunami* (2007), Stern updates a technique with a long tradition: the one adopted in Chinese shadow plays and other proto-cinematic forms of spectacle. His Plexiglas, computer-controlled kinetic shadow sculptures use lions, dragons, snakes, Chuck Norris, and kung-fu to talk about conflict, violence, masculinity, fantasy, and cultural stereotypes. But also play, play, play, with all its pleasures and contradictions.

First published in the catalogue of the show "Eddo Stern: Flamewar", curated by Ilana Tenenbaum for the Haifa Museum of Art (January 24 – June 20, 2009), with the title: "Machine Animation & Animated Machines".

Interview with Tale of Tales

Tale of Tales is a game development studio founded in Belgium in 2002 by Michael Samyn and Auriea Harvey. The name was stolen from a famous collection of Italian fairy tales, Lo cunto de li cunti *by Giambattista Basile (1634). During the nineties, Samyn and Harvey – at first independently (as zuper! and entropy8) and then together (as entropy8zuper) – developed an extraordinary body of work, using internet technologies – from simple html to Flash – in order to tell stories and engage the audience. Variously labeled as Net art or Web Cinema, this work finds a natural continuation in Tale of Tales projects, especially the first one: "8".*

The game, that should have been on shelves in January 2007, was actually never released due to lack of funding, but it's still on its authors' agenda. Inspired by the different versions of the Sleeping Beauty story, it features a deaf mute 8 year old girl as the main character: not a simple avatar, but an half-autonomous character, whose behavior can be modified but not determined by the player.

In the following years, Tale of Tales developed many successful projects, including "The Path" (2009), a short horror game inspired by the tale of Little Red Riding Hood.

HOW DID "TALE OF TALES" COME ABOUT? WHY DID AN ARTIST DUO FEEL THE NEED TO CREATE AN INDEPENDENT TEAM AND WORK TOGETHER ON A VIDEOGAME?

We were never simply an artist duo. We were also a design studio. But we made a point of not distinguishing between the two too much. When we designed a website, we wanted it to be meaningful. And when we made art, we wanted it to communicate. There have always been playful elements in our work. And we have always had an interest in creating virtual environments of one kind or other. When web technology started stagnating and the whole thing started to resemble a shopping street, we turned towards a technology that was still growing rapidly and allowed for much more sophisticated applications: real time interactive 3D [1].

Also we were a bit fed up with the distinction between doing commissioned jobs to earn money and making art without any financial compensation (we famously failed at making pay-per-view art on line with *Skinonskinonskin* [2]). On the web people want everything for free. But they don't mind putting down money for a disc in a box in a store. It's a contradiction that we accepted since it allowed us to make something of our own invention – and get rewarded for it (which means we could afford to be more serious about our work).

"8" WILL TAKE YEARS TO COMPLETE. CAN YOU TELL ME WHAT THE MAIN STAGES OF THE PROCESS ARE?

I think the most important stage of preproduction is behind us now. We have written a scenario, designed the game, made a demo and put together a team for production. That has taken about 2 years. We have also found publishers who are willing to invest in this production (which took another half year). Now all that is left to do is actually make the game. When this is done (in a approximately a year), the publishers will handle the marketing and distribution. And then people can buy the game and hopefully enjoy it.

HOW MUCH IS THE INTERNET COMMUNITY INVOLVED IN THIS PROCESS? WHAT ROLE DOES IT PLAY?

Is there still an internet community? When we started with this medium, around 1995, we were inspired by an ambitious and intelligent group of people with near to utopian ideals. With the turn of the millennium, the internet has started to resemble the so-called real world more and more: loud, boring and dirty. It's no longer the safe haven for the gentle and kind that it used to be.

That being said, we still use it, perhaps nostalgically. It's a nice medium to discuss things and research people's responses to certain ideas. The internet is still part of our work process: our design document is a Wiki for example, and we communicate with all of our team members through various internet technologies.

WHAT DO YOU THINK ABOUT THE INDIE GAME DESIGN SCENE? IN YOUR OPINION, WHERE DOES ITS FUTURE LIE? DO YOU THINK IT WILL MANAGE TO CARVE OUT A NICHE FOR ITSELF ALONGSIDE THE BIG GAME CORPORATIONS?

I don't really see how this independent scene has anything to do with game design. They just seem to use games ironically for one or the other purpose. I see no proof of these people being serious about the craft of making games. I think they have already carved out a niche for themselves. Or better: they are filling a niche that has always been there. Academics researching games are very receptive to this type of stuff. I'm sure they prefer looking at intelligent parodies of first person shooters rather than "Doom" or "Half Life". Whether that entitles them to any authority on the subject of games, game design or game culture is another question.

I think these activities are part of the art world and as such part of a self-sustaining and marginal system that has cut all ties with the world inhabited by humans because it is its only means of survival.

Within the games industry, there is also an independent games scene. Usually this is about games that can be made cheaply and sometimes they contain innovative designs that are so extreme that only other designers can appreciate them. In general, much like the open source community for other software, the independent games scene is an excuse for the games industry not to have to do anything moral, ethic or even aesthetic.

DO YOU THINK THE VIDEOGAME INDUSTRY AND THE WAY WE THINK ABOUT VIDEOGAMES AS CULTURAL OBJECTS ARE CHANGING?

I see a certain polarization happening. The big publishers are getting even bigger. And their products are mostly crap that appeals to the masses. Since they are getting so huge, a lot of smaller publishers simply cease to even try and compete with them. As such, I think, there will be more opportunities in the future for more original and experimental games to be made. As long as we can find ways of making these for relatively modest budgets. I'm not sure what you mean by "videogames as cultural objects" and what it means to think about them as such. Can you explain?

WELL, LET'S PUT IT THIS WAY. I THINK I AM A VICTIM (MORE OR LESS CONSCIOUS) OF THE IDEA THAT VIDEOGAMES ARE A "LOW" FORM OF CULTURE, BUT THAT THEY ARE GROWING UP AND BECOMING ONE OF THE "ARTS", DEVELOPING MORE FASCINATING AND ARTICULATED NARRATIVES. OR, TO USE A COMPARISON, WE ARE MOVING FROM THE LUMIÉRE BROTHERS' TRAIN TO JOHN FORD'S INDIANS. I GUESS YOU DON'T AGREE...

Well, to make the link to cinema complete, we also have to be aware of the fact that early Hollywood cinema was considered low popular culture at the time. But now all those Bogart movies are considered to be great classics. We think to some extent that society needs to develop an understanding of new media before it can appreciate them.

That said, we totally agree with you that most videogames are of poor artistic quality. But we don't think this will get better in general. I think there will indeed be more highly artistic videogames in the future but there will also be crappier ones. We would argue though that the crap videogames are as much part of the culture as the good ones. It's a sad fact that in modern society everybody's opinion is valued equally and since, statistically speaking, most people only have average intelligence or sensitivity, most of modern culture will be of low quality. Especially now that education on aesthetic and intellectual issues is not a high priority, since our democratic rulers have discovered mass media.

"8" IS AN AMBITIOUS PROJECT THAT COMBINES A REFINED NARRATIVE WITH GAMING AND INTERACTION. IS IT ART THAT TRIES TO EMERGE THROUGH VIDEOGAMES OR A VIDEOGAME THAT TRIES TO RISE TO THE LEVEL OF ART?

That's a good question. I think it is both but also more than that. I think "8", like a lot of our older work, is an attempt for a non-modern kind of art to come to the surface. We think that modern art is at a dead end. Postmodernism pointed this out already but has been unable to provide solutions. I don't think future art historians will care much about the museums and galleries of the late 20th century. They will look at cinema and advertising and design to find out about our culture. And as you are probably aware of, a lot of rubbish is being created in these media. One of the reasons for this is that too many truly creative people are hiding gutlessly behind their barricades of art magazines and gallery display windows.

In other words, we try to bring an artistic experience to a larger audience, yes. I think video games are art. In most cases they are bad art. But most fine art is also bad art. So "rising to the level of art" is not something videogames need to do. They are already low enough. Some games are even better than a lot of art. Some art is better than a lot of games. If anything needs to rise to the level of art, it's art itself.

"8" IS A STRANGE GAME: NO LEVELS, NO SCORES, NO COMPETITION, A REFINED DESIGN BASED ON ORIENTALIST PAINTING, A NARRATIVE INSPIRED BY SLEEPING BEAUTY FOLKTALES FROM AROUND THE WORLD, AN AUTONOMOUS CHARACTER WHO EVOLVES THROUGHOUT THE GAME IN RESPONSE TO THE BEHAVIOR OF THE PLAYER: IS THIS YOUR ANTI-IDEOLOGICAL AND AESTHETIC WAY OF REACTING TO THE AGGRESSIVE AND MILITARISTIC IDEOLOGY OF MAINSTREAM VIDEOGAMES?

I wouldn't call "8" anti-ideological. The fact that we chose to make a non violent and non competitive game that focuses on pleasure is very much an ideological statement. The fact that it displays a positive image of a culture inspired by Islam is also not without ideological implications these days. I would even say that making a game that attempts to be aesthetically pleasing is even an ideological decision.

Mainstream videogames, like all other mainstream cultural expressions are only mirrors of a society. I don't think George Bush attacked Iraq after playing "Counter Strike". If an industry behaves aggressively, it is because there is a large tolerance (if not appreciation) for this type of behavior in society. So if we counter that in our work, we are not just attacking the videogame industry but society at large, I guess.

Western countries are becoming more and more conservative and aggressively right-wing. In Belgium this is referred to as people's mood turning more "acid". With our work, we are trying to counter this acidification by allowing people to have pleasure. Pleasure is the sweetness than can dissolve acidity.

WHAT DISTRIBUTION SYSTEM WILL YOU ADOPT FOR "8"?

"8" will be distributed by various publishers. So we're not alone in making decisions about this. It will definitely be available in stores where people can buy boxes with discs in them, since this is something many people still like to do. But if we can help it, we would like to have it distributed electronically as well, for the people who have the luxury of broadband internet.

First published in *A Minima*, issue 10, 2005, pp. 138 – 151 with the title: "A Game for Pleasure. Interview with Michael Samyn & Auriea Harvey".

[1] Cf. Auriea Harvey & Michaël Samyn, "Realtime Art Manifesto", 2006, online at www.tale-of-tales.com/tales/RAM.html.

[2] *skinonskinonskin* (1999) has been described by Wired as a «a poetic multimedia documentary of a real-life love affair between two members of Hell.com, launched 13 May for private guest preview only.» The project was a kind of private dialogue made public as an ever-growing collection of Web pages. It was released by Hell.com, a community of artists and designers that Michael and Auriea were part of. Cf. Reena Jana, "Neither Art Nor Porn", in *Wired*, May 28, 1999, online at
www.wired.com/culture/lifestyle/news/1999/05/19908.

Reality is Overrated. When Media Go Beyond Simulation

«Where is reality? Can you show it to me?» Heinz Von Foerster [1]

Reality Construction and Simulation

The relationship between media and reality has been debated since the very beginning of Western culture. The two main keywords at stake here are: representation and construction. According to the first, media portray reality; according to the second, media construct reality. Of course, these two approaches are strictly connected to the model of thought you are adopting in order to describe reality itself: a realist model (reality is something that exists "out there") or a constructivist model (reality does not exist; it is only a construction in the mind of a given "agent").

Constructivism is an epistemological perspective according to which knowledge is the result of an act of creation, and not of a process of discovery [2]. It was started in the mid-1990s by Jean Piaget, even if it has many roots in Western philosophy, from Protagoras to Vico and Kant; and in its more radical iteration it becomes a claim that "ontological reality" does not exist at all, or is, at least, utterly incoherent as a concept. "The environment as we perceive it is our invention" because "the nervous system is organized (or organizes itself) so that it computes a stable reality," demonstrates scientist Heinz von Foerster in a 1973 article titled "On Constructing a Reality." [3]

However, today's catch-phrase "media construct reality" rarely shares this kind of radicalism [4]. In most cases, it either means "if something is not on TV, it doesn't exist" or "media manipulate reality in order to make us believe in an altered version of it." It works as a complaint about the power of the media to modify the perception of something that exists out there, rather than to claim that no reality exists outside of the media. Even Jean Baudrillard's theory of simulacra, probably the most advanced theory on the power of media still available today, does not go much further. Even if he draws distinctions between representation and simulation, and writes that «the age of simulation [...] begins with a liquidation of all referentials» [5]; even if he claims that there is no difference anymore between the map and the territory, and that the map actually precedes the territory; simulation as he describes it neither deletes nor negates ontological reality; it just takes its place. The real is still there, yet it has been substituted in our perception by «signs of the real». So, this is how Baudrillard explains the notion of «the successive phases of the image»:

«(1) it is the reflection of a basic reality (2) it masks and perverts a basic reality (3) it masks the absence of a basic reality (4) it bears no relation to any reality whatsoever: it is its own pure simulacrum» [6].

The common-sense interpretation of the sentence "media construct reality" lies between points 2 and 3; Baudrillard continues on, introducing point 4.

The Desert of the Real

Some years later, Slavoj Žižek framed the problem of the relationship between media and reality in a completely different way, talking about the "virtualization of the real" and explaining that today reality imitates the media. He wrote:

«... in the same way decaffeinated coffee smells and tastes like the real coffee without being the real one, Virtual Reality is experienced as reality without being one. However, at the end of this process of virtualization, the inevitable Benthamian conclusion awaits us: reality is its own best semblance». [7]

According to this approach, 9/11 is the best application ever of «digitalized special effects» developed by the cinema industry in recent years: a real event designed to be televised, a terrorist act perpetrated not «to provoke real material damage, but FOR THE SPECTACULAR EFFECT OF IT».

In my opinion, the effectiveness of both Baudrillard's and Žižek's thoughts on this subject is today undermined by the fact that, when talking about the media, they are basically talking about TV and mass media. The fact that Žižek refers to virtual reality and to *The Matrix* (1999) has little importance here, because he understands virtual reality as a "simulation" (an indication of the real misunderstood for the real thing) and because *The Matrix* itself is strongly grounded in Baudrillard's theories. *The Matrix* is nothing more than a convincing simulation built by intelligent machines in order to persuade us that we are still living in the good old world, while in fact we are convicted slaves in a desolate, post-atomic landscape, kept alive in order to provide energy to the machines. A nice story, but is it able to picture the contemporary media environment? Or is it just updating twentieth century paranoia, which claims that media replaced religion as "the opium of the masses"?

Computing a Reality

Picture this: a teenager cooped up in his bedroom, sitting down in front of his computer. He stays there all the time, does not participate in any sports, has no friends apart from those he meets in World of Warcraft, and the long list of contacts featured in his Facebook account. His parents think he is a good guy, maybe a little bit shy and antisocial, until they discover that he defecates on the floor. Guys like this are called, using a Japanese term, hikikomori. It means "withdrawal," and is used to describe reclusive people who have chosen to withdraw from social life, often seeking extreme degrees of isolation and confinement [8]. Actually, the term worked very well when the hikikomori did nothing else but read manga comics, watch TV and play computer games. Today, the hikikomori are rarely hermits. They withdrew from their social life, yet they have a social life; they left the world, but they have a world. The problem is that they are mediated by a sophisticated machine called "the computer," designed in the 1960s and 1970s by a vast community of people. Some were involved with LSD experiments; others shared constructivist ideas. However, it is still difficult to prove that these had any influence on the final product. What we can be sure of is that this machine, especially in its networked version, completely redefined the usual relationship between media and reality, escaping both the logic of representation and the logic of simulation, giving birth to a new reality, which is neither a reproduction nor a simulacrum.

It is a cultural landscape with its own habits, rules, cultures, jargon and iconography. It is a social landscape with its own communities and parties. It is a place where you can talk, work, have sex, enjoy art, waste your time, and die. It is a "reality." Let us call it "media reality" or "digital reality" if you like. It did not replace ontological reality; it simply asked to occupy a place next to it - to improve it. The map does not precede the territory, as Baudrillard claimed; the real still exists, and the map is now part of it. Sure, the hikikomori chose to completely "retire" into it, but hikikomori is a disease. Every new lifestyle has produced its own diseases, and media reality is no exception.

However, most people simply agreed to integrate it into their lives, learned to switch from one level to another, and enjoyed the enhancement. You either contribute to Wikipedia or build real estate in virtual worlds, spend hours managing your parallel life on social networks or dig into GIF repositories, browse through Youtube in search of your favorite video ever or download movies from peer-to-peer networks. You either write code for Linux or travel the world through Google Maps, play with Photoshop filters or with text-to-speech software, and you can be a producer, a user or a prosumer; all this is now part of your life. You took the last train to the world of Perky Pat, and there is no turning back.

Media Constructivism

How does artistic activity react to this shift? How are artists dealing with their "improved life" and with the expanded reality they are living in? Just like anybody else? My answer is: by tackling the so-called "digital medium" as it was described above - not just a medium, but a new level of a "reality" that is more and more layered, more and more "constructed," and where, between ontological reality, simulated reality and media reality there are no barriers anymore, but only the translucent, easily penetrable sheets of shadow theater: by exploring it, sometimes contributing to building it and adding layers to its own narratives; by referring to its aesthetics; by digging deep into it. In the early days of the medium, both those who embraced it and their opponents described this approach as "self-referential" and "formalist." It was a misunderstanding, the consequence of another misunderstanding: interpreting the digital media environment as a "medium." In recent months, I have started filing different artworks under the working label "media constructivism." That seems to work quite well for works that understand the digital media environment as a reality, and that consider what is constructed by media to be "real." The following are some examples.

After portraying avatars as real people and re-enacting art performances of the past in virtual worlds, Eva and Franco Mattes shot pictures of landscapes in an ultra-violent first-person shooter. When the spectator faces these silent "topographies," which call to mind the sublime landscapes of Caspar David Friedrich, as well as the urban atmospheres of Edward Hopper and the magical realism of the 1920s, she can hardly imagine that to attain this peace the artists had to fight off hundreds of aliens and human enemies.

The sublimity of the virtual landscape has been explored recently by the Spanish artist Joan Leandre in his video *In the Name of Kernel* (2009 - ongoing), which hacks corporate flight simulators, while identity construction in digital realities finds its master in Gazira Babeli, an avatar artist who plays the role of a virus in the system with a Keatonian sense of comedy. Babeli is living proof that the separation between the so-called "virtual" and the so-called "real" is just a matter of perspective; and probably Brody Condon, who took part in the 10th Sonsbeek International Sculpture Exhibition (2008) with a series of physically and psychologically intense live games involving 80 players and a whole forest, would agree with her on this point.

For years, Miltos Manetas has been portraying characters from videogames, as well as painting webpages and people living too close to their machines. For some weird reason, he never did it with Cory Arcangel, who enjoys and subverts almost every machine, from old Ataris to Quicktime, from VHS to plasma screens and Adobe Photoshop. One of his last works, and a beautiful example of media constructivism, is a series of abstract prints which are the result of a dumb, literal application of Photoshop gradient tools. Arcangel's work represents, at its best, a double concern that we may find in the work of many artists belonging to the second generation of Web users: the interest in what artists Olia Lialina and Dragan Espenschied called in a recent, inspiring book, "digital folklore" [9] and the will to explore the conceptual potential of simple software tools and processes.

In his recent work Paul B. Davis deploys the aesthetic and conceptual implications of video compression errors; Oliver Laric appropriates a web vernacular and its modes of expression, from clipart to homemade remakes of pop videos, and makes a powerful statement on customization, manipulation and versioning in his recent video essay *Versions* (2009), which makes us miss some of the artists' essays from the 1970s less. Damon Zucconi is interested in what lies under the surface of our visual culture: an "underlying problem" that a little manipulation of the surface brings to the fore. For example, in *Morris Louis; Dalet Kaf (Horizontal and Vertical blur)* he appropriates a painting by Louis, applying a simple editing filter to it and then printing it out quarter-scale.

In these works and in the work of many other artists, all the layers of reality collapse. They are not about reality, like a painting by Courbet. They are not about media reality, like Andy Warhol's *Car Crashes* or Richard Prince's *Cowboys*. They are not about the map or the territory. They are about both, because the two have become one and the same.

First published in *Artpulse*, Vol. 1, N° 3, March – May 2010.

[1] *Das Netz. The Unabomber, LSD and the Internet*. Dir. Lutz Dammbeck, 35 mm, 121 min., (Germany), 2003.

[2] See Edward Craig (ed), *Concise Routledge Encyclopedia of Philosophy*, Routledge, 2000, p. 171.

[3] Heinz Von Foerster, "On Constructing a Reality", in *Understanding Understanding*, New York, Springer-Verlag, 2003, pp. 212 – 225.

[4] See Stefan Weber, "Media and the construction of reality", in *Mediamanual.at*, 2002, online at www.mediamanual.at/en/pdf/Weber_etrans.pdf.

[5] Jean Baudrillard, *Simulations*, New York, Semiotext[e], 1983, p. 4.

[6] Ivi, p. 11.

[7] Slavoj Žižek, "Welcome to the Desert of the Real", in *The Symptom*, Issue 2, Spring 2002, online at www.lacan.com/desertsymf.htm.

[8] See Maggie Jones, "Shutting themselves in", in *The New York Times*, January 15, 2006.

[9] Olia Lialina, & Dragan Espenschied (eds.), *Digital Folklore*, Stuttgart, Merz & Solitude, 2009.

Interview with Joan Leandre

Joan Leandre defines himself as a "media interpreter." Active as a video artist in the field of independent media from the early 1990s, he won international recognition from 1999 thanks to retroYou *(RC) (1999 - 2001), a progressive modification of the parameters used to construct the 3D graphics of a car racing video game. With* retroyou nostal(G) *(2002 - 2003) he goes on to deconstruct a flight simulator. In both cases, Leandre utilizes software to subvert and re-write a powerful ideological machine, translating a rather conventional generator of reality into a medium for illusions. The Dr. Strangelove of computing, Leandre loves the bomb and knows its mechanisms well enough to transform them into the workings of a multi-layered ambiguous narrative, esoteric and seductive at the same time. This aspect of his work is apparent in his latest project,* In the Name of Kernel *(2006 - ongoing). The kernel, the heart of every operating system, becomes the myth around which coagulates a symbolic event combining travel literature, the alchemy tradition and science fiction, terrorism and conspiracy theories, programming and mountaineering, 3D modeling and satellite mapping, hallucinations and revelations.*

YOU SPENT TEN YEARS HACKING A FLIGHT SIMULATOR. WHY? YOU MAINTAIN AN INTEREST IN THE INTERSECTION BETWEEN MILITARY RESEARCH AND ENTERTAINMENT, AS EVIDENCED BY THE BABYLON ARCHIVES CYCLE, SO WHY NOT CHOOSE AN FPS (FIRST-PERSON SHOOTER), LIKE MANY OTHER ARTISTS?

You could say, I was waiting for the right moment, letting things come into themselves, in a way. I don't have a special fetishistic need to use specific tools. I mean, most of the tools we all use are produced within the intersection between military research and entertainment-- but that doesn't mean you have to narrowly direct your energy towards such a closed territory for research or as a personal manifesto. In response to your question about FPS, I already worked with it in *the Babylon Archives* series together with Abu Ali and *Velvet Strike* with Anne Marie Schleiner and Brody Condon, those projects were deeply immersed in that time for me, so there's no need to continue on that path. But it's not easy to break the links connecting what you've produced at different times, something always continues.

I've tried, on several occasions, to infiltrate software itself. In the case of *In the Name of Kernel!: Song of the Iron Bird,* the starting point is not crucial, except for being simulation software with text. I was especially struck by the stillness of watching aircrafts fly on the auto pilot mode, I use to go and then come back and everything seemed to be the same.... with maybe some unexpected clouds down on the horizon. Time was very slow, almost like physical time. I felt attracted by this artificial sense of time, one which you can accelerate or slow down at your own will.

PUTTING TOGETHER IMPRESSIVE VISUAL OUTPUT AND HARD CODE WRITING, HYPER REALISTIC 3D IMAGERY AND TEXT-ONLY DOCUMENTS, IN THE NAME OF KERNEL SEEMS TO GROW AT THE INTERSECTION BETWEEN TWO PREVIOUS PROJECTS, RETROYOU NOSTAL(G) (2002-2003) AND RETROYOU NOSTALG(2) (2002-2004). WHAT'S THE CONCEPT BEHIND RETROYOU NOSTAL(G)?

retroyou nostal(G)'s main axis consists in the operation of reducing a very heavy complex software to the minimal expression. The software is a simulation in which the geography is eliminated, except for a location 100.000m high, the physics are reversed and the graphical interface is reduced and recombined. You could say it has become the simulation of a world collapsing in on itself through the physical hacking of the program. But *retroyou nostalg(2)* goes toward quite the opposite direction, it is the amplification of a modest terminal application to the level of an unknown, very cryptic sort of software. It is composed of a DOS terminal program series based on the use of old programming resources, it is a compilation of terminal applications for Windows dealing with system interruptions and archaeological software stuff such as the .bat virus from the 80's and the heritage of the early NFO and Demoscene. *retroyou nostalg(2)*'s main premise plays on the limits of a corporate software environment for fun, without becoming lethal for a modern OS but enough to be included in the black definition lists of AV applications. Some of the *retroyou nostalg(2)* .exe(s) are not usable anymore because of their ephemeral nature or because they no longer work within an OS environment. The whole series is located in this sort of very unstable context. Again, by it's own definition the series is very ephemeral in time. I thought, better let it go, there's stuff I compiled some time ago which now is really unknown to me, I don't even know what payloads they can trigger on a given machine: they might sleep in your system for 300 years and then sometime in the future they might wake up and trigger a great brute force event. That makes no sense, I love it. Some of *retroyou nostalg(2)* is very much related to the recovery and assembling pieces of almost vintage C code written by others, those you can find in forums. Others are written from scratch with the goal of compromising data itself. The series looks backward to understand forward, the roll of the programmer here would be something closer to the practice of an archaeologist collecting forgotten data. *retroyou nostal(G)* starts before transformation, some sort of memory of something which will never be the same anymore, not even in a descriptive or metaphoric way. The whole thing would be about a mood, it's not so much about the construction of a transparent conceptual icon but about the memory of instants gone.

I WOULD SAY THAT YOUR "USER UNFRIENDLY" APPROACH MUST BE UNDERSTOOD IN THIS CONTEXT. I MEAN, "USER FRIENDSHIP" IS USUALLY JUST A WAY TO CONTROL THE USER, AND THE WAY HE OR SHE INTERFACES WITH THE WORK. SINCE RETROYOURC, ALL YOUR WORK CAN BE ACCESSED UNDER A HUGE FRAME OF INFORMATION, CODE, APPARENTLY USELESS TUTORIAL, FRAGMENTS OF NARRATIVE. THE USER MUST NAVIGATE A LOT, UNDERSTAND WHAT IS NOISE AND WHAT IS INFORMATION, PUT TOGETHER THE PIECES AND BUILD HIS OR HER OWN NARRATIVE. AM I RIGHT?

Of course this sort of "user friendship," as you put it, is very often the worst enemy for the average computer user, especially if we talk about this euphoric understanding of technology where the machine is promised to be almost self-sufficient. You hear this promise from the monopoly of the "happy software" industries and this perception has become massive. It should be refused by all means. Now you have millions of almost blind, bewildered users. This is one of the central problems when trying to migrate to an open source OS for instance...then you are the driver, not the machine...The illusion is gone. We should not forget that there was an era in which a computer was a tool for specialists, now millions sit there for hours with fear or at least ignorance of what they are really dealing with. Perhaps, in this context, "unfriendly" means to be aggressive against the mainstream corporate monopoly of computer interfaces. I say let the computer exist by itself, some unfinished stuff here and there which one recovers after years. You then discover that what exists is something circumstantial but not casual. All together, these elements would work as a container hosting data which reflect some sort of cryptic anti-pessimism in strong opposition to a euphoric, permanently updated world. It might look as some ironic approach when very often these days irony is counter-revolutionary. The key could just be to keep an exalted consciousness which allows you to develop your life into a state of permanent observation and then participation. All, of course, with the goal of not capitulating to monoculture in a moment when mainstream and counter imagery is so mixed that it conforms into one single mass self-consumed environment.

RETROYOU NOSTAL(G), LIKE RETROYOURC, HAS OFTEN BEEN DESCRIBED AS AN AESTHETIC SUBVERSION: YOU TAKE A GAME - BE IT CAR RACING OR A FLIGHT SIMULATOR - AND YOU TURN IT INTO A FUTURISTIC PAINTING. CAN YOU EXPLAIN THE WORK FROM AN AESTHETIC POINT OF VIEW?

It might be convenient not to understand things only from either an aesthetically or conceptual point of view, it could be that this duality is a convention with a visible path to follow. So, these mutations of corporate software come with one main aim: the single act of reversing a preexisting object, the aesthetic quality comes afterwards, as an enjoyable game. The end result is one of a thousand possible consequences of the intervention. That is for me where the real game starts, after discovering how to ride the software off of the track. The so-called aesthetic experience is assumed to deal with sensorial perception, about the stuff you don't see: the mutation of the structure of the program, the names of the files, the reversed .exe application, the physics of the software... all of this decoding and recoding experience... and, yes, that is less common to notice and understand, perhaps because of this monochrome approach to the machine-bunker.

IN *IN THE NAME OF KERNEL!* THERE IS A SHIFT FROM PREVIOUS PROJECTS. IN A WAY, YOU SEEM TO GO BEYOND THE FORMAL SUBVERSION OF THE SOFTWARE ENGINE AND USE IT TO CREATE A NARRATIVE, COMPLEX, FICTIONAL WORLD. CAN YOU EXPLAIN WHAT EXACTLY YOU DID WITH THE FLIGHT SIMULATOR FOR THIS PROJECT?

Again, I don't see how to draw a boundary between formal or beyond formal. *retroyouRC* was, in the first place, an interruption of a given entertainment software, in the sense of letting the program go beyond the mainstream standards. Even more with *retroyou nostal(G)*-- the flight sim reduction project. I am also concerned by the trends and the fast consumption update of technology, and this is always a risk when using tools dictated by the mainstream. And, after all, what is a formal subversion? It is either a subversion or not at all. So, I tend to believe in long term projects, which sometimes are unfinished because I believe it takes time to allow projects to emerge, to think and review what you do. My goal is not to produce an objectual product but to use it as a transport for understanding and to overcome things. Time makes things go into their corresponding location. I guess it's all about a balance, the narrative has always been there in opposition to the self running machine. Narrative creates an additional mood and a context in which other elements can exist, but it also exists by itself and it's part of this unknown perhaps organic structure.

When I first started *In the Name of Kernel! Song of the Iron Bird*, I learnt how to fly the big heavy birds and recorded some of the best landings and takeoffs, then I reprogrammed all flying aircrafts in the world to fly routes inside a given closed relatively small area- thousands of aircrafts randomly flying over an empty land of maybe 50.000 square meters. By doing so, the aircrafts lost their geometry and became powerful flashing lights. So, the airplanes became only light emitters, like big heavy ships falling from the sky over high resolution satellite data. Anomalies are everywhere in the *Song of the Iron Bird*. Locations are not casual but they are all intoxicated. *In the Name of Kernel! Song of the Iron Bird* puts together some distant representation layers all included in the original program, impossible events and unknown landscapes, it is the documentation of a software transformation which takes the form of a highly calm energetic mood.

COMING TO THE NARRATIVE DIMENSION, IN THE NAME OF KERNEL! IS A COMPLEX HYPERTEXT IN WHICH MOUNTAINEERING, AUTOBIOGRAPHY, PERSONAL DATA, COLLECTED DATA, CONSPIRACY THEORIES AND HERMETIC TRADITION ALL MIX TOGETHER. IN THE TEXT WRITTEN FOR THE PROJECT, YOU -- WELL, MR. KUBASIK -- USE TERMS FROM PROGRAMMING CULTURE, SUCH AS "KERNEL", "SYSTRAY", "WIPE", "SHRED", "RENDER", "FIREWALL" TO NAME PLACES AND CHARACTERS: THE KERNEL PEAK, THE GREAT ICE-FIRE WALL, THE GREAT SYSTRAY GLACIER. I READ IT AS REVERSE ENGINEERING ON DUCHAMP'S GREAT GLASS: INSTEAD OF USING A CHOCOLATE GRINDER TO TELL OF A MYSTICAL/ALCHEMICAL EVENT, YOU USE A MYTHOLOGICAL NARRATIVE AS A METAPHOR FOR A COMPUTATIONAL PROCESS. YOU'LL PROBABLY ANSWER "NO" BUT... CAN YOU HELP US GET INTO THIS METAPHOR?

It is a map to reach the impossible. Thanks to Julie and Kurt, Reinhold, Herman and Juanito, among many others, whose vision helped create the piece. And thanks to Robert and Beni, with whom we did and still do some climbing while my computer is rendering by itself in Barcelona. Without them, this mad representation of nature would have been impossible. I always wanted to climb a big mountain and, still, I dream every day of the feeling of absolute peace which comes when you are almost done with the climb, and your body is exhausted. I remember last summer we were climbing a modest 3.400m mountain, there was a turn over the remains of the glacier and then you could see the summit peak... all those very tiny people slowly climbing the 45 to 50 degree angle final summit ramp... there was at least fifty people there going up... I was frozen, marked by this picture and by the fact of your own transformation when you reach your limit in a spiritual or physical way. We all missed the train. *The Kernel Peak* is a celebration of these instants when going beyond seems almost impossible, when there is a line of so many people going nowhere, when you forget your reason for being there. From then on, I dreamed of stressing my computer to its kernel peak by rendering a huge impossible mountain like Nanga Parbat, Lamba Pahar or Sagarmatha.

IN AN AGE WHEN "UNMONUMENTAL" SEEMS THE KEYWORD, AND WHEN, FOR EXAMPLE, AN ARTIST LIKE MARK NAPIER IS USING SOFTWARE TO GENERATE A SOFT, MALLEABLE VERSION OF THE MODERNIST, IRON AND CONCRETE SKYSCRAPERS, YOU SEEM INTERESTED IN A NEW KIND OF MONUMENTALITY: YOU CALL YOUR 7 COLUMNS MEGA NFO FILE A MONUMENT, BUT ALSO THE IMPRESSIVE 3D OF THE KERNEL PEAK, AND THE AMAZING ENERGY OF THE HD VIDEO, GO IN THE SAME DIRECTION. IF IN THE NAME OF KERNEL! IS A MONUMENT: WHAT IS IT A MONUMENT TO?

Almost anything can trigger a deep commotion. We live in the age of the ephemeral monument and fast consumption spectacle where sameness is all around-- it is the common rule. Again, I always wanted to render a huge mountain which I could not climb.

In the Name of Kernel! is a triple serial project. It is composed of *The Song of the Iron Bird*, based on a reversed flight simulator, *The Kernel Peak*, a celebration of the impossible, and *The 7 Columns MEGA NFO FILE*. I call the last one *The 7 Columns MEGA NFO File*, and understand it as a monumental, but very small, excerpt from the Disinformation Age. *The 7 Columns NFO* is an artificial emulation of a regular common NFO file as those have become in my opinion a very important computer history reference. It is a 150x120 cm print signed by a unique serial number. It is close to several related topics, for instance, to data property, privacy and identity on the net. It is about the limits of what is usually both accepted and banned in the society of disinformation. It is similar to *the Kernel Peak*, both share common elements and refer to our isolation from the most basic elements in life. In this sense, *The Kernel Peak* would be the topmost imagery of a deeply impressive nature. It points to historical and contemporary approaches to the representation of nature, it is revealing in its own synthetic nature.

COMING TO THE VIDEO, TWO PATHS SEEM TO CROSS THE MAIN NARRATIVE, WHICH IS CENTERED AROUND THE SIGHTING OF LIGHT GLOBE UFOS DURING A FLIGHT MISSION: THE VIEWPOINT FROM ABOVE OF HIGHLY RECOGNIZABLE LOCATIONS, FROM DISNEYLAND TO CHERNOBYL; AND A CLOSE LOOK AT THE STRANGE HUMANITY ON THE SURFACE. THIS INTRODUCES ANOTHER ISSUE THAT SEEMS QUITE RELEVANT FOR YOUR WORK: SURVEILLANCE (FROM SATELLITE SURVEILLANCE TO DATAVEILLANCE ADDRESSED IN THE 7 COLUMNS MEGA NFO FILE) AND WHAT WE COULD CALL THE POLITICS OF VISION. CAN YOU TALK ABOUT THAT?

Those are two different layers in the video among many others. I didn't really think about it in terms of data surveillance as that comes very often out of the box and it might be obvious and understood almost as a must nowadays. I think about *In Song of the Iron Bird*, somehow as a glimpse of the future as much as a representation of machine pleasure. Perhaps the key point *In the Song of the Iron*

Bird is the debris recovery from the simulator itself, hidden tiny objects such as the puppets you mention, hiding in the program libraries, too tiny to be seen, only present in some specific geographical areas, hard to see from high above. I took and resized them to a very big scale, made them visible. Same with other stuff, just took and slowly brought it to a higher scale. That is all, a balance between different recombined elements. There seem to be some sort of continuity, not at all a narration but a recombination transported by the video and audio streams. In words of the airplane's captain Prefect Fatal Error: «I love my 747, she's my personal queen. I love to let her fly automatically while smoking pod in the cop-kit. I ask then the passengers if they are into having a good ride and push the throttle forward. I take control and start a sharp descent into the landscape. There are a million flashing lights in the sky, all the aircrafts of the world flying in harmony. There are boats and cars falling from up-there and the smoky cabin tastes sweet. Passengers are now screaming of joy while we all together celebrate this piece of iron wonder. When we are back on earth we will show the picture of velocity and thank god for still being sort of alive.»

First published in *Rhizome*, May 21, 2008 with the title "A Map to Reach the Impossible: Interview with Joan Leandre".

Is the Future What it Used to Be?

I recently read *Wired's* interview with Andrej Ternovskij, the man behind Chatroulette [1]. I knew that he was really young, and yet I was struck when I read his birth date: April 22, 1992. In 1992 the Web was just coming to life, the Internet was already 23 years old, and the Cold War (one of the main reasons that originated it) was a thing of the past. Ternovskij doesn't know a world without computers - and I'm almost sure he has never seen something older than Windows 98 or Mac OS 9.

Today Chatroulette [2] is one of the hottest sites of the contemporary internet. It is a video based random chat-room, where you don't go to meet the people you know, but to discover new friends. The website mixes a utopian social model – through the Internet, I can meet people I couldn't meet otherwise – and a discomforting, sometimes cruel shallowness. You are invited to judge your partner in the blink of an eye. You can meet the worst people in the world: exhibitionists, deviants, pedophiles, etc. If you spend a couple of hours out there, you'll come out thinking that it's a really bad place.

The same will probably happen if you spend some time on 4chan [3]. In 2008, Lev Grossman described it in *Time* as «a wretched hive of scum and villainy. Spammers don't even bother to spam 4chan; Google started searching it only six months ago […] If you're looking for obscenity, blasphemy, homophobia, misogyny and racial insults, you don't have to dig too deep» [4]. 4Chan defines itself as «a simple image-based bulletin board where anyone can post comments and share images». The loosely designed platform features many boards, on specific topics such as Japanese culture, video games, television, technology, weapons, fashion, sex and the random board /b/. On /b/ all posts are anonymous, which is why "Anonymous" has become the main character on 4chan, and the name behind many of the "raids" perpetrated by 4channers both online and offline. With a critical mass of users, 4chan is in fact a strong online community, where bad behaviors and collective practices are rooted in a radical sense of freedom. 4Channers use their skills to defend their freedom. Acting under the name Anonymous, under the movement label "Project Chanology" and behind Guy Fawkes masks, many often gather in public spaces to protest against the Church of Scientology. Furthermore, many infamous Internet memes originated on 4chan. That's why 4chan has been recently described as a true example of relational aesthetics [5].

4chan was started in 2003 by a then-15 year old student who uses the screen name "moot". His real name, now widely advertised, is Christopher Poole. Interviewed by Grossman, he said: «My personal private life is very separate from my Internet life. There's a firewall in between». This makes me wonder when the word "internet" became a substitute for "public?"

Bruce Sterling said "The future is this place at a different time." [6] The place I'm concerned with is the Internet – or, more specifically, the computer environment the Internet is a part of. This place was dreamt, and shaped by the counterculture of the Sixties. Today, it's the reality we all live in. Their future has become our present.

Few generations can claim such a direct responsibility for their own future.

But can they still recognize their dream in our reality? Is the future what it used to be for them? What happens to their ideals when they are taken over by a generation that takes them for granted? And, last but not least: what is the relationship between the generation that shaped this environment and the generation that's inhabiting and implementing it today? What is the difference between the Californian engineer, with his lysergic dream of an expanded mind, his sense of community, his belief that information wants to be free, etc. and the teenager Andrej Ternovskij, lazy, bad at school (especially in math), without friends (except those he met online), without ideals (besides the vague wish to "explore other cultures").

My obsession with these questions began about one year ago, when I was trying to understand how the so called "surfing club" generation of Internet artists were "living" the computer environment and the Web. My interest has been nurtured recently by the simultaneous reading of two books: *What the Dormouse Said. How the Sixties Counterculture Shaped the Personal Computer Industry* (2005) [7], by John Markoff, and *Born digital. understanding the first generation of digital natives* (2008), by John Palfrey and Urs Gasser [8]. I downloaded them both from *Monoskop* [9], a wonderful website sharing books about digital and media culture. This website is, incidentally, a beautiful example of my argument. Since its very beginning, the Internet has been used for two main things: communication (Hello, world!) and file sharing. This latter practice is the outfit of three different approaches to culture: the academic habit to share knowledge; the anti-copyright ideals of the counterculture ("steal this book!", as Abbie Hoffmann wrote); and the hacker ethos that "information wants to be free". The first generation of computer users were the children of an age when copyright ruled: for them, file sharing was a strong political statement. The second generation of computer users – the one I belong to – faced the downfall of copyright, but also its strenuous fight to survive. For us, file sharing is a habit: something we do because "everybody is doing it", but with a creeping sense of guilt, because it's against the law and because we lack the ideals of the previous generation. As for the digital natives, well... they just don't give a fuck. It's always been there, and even talking about it makes you look like an old and boring guy.

The most interesting thing is that probably the lazy, apparently vacuous Andrej Ternovskij – as well as the polite, skinny moot – would be probably more likely than me to fight to defend their right to download what they want, if needed. I discovered it reading *Little Brother* (2008), a nice *bildungsroman* by Cory Doctorow [10]. In the book M1k3y, a "happy nerd" from San Francisco, fights against to defend his rights – and, in doing it, reconnects to the glorious past of his hometown. Is it so surprising that, while we are all getting used to the "transparency" of systems such as Facebook and Google, the "radical opacity" of 4chan was conceived by a teenager? «People say some disgusting, vile things. But just because we are hosting it doesn't mean we agree with it. I don't support what they are saying; I just support that there is a site like that to say that», said moot to the *New York Times* [11]. Doesn't it sound so Seventies?

I have to be sincere: I still don't have a single answer to my questions. I still don't know whether our present is more likely to produce the dreams of the Merry Pranksters or to the nightmares of the Unabomber. What I know is that media became a consistent part of our world. On the one side, in their effort to mediate "the real world" (whatever it might be), they media became our main experience of it, making more and more difficult to distinguish between mediation, simulation and construction, and to go back to the real thing. On the other side, they were starting to set up "realities" themselves. Virtual worlds, videogames, websites, chatrooms, and the Internet as a whole are increasingly experienced as "places" instead of media: places where a growing number of people are spending a growing portion of their own life [12].

Most of the works in this show exemplify this shift. In *Facebook Reenactments* (2009), Austrian artist Ursula Endlicher selects some "Facebook names" shared by different people, and re-enacts them. The project raises issues of privacy and identity construction. The artist uses publicly available private information about individuals she doesn't know as the starting points for the creation of a "virtual identity" enacted in the real world, implicitly suggesting that every Facebook account is a story in itself.

The way people use the Internet to reveal something about themselves, interpreting a potentially broadcast medium as a private communication medium, is a subject of research for many artists. Since he started using Chatroulette, Tamas Banovich took a picture of any partner he met online, trying to capture «the moment of intense anticipation, curiosity mixed with apprehension [...] when one comes face to face with a stranger». Looking at those faces, we imagine what will happen next. But those images, isolated from their context, show us much more than the multitudes of humanity spending time online in search of something – a partner, a friend, an audience, a surprise. We can enter their bedrooms, know how they live and how they experience the Internet.

Something similar happens looking at the photos appropriated by Mikolaj Dlugosz in such places as eBay and Allegro, Poland's most used online auction website. In these flea markets of the XXI century, people post amateur pictures of items they want to put on sale. When they are featured in the photos, they usually put a blur or an abstract spot on their faces. Nevertheless these pictures, isolated from their context, can still tell a lot about them. What is that guy selling? His car or his dog? And what's on sale in that wedding photo? The man's tuxedo? The woman's veil? Are they still in love?

While Dlugosz looks for life where it isn't supposed to be, in *Best Day Ever* Zach Gage created a program that looks for happiness on Twitter, and then reposts it on a dedicated Twitter account. The project is an ironic take on the sharp contrast between text messages as a "cold medium" and the hot content we often spread through them.

Other projects either address media reality as a consistent part of our daily life or try to unmask it, revealing how the illusion of a real experience was constructed. This is the case of Joe McKay, who explores tools such as Google Streetview or Mapjack looking for reflections of the cars or vans used to take the pictures later compiled in a 3D panorama. McKay appropriates these "phantom images", and reconstructs them by means of a digital collage. The final result is a "lie", but a lie that tells the truth about a complex system of simulation. He finds the bug in the Matrix, and reveals it to the poor everyman fully immersed in the illusion. In these works, we can find an interesting conceptual reference to the hyperrealism of the Seventies, which often uses store window reflections in order to show us the artifice that produced the image, and to demonstrate that actually every image is a construction.

On the other side, Kevin Bewersdorf turns some of the results of his Google image searches into real objects. Rather than unmask the illusory power of media, he wants to show how much the digital environment is actually affecting our daily life. The way these objects are produced, however, suggest other considerations. Bewersdorf orders his objects from online services such as walgreens.com that follow his instructions and mail him the final product. So, these apparently real objects are, in fact, the output of a digital environment and an immaterial economy – they only become real when Kevin opens the package.

Eva and Franco Mattes (aka 0100101110101101.org) are concerned with another form of translation. In the attempt to better understand what it really means to live in a virtual world, they started re-enacting seminal works of performance art from the Sixties and Seventies in the synthetic environment of Second Life. This project, conduced with the rigor of a scientific experiment, made them experience and show not only the differences between one world and the other(s), but also the shifting meaning of concepts such as "life", "sex", "violence", "society" and "environment" in the present, hybrid way of life.

It's easy to see that most of these works are concerned with appropriation as an artistic strategy. The Mattes appropriate performances from the past; Bewersdorf, McKay and Dlugosz appropriate found images, steals faces and emotions, Endlicher re-enacts Facebook accounts. A master of stealing and recycling is, no doubt, Kenneth Tin-Kin Hung: his satirical animations are sophisticated collages of images found on the Web. Even more radically, The Yes Men appropriate real identities and play them out on the public stage. After acting as the representatives of giant institutions and corporations such as the WTO and Dow Chemical, The Yes Men collaborated with a wide network of activists and journalists to release a fake *New York Times*, printed in thousands of copies and distributed them for free in New York City. The headline news read: "Iraq war ends". The stunt plays with our usual confidence in the news media to release a lie and to temporarily hijack people in a parallel world: the world where that lie is true.

One of the virtues of a fake newspaper is that it never gets old. Today, printed newspapers are quickly made obsolete by the continuous flux of news we can experience on the Internet; encyclopedias have to confront databases and user generated content. A previously monolithic truth became negotiable and fluid. As the Romans did with emperors and generals fallen out of favor, artist Michael Mandiberg translates this "damnatio memoriae" into a physical damage inflicted to freshly printed newspapers ("Old News"), encyclopedias and dictionaries ("Database") in the form of laser-cut graffiti. Whatever the future will turn out to be, they are marked. Maybe.

First published in the catalogue of the show "The Future is Not What It Used to Be", curated by Magdalena Sawon at the Centrum Sztuki Współczesnej Zamek Ujazdowski, Warsaw 2010.

[1] Julia Joffe, "Roulette Russa", in *Wired Italia*, Issue 18, August 2010, pp. 62 – 69.
[2] Cfr. www.chatroulette.com.
[3] Cfr. www.4chan.org.
[4] Lev Grossman, "The Master Of Memes", in *Time*, July 9, 2008, available at the URL www.time.com/time/business/article/0,8599,1821435,00.html.
[5] Cfr. Anonymous (Brad Troemel), "What Relational Aesthetics Can Learn From 4Chan", in *Art Fag City*, September 9, 2010, available at the URL www.artfagcity.com/2010/09/09/img-mgmt-what-relational-aesthetics-can-learn-from-4chan/.
[6] Cfr. Hans Ulrich Obrist, "Hurricane List of Futures", M/M, Paris 2007.
[7] John Markoff, *What the Dormouse Said. How the Sixties Counterculture Shaped the Personal Computer Industry*, Penguin Books, London 2005.
[8] John Palfrey, Urs Gasser, *Born digital. Understanding the first generation of digital natives*, Basic Books, New York 2008.
[9] Cfr. http://burundi.sk/monoskop/log/.
[10] Cory Doctorow, *Little Brother*, Tor Books, New York 2008.
[11] Nick Bilton, "One on One: Christopher Poole, Founder of 4chan", in *The New York Times*, March 19, 2010, available at the URL http://bits.blogs.nytimes.com/2010/03/19/one-on-one-christopher-poole-founder-of-4chan/.
[12] Cfr. Domenico Quaranta, "Reality is Overrated. When Media Go Beyond Simulation", in *Artpulse Magazine*, Issue 3, March – May 2010. Available online at http://artpulsemagazine.com/reality-is-overrated-when-media-go-beyond-simulation/.

The Unbearable Aura of a Website. Originality in the Digital Age

With the digital medium, Benjamin's theory about the work of art in the age of mechanical reproduction seems to have reached a dead end. When there is no difference between copy and original, the aura fades and rarity can only be artificially simulated. Yet, is this always true? Playing with Benjamin and Groys, this article shows how, like the mythological Phoenix, the aura can resurface in the most replicable digital artifact: the website.

Copy and Original

On July 8, 1999, the *New York Times* published a story [1] reporting on a mysterious European activist group, whose practice consisted in copying art websites and publishing them on the address 0100101110101101.org. The article described this practice as an «attack on the commercialization of Web Art», yet it was more than that. With their thefts, 0100101110101101.org wanted to state clearly, on the one side, that the Web was – and should always be – the place of free access to knowledge; and, on the other side, that the digital medium finally turned the word "original" into a nonsense.

This is true, of course. Take a given file, copy it, and you'll have a perfect copy of the "original", described by the same long string of 0s and 1s. Copy it again, and again, and again, and you'll get the same. No loss of quality, no material difference between the first file and the last one. Put this file online, and everybody will make a perfect copy of it just viewing it on their browser.

If the difference between copy and original fades, the concept of the "limited edition" turns into a convention as well. In visual arts, limited editions were introduced with print. Printing technics such as xylography or lithography used a matrix that deteriorated over time, and the number of good prints that you could get from a single matrix was limited. Modern printing technics, photography and video turned the limited edition into a mere convention: an artifice that still made sense someway, related as it was with access to the means of production and to the "source" of a given content – i.e. the negative in photography.

But what does it mean to edition a website, a digital video or a digital image? If I copy an editioned DVD, I will have a perfect copy of it – no loss of quality, no material difference. If I have access to the same image file and the same printing machine, I can make a perfect copy of a digital print. In the digital realm, rarity doesn't exist: it can only be artificially simulated.

The Invisible Original

Yet, this is only part of the truth, the macroscopic difference between the digital realm and the material world that made some enthusiasts announce the end of intellectual property and of any cultural market at the end of the 20th century. In actual fact, the digital medium doesn't destroy concepts such as "original"; "rarity" and "aura": it just forces us to reconsider them. In his essay "From Image to Image File – and Back: Art in the Age of Digitalization" [2], Boris Groys does it discussing the difference between the digital image and the image file. According to Groys, there can't be a copy without an original. In the digital realm, the original is the image file. Yet, «the image file is not an image – the image file is invisible» [3]: an invisible string of digital code that turns into an image only when "performed" by a machine. The digital image is just a copy (a documentation) of an invisible original. In the process of visualization, «the digital original […] is moved by its visualization from the space of invisibility [...] to the space of visibility [...]. Accordingly, we have here a truly massive loss of aura – because nothing has more aura than the Invisible.» [4]

For Groys, visualizing a digital file is a sacrilege. In the computer environment, this loss of aura is permanent, and can be "cured" only by curating: bringing it to the exhibition space, adopting the sacerdotal role of visualizing the Invisible. In other words, the digital image is only apparently ubiquitous and infinitely reproducible in any place: in order to «guarantee its own identity in time» [5], the digital image has to be located in a specific place (the exhibition space).

The Topological Aura

Groys is here relying on Walter Benjamin's «topological definition of aura», as he calls it in another essay, discussing how the medium of installation can turn art documentation into art again [6]. According to Benjamin, «even the most perfect reproduction of a work of art is lacking in one element: its presence in time and space, its unique existence at the place where it happens to be. […] The presence of the original is the prerequisite to the concept of authenticity.» [7] Benjamin calls this presence (better translated as "its here and now") the aura of a given artwork. So, mechanical reproduction doesn't destroy the aura: it just depreciate «the quality of its presence», because «by making many reproductions it substitutes a plurality of copies for a unique existence. And in permitting the reproduction to meet the beholder or listener in his own particular situation, it reactivates the object reproduced.» This is a crucial point: aura is not lost – we just lose the ability to perceive it, because we depreciate the here and now. But aura can be restored, thanks to the increasing importance of what Benjamin calls the «exhibition value» of a work of art; or, in Groys' words: «(post)modernity enacts a complex play of removing from sites and placing in (new) sites, of deterritorialization and reterritorialization, of removing aura and restoring aura.» [8]

Now, let's go back to the digital file again. According to Groys, the aura of a digital file is the consequence of its own invisibility; any visualization of the invisible original sacrifice its aura to the needs of documentation; and the only way to restore it is to locate the piece in an exhibition. Thus, a digital image is translated into a print, a digital animation into a video installation, a 3D model into a sculpture, etc. Let's take, for example, Thomas Ruff's recent series *Zycles* (2009). The project includes a series of large-format inkjet prints on canvas displaying abstract images generated by a computer program. The "invisible original" is an algorithm (probably not written by the artist) visualized on a computer by a specific 3D program. The artist takes hi-res screenshots of the computer-generated image and translates them into editioned, high quality digital prints: the photo documentation of a performance (the computer performing the program written by a programmer), turned into "original art pieces" by virtue of the way they are produced and displayed (localized in an art space).

The Unbearable Aura of a Website

Of course, this process is totally legitimate, and, in a way, it's embedded in our (post)modernity. Yet, we shouldn't forget that these prints are surrogates. And we should also wonder: is it possible to preserve the initial aura of the digital file or to restore it in a digital environment? Is it possible to create an auratic, digital original? At this point, we may be able to translate this question into another: is there a "here and now" for a digital artifact? Can it be located, and where?

Any file has, of course, a specific location on a computer, described by the file path: Apple/Videos/Cremaster.mov. But this is a private location, that can't be perceived as an "exhibition space". It's just a file on a computer. Now, open a web address. The same artifact appears in front of your eyes. It's not a file on a computer: it's an object you meet during a trip, in a specific place called, let's say, Youtube, situated in a bigger place called World Wide Web. You can see all this in the location bar of your browser, where the URL of the site is displayed. Now, please read Benjamin's definition of the aura of a natural object. He writes: «We define the aura of the latter as the unique phenomenon of a distance, however close it may be. If, while resting on a summer afternoon, you follow with your eyes a mountain range on the horizon or a branch which casts its shadow over you, you experience the aura of those mountains, of that branch.» [9] Can you find somewhere a better description of Web surfing? Can you find another place that can be, at the same time, so close to the visitor and so far away from her? When you visit a website, it's simultaneously on your computer and on a server somewhere else in the world. If you are lucky, a bunch of other people are visiting it at the same time: an old German lady, sitting on her sofa; a Japanese secretary in her office; a Swedish teenager in his bedroom. This is the "here and now" of a website: download it onto your desktop, and you'll lose it.

In other words, a Web address gives to any file a presence, an aura. A website – or any file experienced through the Internet – is an auratic, digital original. Technically, a website is a collection of files located on a shared computer space, associated to an IP (Internet Protocol) address (a numerical label assigned to any device participating in a computer network) and to an URL (Uniform Resource Locator). If a website is a building, the IP is its position on the map (i.e. 1071 Fifth Avenue New York, NY 10128-0173) and the URL is the name currently used to identify it (i.e. Solomon R. Guggenheim Museum). As a whole, a website can be described as an installation: it locates a series of fragments (documentation of invisible originals) in a specific, unique place. You can go to that place using a browser and clicking on a link. As any real original, if the link is wrong, or the website is not there anymore, you can't experience it. You may experience an identical copy locally, but it won't be the same thing: you will miss the aura of the original piece [10].

This "aura" is the result of a unique relationship: the one between the content of the website and its location. I'm not the first to say this. One of the first sites cloned by 0100101110101101.org in 1999 was Art.Teleportacia, described by its author, the Russian artist Olia Lialina, as "the first online art gallery". Opening a Web gallery, Lialina was not contributing to the commodification of the Web, but she was making a statement, at the time provocative, about the unique aura of a website. In a later text, she defines the URL as «the only parameter which protects copyright» [11] of an online work, and makes a series of examples where the location bar becomes an integral part of the work. One of her works is particularly useful to show it. *Agatha Appears* (1997) is a short metaphorical love story between Agatha, the main character, and the Sysadmin, a term describing a person employed to maintain and operate a computer network. The central part of the story is a "trip through the Internet", told using the location bar content in a literary way. Agatha and the Sys move from server to server, from country to country, only by means of a click. The work is full of Internet jargon and displays the formalism typical to early net.art, but it's still one of the best and more enjoyable online works ever made, also thanks to a recent restoration.

Another artist who got the importance of the relationship between the location and the content of a website was Miltos Manetas. In 2000, Manetas launched the Neen movement, a label that gathered a wide number of artists [12]. Most of them were working online. As Manetas wrote in a prophetic essay: «Websites are today's most radical and important art objects. Because the Internet is not just another "media", as the Old Media insists, but mostly a "space", similar to the American Continent immediately after it was discovered – anything that can be found on the Web has a physical presence. It occupies real estate.» [13] A typical Neen artwork can be described as a dedicated web address displaying a single content: a sound file, an animation, a video, an image, an interactive piece of software, a text. Thus, francescobonami.com is a website displaying a theoretical text about Neen; jacksonpollock.org is an interactive Flash animation allowing you to paint a Jackson Pollock; jesusswimming.com is a silly animation displaying exactly what the URL says; so does jesusdrowning.com, an homage to Manetas by Rafael Rozendaal, one of the best and more prolific authors of Neen websites. Neenstars (as Neen artists call themselves) create "places" for the Internet, where one can stop for a few seconds, take a rest from the information overload, be surprised, and go ahead.

In the following years, many young artists, little or no connected with the Neen movement, started making "single serving sites" [14] like these. Sometimesredsometimesblue.com, for example, is a monochrome website by Damon Zucconi; etherealself.com, by Harm Van Den Dorpel, is a site that captures the video streaming of the user's camera and displays it on a diamond; and etherealothers.com is a parent website where all the faces of the visitors of etherealself.com are displayed in a grid.

Apart from this, an increasing number of artists, more or less known, has a consistent web activity. Paul Chan, Ryan Trecartin and Cory Arcangel are probably the most visible examples. Most of Paul Chan's publications, animations, fonts and sound works can be downloaded for free from nationalphilistine.com, his place on the Internet. Trecartin doesn't even have a website, but he got well known through Youtube before starting building a reputation in the contemporary art world. One might wonder which version of *I-be Area* has more aura: the online, low-res version, visited by up to 50.000 people, or the hi-res, editioned gallery version of the video.

Another legitimate question might be: why websites didn't become the ultimate collectible? Why collectors still prefer to buy offline, editioned versions of a digital piece instead of websites? Both these choices require faith: you need faith in the workings of the art world in order to believe that the editioned DVD you bought for 10.000 euros is more valuable than the online version of the same video. This is a kind of faith a collector can deal with. But what happens when you buy a website? You have, at a first level, to get used to a different concept of owning. You own something that is – and must be, in order to keep its aura – accessible to everybody; something unique, but whose content can be easily copied by everybody; something living in the public arena, that you can't protect as if it were in your storage space; something subject to the variations of its own environment and of its visualization software. Furthermore, you need faith because you are buying an invisible original: a bunch of data stored on a server and accessible from a specific online location. In other words, you need the faith required to recognize art out of the context that, along the last century, acquired the ability to turn everything that is shown there into art: the exhibition space.

First published in *Artpulse*, Vol. 2, N° 3, Spring 2011.

1. M. Mirapaul, "An Attack on the Commercialization of Web Art", in *The New York Times*, July 8, 1999, available at
www.nytimes.com/library/tech/99/07/cyber/artsatlarge/08artsatlarge.html.
2. In B. Groys, *Art Power*, The MIT Press, Cambridge: Massachusetts and London: England 2008, pp. 83 – 91.
3. Ibid., p. 84.
4. Ibid., p. 86.
5. Ibid., p. 84.
6. B. Groys, "Art in the Age of Biopolitics: from Artwork to Art Documentation", ibid., pp. 53 – 65.
7. W. Benjamin, "The Work of Art in the Age of Mechanical Reproduction", 1936, § 2, available online at
www.marxists.org/reference/subject/philosophy/works/ge/benjamin.htm.
8. In B. Groys, "Art in the Age of Biopolitics...", p. 64.
9. In W. Benjamin, "The Work of Art in the Age of Mechanical Reproduction", § 3.
10. A copy uploaded on another website can, in turn, acquire a new aura by virtue of its relocation. When Slovenian artist Vuk Cosic put a copy of the Documenta X site on his website, declaring it an Internet readymade, he added the aura of art to an object that up to then only had the aura of the "natural object", in Benjamin's terms. We could develop this even further, and say that the Internet is probably the only place where aura is not connected with authenticity. A work by Vuk Cosic has the aura of the original artwork and of the located object; a copy of the same work by 0100101110101101.org has, again, the aura of the located object and of a work of appropriation art.
11. Olia Lialina, "Location = YES", available at
http://art.teleportacia.org/Location_Yes/index.html.
12. For more about Neen, cfr. www.manetas.com/eo/neen/.
13. Miltos Manetas, "Websites Are The Art Of Our Times", 2002 – 2004, available online at
http://manetas.com/txt/websitesare.htm.
14. The definition was coined by Jason Kottke, who runs the blog kottke.org. Cfr. http://kottke.org/08/02/single-serving-sites.

Petra Cortright

«It takes strength to be gentle and kind», the Smiths said in one of Petra Cortright's favorite songs. It takes strength to take the usual, dumb, stereotyped, commodified imagery of prettiness and kindness and use it in a way that doesn't look dumb or critical. It takes strength to adopt custom software effects, user friendly tools and vernacular genres and use them to make things that make you talk about art without apparently being anything more than what they are expected to be – a Youtube video or a Photoshop exercise. It takes strength to make art «about beauty and craft», as Ed Halter wrote.

Petra Cortright's work has this peculiar strength. Take, for example, *When You Walk Through the Storm* (2009). In this video, a girl – the artist – is looking at you from the screen. Like you, she is sitting down in front of her computer. She looks sad – an impression enforced by the cold palette of the video. Slowly, she starts moving her hand up and down in front of her face. The movement activates a video effect that makes her appear underwater, fading her face in a myriad of pixels. At the same time, the intimacy created by the webcam gaze fades as well: she is close to you, on your computer screen, but the water effect makes the space in between you and her appear physical, and the sound – the song of the title – seems to come from the deep.

Most of Petra's videos follow the same basic rules. In the diptych *Sparkling I and II* (2010) the artist wears sunglasses, walks through a garden and scrolls a tree, producing a beautiful rain of sparkling digital symbols; in *Footvball/Faerie* (2009) she plays football covered with a digitally-added pink cloud; in *Das Hell(e) Modell* (2009) she dances to the music of a Kraftwerk song, while a video filter alters our perception of time and makes her appear more angelic than usual; in *Bunny Banana* (2009) she eats a banana wearing bunny ears; and in *Holy Tears* (2009) she sheds digital tears ironically posing as a saint. All these videos are shot with a custom webcam, and use simple effects available to anyone. What makes them different from the amount of ego-clips we can find on Youtube? What gives them the power of a revelation? What makes them significant for the thousands of people that watch them online, but also for people that, for generational or other reasons, don't share the internet and juvenile culture she refers to (in spare order, cyberpunk, psychedelia, kawaii, electronic music, sharing, exhibitionism)? Probably, the answer is: the way she is able to add all these levels, kindly and gently, to an object that doesn't lose the authenticity of a teenager's secret diary, or a student's sketchbook.

Most of Petra's gif animations and static images look like sketches at first sight. They are, again, about beauty and craft. But beauty is unconventional and craft doesn't mean that she uses image editing tools in the way a professional does. Quite the opposite. In her animated gifs, she either modifies vernacular material or explores animation effects and low-res aesthetics creating her own abstract gifs. In her still image pieces, she creates photo-collages where the complexity of the landscape is contradicted by the geometrical nature of the cuts; she employs different filters for different image layers; and she explores the liquid nature of the digital image literally liquefying found photographs of models, still lifes or landscapes. All this converges in *The Infinite Sculpture Garden...* (2010), her last and, up to now, most complex work: an abstract, suggestive landscape where geometrics, reflections, patterns, shadows and transparencies all conjure in the development of a hermetic, hyper-textual visual poem.

All these references to layers, effects and tools do not mean that Petra Cortright's work is formalistic and medium-related. Petra belongs to the first generation of digital natives. For her, referring to internet culture and desktop metaphors is as natural as, for any aboriginal, referring to her traditions. She lives online. Let's spend half a day on Google searching for her and we will know almost everything about her: that she loves pets and trees, that she hates New York, that her father died of a melanoma, that she had a wonderful love story and that she broke up. Her life is a continuous online performance taking place every day on her Twitter, her Facebook, her Flickr account. Her work is not about the medium: it's about Petra Cortright. And it takes strength to be Petra Cortright.

First published in the exhibition brochure of the solo show of Petra Cortright at Gloria Maria Gallery, Milan, April 2010, with the title "It Takes Strength to Be Gentle and Kind".

Interview with Oliver Laric

In the past few months, when people have asked me to suggest something inspiring to read, I've always replied: "Go to oliverlaric.com and select Versions." True, Oliver Laric is not a writer but an artist, and Versions is not an essay but a video – or, better, an ongoing art project involving two videos, "a series of sculptures, airbrushed images of missiles, a talk, a PDF, a song, a novel, a recipe, a play, a dance routine, a feature film and merchandise". But if you are looking for a brilliant statement on the visual culture of the Internet age, or an in-depth analysis of its historical roots in Western culture, I couldn't suggest anything better.

Oliver Laric is a young Austrian artist currently living in Berlin. In 2006, together with a group of friends, he founded VVORK, an art blog that acts as an exhibition space and, occasionally, a curatorial platform that organizes events in brick-and-mortar venues. While the website - one of the most successful art blogs ever - features art from any time and place, using text only for technical descriptions, elevating the status of the "mechanical reproduction" – usually a JPG or a video – to give it the legitimacy of the real thing, and working as a collaborative flow of consciousness where associations are never explained but simply offered to the user, the shows concentrate on contemporary art responding to the cultural shift introduced by the information age. And they both do it in an original way, escaping common categorizations and frameworks.

In October, Laric will present the last iteration of Versions at Frieze Art Fair. In this interview, we talk about this ongoing project, VVORK, and much more.

ACCORDING TO MY GOOGLE SEARCHES, YOU WERE BORN IN LEIPZIG AND INNSBRUCK, YOU ARE BLACK AND CAUCASIAN, AND YOU HAVE SAID: "I USUALLY GIVE FAKE CVS WHEN I AM ASKED TO GIVE A CV. RECENTLY I STARTED GIVING REAL ONES." AND NOW?

I am hiring a writer to develop multiple biographies.

IN YOUR WORK, THERE IS AN INTERESTING BALANCE BETWEEN TRANSPARENCE AND OPACITY. ON THE ONE HAND, YOU REVEAL LITTLE ABOUT YOURSELF THROUGH YOUR WORK AND YOUR WEBSITE. ON THE OTHER HAND, HOWEVER, VERSIONS IS PROBABLY ONE OF THE MOST STRAIGHTFORWARD ARTIST'S STATEMENTS I HAVE EVER SEEN. IN A WAY, IT IS EVEN TOO MUCH, SINCE IT LEAVES LITTLE SPACE FOR INTERPRETATION. WHAT DO YOU THINK?

I enjoy interpretations and mediated experiences: books about books, exhibition catalogs, interpretations of films. Some of my favorite artworks and movies have only been described to me. A description can generate new work while acting as a portrait of the person retelling the idea, plot, etc.

There is a novel titled *The Weather Fifteen Years Ago* (2006) by Wolf Haas, written as an interview between a literary critic and the author. There are two layers: the fictional interview and the fictional novel. Over the course of the interview all details of the plot are revealed through the subjective interpretations of both critic and author. Versions is an interpretation open to interpretations. The first incarnation has been reinterpreted by Momus, Dani Admiss, and Guthrie Lonergan, and I just found another reinterpretation of the last version on YouTube. They are permanently in a beta state and affect each other.

> YOU OFTEN ACT NOT ONLY AS AN ARTIST BUT ALSO AS AN ART CRITIC AND CURATOR. MANY ARTISTS WORK IN THE SAME WAY TODAY, BUT I AM STILL QUITE CURIOUS ABOUT HOW YOU DEAL WITH IT. HOW DO YOU DEFINE YOURSELF?

Sometimes it is hard to distinguish between VVORK work and work. For example, working on *Versions* was similar to working on an exhibition. The outcome was a selection of works placed in the same space.

> YOU HAVE SAID: "I DON'T SEE ANY NECESSITY IN PRODUCING IMAGES MYSELF — EVERYTHING THAT I WOULD NEED EXISTS, IT'S JUST ABOUT FINDING IT." IS THE ARTIST AS CREATOR A THING OF THE PAST?

Using an existing image creates a new image, just as with iconoclasm: the destruction of an image creates an image. Or with translation: as Jorge Luis Borges described in the often-quoted *Pierre Menard, Author of the Quixote*, translations produce new works.

> FOR YOU AND MANY ARTISTS OF YOUR GENERATION, USING "FOUND MATERIAL" MEANS USING THE KIND OF VERNACULAR MATERIAL (FOR LACK OF A BETTER TERM) YOU CAN FIND IN PLACES SUCH AS YOUTUBE, 4CHAN, FLICKR, GOOGLE, AND 3D WAREHOUSE. IS THE RELATIONSHIP BETWEEN ART AND NON-ART, HIGH CULTURE AND POPULAR CULTURE, DEFINITELY CHANGING?

Some of my favorite exhibitions don't make clear distinctions between those fields, incorporating works by journalists, architects, musicians, etc. I think it is a more interesting strategy to curate works, instead of being involved in a scene or a CV.

As VVORK, we were invited to curate part of the Photo Biennale in Mannheim and selected works by photographers that we found on Flickr, Reuters, and stock photography sites, along with the works of artists. It would have been impossible to distinguish the selection.

> YOU HAVE SAID: "I THINK IT IS NECESSARY TO IGNORE AUTHORSHIP, TO CREATE A SPACE FOR SOMETHING THAT IS INTERESTING AGAIN." HOW CAN YOU RECONCILE THIS APPROACH WITH THE RULES STILL FOLLOWED IN THE ART WORLD?

I think ignorance of copyright and art market debate is beneficial to my health and happiness.

FOR YOU, WHAT IS *VERSIONS*? ART OR THEORY?

A series of sculptures, airbrushed images of missiles, a talk, a PDF, a song, a novel, a recipe, a play, a dance routine, a feature film and merchandise.

CONTEMPORARY ART IS A LITTLE NICHE, BUT ARTISTS WITH A STRONG ONLINE PRESENCE HAVE THE POSSIBILITY TO ADDRESS A BROADER - AND VERY DIFFERENT - AUDIENCE. HOW DO YOU DEAL WITH IT?

One of the first works I uploaded to my site (*787 Cliparts*, 2006) spread to numerous other websites. On some days it had more than 30,000 viewers. This was an exciting experience and made me realize that my website is not a space of representation but of primary experiences. You are viewing the real thing. And when the work travels to other sites, it is still the real thing.

It also landed on the front page of YouTube. By now there are over 1,500 comments, a type of feedback that I have never experienced in a gallery context.

"NOT A SPACE OF REPRESENTATION BUT OF PRIMARY EXPERIENCES" - YOU HAVE SAID THE SAME ABOUT VVORK. STILL, I HAVE SOME PROBLEMS WITH APPLYING THIS MODEL TO A SCULPTURE OR AN INSTALLATION. CAN YOU HELP ME?

Walking around a sculpture and viewing a single perspective in a catalog are different experiences, but both are authentic and vivid experiences. My favorite sculpture is easy to experience as a description. It is a Virgin with child built around 1510 out of sandstone in Basel. Reformation iconoclasm came and the baby Jesus was replaced with a scale in 1608. She [the Virgin] is now Justice. The first part of her life was very spiritual; the current [one] is more pragmatic. I am curious to witness her upcoming incarnations. Out of love for this statue, I asked a 3D modeler to reconstruct her digitally, coating her in a Terminator-esque chrome texture. In *Terminator 2: Judgment Day*, the antagonist T1000 was capable of assuming any shape, just like Barbapapa [1]. I made a pilgrimage to see the statue and it was an underwhelming experience, like seeing the movie after reading the novel.

You can also imagine the parts that a mediated experience is lacking - the sound, the smell of the space, and the tourists around you. This lack of information triggers productive speculation. In Japanese porn, the genitals are pixelated, but a frequent consumer doesn't see the pixels anymore. There is a similar internal projection with small online videos; at some point you automatically assume the Dolby surround sound and the crisp HD resolution.

We did an exhibition in 2009 at MU in Eindhoven (The Netherlands) titled "The Real Thing" after a short story by Henry James on an artist who prefers representation over reality. We showed a series of press releases selected by Daniel Baumann, tourist photographs of Jeff Koons' Balloon Dog at Versailles, a *New York Times* back issue with an article debating the existence of Gelitin's balcony mounted on the World Trade Center in 2000, a video sampler of Seth Price's editioned videos, a PDF version of a performative talk by Cory Arcangel, acoustic versions of Claude Closky's text pieces, and cam versions of the current Hollywood blockbusters, among other works.

ARE YOU INTERESTED IN THE WAY THE ONLINE COMMUNITY REACTS TO YOUR WORK AND HOW THEY USE AND ABUSE IT?

It is the most interesting part. It happened often with *787 Cliparts*. The visual material was modified, shortened, extended, or scored with music. An advertising agency even reconstructed the video by producing their own clip art.

These reactions led to the Mariah Carey video *Touch My Body (Green Screen Version)* (2008), in which everything but Mariah was turned green, enabling anyone with some video editing knowledge to adapt the video and substitute backgrounds. My activity was a technical preparation and the modification part was outsourced to Mariah Carey fans.

YOU STARTED VVORK IN 2006 WITH CHRISTOPH PRIGLINGER, GEORG SCHNITZER, AND ALEKSANDRA DOMANOVIC. YOU ALL ATTENDED THE SAME SCHOOL (THE UNIVERSITY OF APPLIED ARTS IN VIENNA). IS A COMMON BACKGROUND STILL SO IMPORTANT IN THE INTERNET AGE?

Maybe the common background is more about interest. Google can aid in finding counterparts and bringing the most niche fetishes together. But you still might need to relocate to the ideal environment.

I READ SOMEWHERE THAT YOU HAVE ABOUT 9,000 VISITORS EVERY DAY. WHO ARE THESE PEOPLE?

By now there are about 15,000 viewers a day. Our understanding of the visitors comes primarily through e-mail contact and web statistics about geographic location, duration of visits, frequency, and so on. It so happens that most readers are from unsurprising places like New York, London, Paris, and Berlin. The statistics confirm our expectations.

IN OCTOBER, YOU WILL TAKE PART IN "FRAME," THE SOLO SHOWS SECTION OF FRIEZE ART FAIR. WHAT ARE YOU GOING TO SHOW THERE?

(1) A bootleg of a book titled *Ancient Copies*, (2) a version of *Versions*, (3) a reproduction of a relief defaced by Reformation iconoclasm.

First published in *Artpulse*, Vol. 2, N° 1, Fall 2010, with the title "The Real Thing / Interview with Oliver Laric".

[1] Barbapapa is a character created by Annette Tison and Talus Taylor in the 1970s for their series of cartoons and children books which were very popular in Europe.

The Art of the Netizens

In the beginning was jodi.org, and jodi.org was within the Internet, and jodi.org was the Internet. No joking. It was 1995 when jodi.org appeared in a still relatively small, slow and amateurish World Wide Web. If you were unlucky enough to get into it by chance, you would never forget it. Jodi.org was a trap, a black hole into an under-construction universe, a trash bin, a dumpster. It was a place that you had to navigate without a map, without directions, and without knowing how to get out. It was a place where all the history of the Internet collapsed into a dada collage, an overgrowing Merzbau showing us what the Internet has been, was and would be in the future.

This place was built by a Dutch-Belgian couple, Joan Heemskerk and Dirk Paesmans. Some of the people who were trapped into its sticky web thought it could be understood as art, and started thinking that a specific "Net Art" was possible. The term was, and still is, quite problematic. Along the Twentieth Century, we got used to terms such as Video Art, Performance Art, Land Art and so on. This may lead us to think that the term "Net Art" describes a practice defined by the medium it uses. Big mistake. The Internet is not a medium: it is a place. Thus, the term Net Art doesn't describe a medium, but a citizenship. It is more similar to "American Art" then to "Video Art". But, while terms such as "American Art" make little sense today, since we live in a global village where local identity has often to fight against a global mass culture; the term "Net Art" makes more sense then ever, because more and more people think about themselves as netizens, that is "citizens of the Internet". Net Art is the art made by netizens. You make Net Art because you are a Net artist, not the other way around. Sometimes it takes the shape of a website, more often it doesn't. This is not really important, however: what defines Net Art is not the medium used, but the cultural background and habits of those who make it. Thus, the term Net Art describes something more similar to Dada or Fluxus than to Video Art: not a medium-based practice, but a community sharing a common culture and a common approach to art.

Net Art

This is, by the way, the reason why the term was often replaced by other labels, such as net.art, Neen and, more recently, "Post Internet". net.art was actually the first term adopted, in 1996, to define the practice. Even if it looks quite similar, the little dot in it makes a big difference. If Net Art is an art label, net.art is the parody of an art label. The dot refers to domain and file names, and thus to the computer culture shared by netizens; and turns the word "art" into nothing more than a file extension (like .txt) or a top level domain (like .com).

Neen was a term chosen by the former artist (since then, Neenstar) Miltos Manetas in 2000, in order to describe the work of a «still undefined generation of visual artists». According to Manetas, «computing is to Neen as what fantasy was to surrealism and freedom to communism. It creates its context, but it can also be postponed [...] Neen is about losing time on different operating systems». Finally, "Post Internet" was born quite recently out of the same need that produced net.art and Neen: describe the art of the Netizens without forcing them into the straitjacket of an (apparently) medium-based definition.

However, both "net.art" and "Neen" ended up to be identified with a specific community of people; and "Post Internet" is too a bad term to work as an art label. So, I will go on using the term Net Art, meaning "the art of the Netizens".

Pioneers

The first Net artists were, indeed, very similar to the first Mormon settlers going West in the Seventieth Century. It was a generation of immigrants: they came from a world were art was a product and they entered a world where art could either be a process, an action and a place. They came from a world of objects, and they entered a world of digital data. They came from a world with borders and they entered a free and wild West. They came from a world where copying was illegal, and entered a place that Cory Doctorow described as «the world's most perfect and most powerful copying machine». No surprise that, in the beginning, they insisted so much on this: making art that can be experienced from anywhere in the world; making and copying websites, appropriating and simulating identities, coordinating events, playing with codes and inventing new codes. What they were doing was pursuing their own frontier, building places, and making things that were impossible in other places. Building places: black holes like jodi.org, open platforms like Irational.org, online galleries like Teleportacia.org, closed laboratories like Hell.com. Making things impossible everywhere else: such as hijacking thousand of people to your own place, as the etoy collective did in 1996; acting as if you were 200 different artists instead of one, as the German feminist Cornelia Sollfrank did in 1997; playing the role of the Holy See online for over a year, as the Italian duo 0100101110101101.org did in 1998; fighting against a giant corporation and winning the battle, as the whole online community did in 1999 in support to etoy; persuading the American media and intelligence that you were going to auction actual votes online, as the Austrian collective Ubermorgen.com did in 2000.

Neen

Of course, many of these early pioneers knew that it was possible to make Net Art out of the Internet, and even without using a computer. Thus, when invited to show in real venues, etoy came up with the Tank System, a large scale installation of pipes that worked as a metaphor of the digital space of the Net; and when, in 2001, Epidemic and 0100101110101101.org decided to use the Venice Biennale as a platform to spread a computer virus, they actually used t-shirts, not computers. However, they were too involved in building places and taking actions to fully explore this possibility. So, we have to thank Miltos Manetas for having stated that clearly, with the Neen Manifesto («computing [...] creates its context, but can also be postponed») and his own work. Manetas made Net Art – or, in his words, Neen – in the form of websites, but also in the form of paintings, prints and videos. Other Neenstars made songs, buildings, installations, games, performances. Let's consider Manetas paintings – something that a "radical" net artist would never have done: physical objects for a luxury market, made with a traditional medium and a quite conventional style. The subjects are cables, computers, videogames, people involved with computers and videogames, websites, navigators, GPS and, more recently, Internet icons such as the Pirate Bay logo. Paintings for a post-digital, post-internet age. On the other hand, his websites are graffiti for the streets of the Internet: instant, one-liner works often consisting in a single page, where a playful animation, or the relation between the content and the address, is enough to turn them into little treasures found out in the trash.

Manetas and the Neen movement are not alone in this process. In the same years the original net.art group starts making things that are not websites: Jodi subverts corporate software and makes installations with hacked hardware; Alexei Shulgin turns an old 386dx into a pop star; Vuk Cosic makes ASCII movies. Other artists, such as Claude Closky and Cory Arcangel, never separated their online activity from their offline works.

Digital Natives

All this opens the path to a second generation: the natives. They are born in a world where any distinction between media and reality doesn't make sense anymore. They are always online, not because they chose it, but because they don't even know an offline status. To say it with a paradox: they wouldn't be surprised to discover that the office desktop borrowed its name from the computer desktop. They always make Net Art, even if their personal homepage is usually built with Indexhibit or Tumblr, and their works are often installations, performances, prints or videos. Does this mean that all contemporary art is Net Art? No, it doesn't. If digital nativity is a condition, Net Art is still a matter of choice. Or, to use Manetas' words: «They are Friends of the information and not Users». Everybody is a user today, but just if you are a "friend of the information" everything you are going to do will bring the Internet watermark in its source code. No surprise that many of them gathered in the so-called surfing clubs: online communities that elevate browsing, copying and recycling to an art form. They are interested in the "digital folklore", to use the term suggested by Olia Lialina and Dragan Espenshied. They browse, copy, edit, share. They often make a professional use of amateurish tools, or an amateurish use of professional tools. To the clean, polished style of "users" they react with their dirty style and their conceptual focus on the tool's basic features. Thus, Petra Cortright makes plain webcam videos of herself where the simple use of a filter is enough to turn them into something magic and disturbing. Harm Van Den Dorpel and Damon Zucconi often play with the layers of an image, modifying found material in order to generate in the viewer new associations and expectations. The duo AIDS-3D makes performances and installations exploring the spiritual side of technology. Rafael Rozendaal makes playful, apparently dumb flash animations, turning interaction into a discovery device. Oliver Laric is interested in versioning as the driving force behind many Internet subcultures. The Italian collective Alterazioni Video turns popular online obsessions – such as making a stack of bowling balls – into sculptures, installations and performances. And Jon Rafman travels the world via Google Street View.

Jodi Again

Of course, the first generation is still there and doing interesting things. I have no room for other examples, so I'd be happy enough to end up with Jodi, our starting point. The ineffable duo never stopped acting as a virus, commenting on the world they are living in and cracking the polished surface of the corporate web, now turned "social". Recently they started thumbing Youtube, replying to the most viewed videos with a simple thumb print. Think digitally, act physically: Net Art is nothing else, after all.

First published in Spanish in the Mexican magazine *La Tempestad* , Issue 72, May – June 2010.

http://domenicoquaranta.com

www.ingramcontent.com/pod-product-compliance
Lightning Source LLC
Chambersburg PA
CBHW070840310526
45793CB00010B/120